COMPLETE SOUS VIDE COOKBOOK

COMPLETE SOUS VIDE COOKBOOK

150+ RECIPES FOR PERFECT MEAT, SEAFOOD, VEGETABLES, AND MORE

SHARON CHEN

PHOTOGRAPHY BY DARREN MUIR

ROCKRIDGE PRESS

For Marcus, the light of my life

CONTENTS

INTRODUCTION

IN EARLY 2018, LIFE TOOK ME FROM AUSTIN, TEXAS, across the Pacific Ocean to Hong Kong. Since I had lived in Asia before, I thought it'd be pretty easy for me to ease into the new environment. What I didn't consider at the time was that the population density of my new home would be 12 times greater than Austin's. Compared to the Texas-sized life I was used to, everything suddenly seemed to be small and crowded. Our 1-bedroom apartment was less than 400 square feet, including a so-called open kitchen with no oven and no counter space for a toaster oven!

How would I cook for my family? No oven means no baking. No baking means no whole chicken, roasts, full slabs of ribs, roasted vegetables, and on and on . . .

And then I discovered sous vide cooking. All I needed was one big pot and a place to rest it. And there began a life-changing cooking journey that quickly turned into an obsession. I started placing whole chicken, steak, bacon, ribs, whole roasts, all sorts of vegetables, potatoes, eggs, cheesecake—you name it—into a water bath to cook, and I haven't stopped since. I have also learned to infuse honey, maple syrup, vodka, and gin using this incredible and modern cooking method. In short, I have spent the past few years experimenting, sharing my developing knowledge, writing about it, and most important, nourishing my family with sous vide cooking.

What better way to express my appreciation for this incredibly versatile and modern cooking method than to share my love with all of you? I present to you 150+ of my favorite sous vide recipes, ranging from basics like Classic Pot Roast (page 175) to creative crowd-pleasers like Lemon and Rosemary Infused Vodka (page 219).

CHAPTER 1

THE ESSENTIALS OF SOUS VIDE

As elegant as it sounds, the direct translation of the term sous vide (pronounced "sue veed") is decidedly less so. It is a French term meaning "under vacuum" and describes a cooking method where you vacuum-seal food in a plastic pouch or jar, then immerse it into a water bath that's kept at a precise temperature for a certain period of time using a gadget called an immersion circulator. This technique maximizes the nutritional value, taste, texture, and aroma of food.

If you are a sous vide beginner, you'll learn the basic and practical skills to get you started in this chapter. If you are already an avid sous vider, this chapter will expand your knowledge and hone your skills, so that you can make almost anything with your sous vide. You may be surprised by what you can make in a water bath.

THE SCIENCE OF SOUS VIDE

There are many benefits to cooking sous vide at home. It yields consistent results and amazing flavors. It allows home cooks to "set it and forget it" while producing gourmet, restaurant-quality dishes in your own kitchen, no matter your experience level.

It may all sound too good to be true, but after you consider the science behind sous vide cooking, you'll realize just how wonderful and practical this invention is. My goal with this science-based chapter is for you to understand the process at work behind the delectable foods you'll find yourself creating.

HOW AN IMMERSION CIRCULATOR WORKS

Unlike traditional cooking methods, sous vide allows you to take complete control of cooking temperature and time. First you need an immersion circulator, sometimes referred to as a sous vide machine. This will heat the water in your container to the desired temperature and maintain that temperature until your food is done.

A typical immersion circulator contains a tube, pump, heating element, thermometer, set of control circuits, and an interface. Here's how it works: When you set your desired temperature for the hot-water bath, the control circuitry powers the heating element. The pump pulls water into the mouth of the tube located at the base of the circulator. Then water emerges from the top of the tube.

The thermometer monitors the water temperature. It feeds the information to the control circuit, which activates the heating element, switching it on and off as needed to maintain the desired temperature. The water continuously circulates through the tube, keeping the water at a precise temperature throughout the container.

WHY IT'S SO DARN DELICIOUS

With sous vide, your food is cooked at a precise low temperature, inside and out, in its own juices, so it's tender and delicious without any waste. This is nearly impossible to achieve with traditional cooking methods.

Let's take steak as an example. The ideal temperature for a medium-rare steak is between 129°F and 140°F. When you cook it in a skillet, the edge cooks first. By the time the center of the steak reaches the ideal temperature, the edges are already overcooked. The meat will also lose some volume thanks to moisture loss while cooking. A steak cooked sous vide at 129°F for an extended period (the cooking time depends on the cut's thickness), on the other hand, is perfectly cooked from edge to edge due to the full immersion and consistent temperature control.

FROM THE LAB TO THE KITCHEN

A heated water bath using an immersion circulator was first used in laboratories for incubating samples in water at a constant temperature over a long period of time and for enabling certain chemical reactions to occur at high temperatures. Although there was an early attempt in 1799 at low-temperature cooking using air as the heat transfer method, it was not until the mid- to late-20th century that the immersion circulator truly made its journey from the lab to the kitchen.

In the mid-1960s, American and French engineers created an industrial food preservation method by preparing food under pressure. Researchers found the flavor and texture of the food to be distinctively improved. Georges Pralus, a French chef, adopted this packing method for his restaurant in 1974, adapting it to cook at high temperatures. Later, Pralus collaborated with scientist Bruno Goussault, who pioneered the combination of vacuum sealing with low-temperature cooking in 1971, and together they continued perfecting the sous vide method. In the mid-2000s, sous vide cooking equipment became available for home use.

HOW TO SOUS VIDE SAFELY

Is sous vide safe? The answer is yes, as long as you keep a few things in mind and follow a few best practices for food safety.

STAYING OUT OF THE DANGER ZONE

You might have heard about the "danger zone," which refers to a food temperature range between 40°F and 140°F. When food sits in this range, potential harmful bacteria can thrive and make you sick.

To avoid the danger zone, the recommended lowest temperature for cooking sous vide is 130°F. But isn't 130°F still in the danger zone range, you ask? That brings us to my next point: Time plays an essential role when it comes to food safety.

THE IMPORTANCE OF TIME

With sous vide, you can actually cook foods at a lower temperature like 130°F and still destroy bacteria, *if you cook them for a longer time*. For example, the most common food pathogen, *Clostridium perfringens*, stops multiplying at 126°F. But at that same temperature, it will take hours of cooking for the most worrisome pathogens (the *Salmonella* species, *Listeria monocytogenes*, and the pathogenic strains of *E. coli*) to reduce down to a safe level. Sous vide takes this timing into account.

Here's an illustration of how time combats the lower temperatures of the "danger zone." The minimal internal temperature for safety for chicken recommended by the FDA is 165°F. When you cook chicken sous vide between 140°F and 150°F, the internal temperature of the bird will never reach 165°F, but the chicken is not only mind-blowingly tender and juicy, it's also totally pasteurized. Why? As soon as the center of a chicken reaches 165°F, 100 percent of *Salmonella* is killed immediately. At 160°F, it takes 14 seconds to kill the *Salmonella*. At 155°F, it takes 50 seconds. When the temperature is brought down to 150°F, the pathogen is killed in 3 minutes. So by adding time, the lower temperature becomes safe.

WHY YOU SHOULD SEAR YOUR MEAT AFTER SOUS VIDE

If you plan to sous vide your meat at a temperature that's lower than 130°F, searing it before sous vide cooking can help kill any bacteria on the surface. But even at higher sous vide temperatures, searing has its benefits.

Searing meat after sous vide cooking is not mandatory, but straight out of a water bath its appearance may be unappetizing. A quick, hot sear will give it a beautifully browned look (thanks to the Maillard reaction, which is a chemical reaction between protein and reducing sugars that gives browned food its distinctive flavor) and will also produce an amazing crust.

USE VERY FRESH INGREDIENTS

The fresher your ingredients are, the better your food tastes. This is especially important with sous vide cooking, where the natural flavor of food is amplified, for better or for worse (i.e. any off flavors from spoilage will also be amplified).

Although it's not recommended to cook sous vide at lower than 130°F for safety reasons, some fish—namely salmon, tuna, and arctic char—are best cooked medium-rare to rare. A lower temperature between 110°F to 122°F can produce the best result. It's extra important to use only very fresh fish for sous vide to bring out the natural flavors. Please remember, however, that raw or undercooked food should not be served to children, the elderly, expectant mothers, and those with compromised immune systems.

NECESSARY GEAR

Aside from the obvious piece of equipment—a sous vide machine—you don't need a lot of gear to make restaurant-quality, delicious sous vide food. Here are the bare necessities.

Immersion Circulator. There are a few sous vide machines that are manufactured particularly for the home kitchen, and they range in cost from $100 to $400. The machines usually come with an app so that you can control them on your smartphone! The most common ones are the Anova Precision Cooker and Breville's Joule Sous Vide. I own an Anova Precision Cooker 2014 version, which is what I used to develop all the recipes in this book. The newer 2019 version is a lot smaller and more powerful, with a very sleek design. While I don't have a Joule because its voltage (120V) doesn't work in Hong Kong (220V), reviews are positive and indicate that people like the size and design.

Large Stockpot or Dutch Oven. In terms of size, as long as your pot can hold enough water that the water line is above the minimal water line on your immersion circulator and you can fully immerse your food when you place it in the water bath, you are in business.

Plastic Bags. Since you'll be cooking in plastic bags, you need to use high-quality, sturdy bags that can handle sub-boiling temperatures for a long period of time. Ziploc brand freezer bags are some of the safest plastic bags to use for sous vide cooking. If you're using a vacuum sealer, you'll need bags designed for your machine. If you're planning to cook above 158°F, however, use sous vide bags and a vacuum sealer. For more on bags, see "What About All That Plastic?" (page 7) and "Sous Vide Bag 101" (page 8).

Cooking Clips. Large binder clips from a stationery store work just fine. Clips keep your bags, especially zip-top bags, from floating. They keep the seal of the bags above the water line and keep the bags from moving around too much.

Trivet, Potholder, or Heatproof Mat. Whether you use a stockpot or sous vide container, the vessel can get quite hot during cooking, so it's good to protect your counter by putting your vessel on one of these protective surfaces.

Skillet. Sous vide food right out of a water bath tastes amazing, but it sometimes doesn't look very appetizing, particularly meats. The easiest way to finish sous vide food is to give it a quick sear on the stove using a flat-bottom skillet, like a nice cast-iron skillet.

NICE-TO-HAVE GEAR

These items, while not essential for success, will help make sous vide cooking easier and more enjoyable.

Sous Vide Container. It's essentially a plastic bin that's heat-resistant and safe to store food in. Cambro is one of the best-known brands and makes containers in different sizes, so while the biggest pot you have might not be able to handle a full rack of ribs, their large container can. Some sous vide machine manufacturers also make sous vide containers that are designed specifically for their sous vide machines.

Reusable Sous Vide Bags. There are two types of reusable sous vide bags: plastic and silicone.

- *Plastic:* The reusable plastic sous vide bags are thicker than Ziploc bags, so you don't have to worry about potential leakage while cooking. They are usually sold in a kit with sealing clips, cooking clips, and a hand pump for you to manually remove air from the bags. I wouldn't recommend reusing bags after cooking meat.

- *Silicone:* The silicone sous vide bags (namely Stasher) are dishwasher-safe and can reportedly be reused more than 3,000 times. They are more expensive but it's a much longer-term investment.

Vacuum Sealer. You can cook most foods perfectly well without a vacuum sealer, but this is the quickest and most convenient way to completely remove air from a sous vide bag. A vacuum sealer sucks out the air and melts the top of the bag together so the food will be protected. Models range in price from $40 to $100.

Hand Torch. A hand torch allows you to sear your sous vide dishes more quickly than a skillet and without worrying about overcooking the center of your dish. There are many hand torch models on Amazon, ranging from $15 to $20, but the most highly regarded one is the Bernzomatic TS8000 (about $40). With a highly recommended Searzall attachment from Booker and Dax, it brings the total cost to a little over $100.

Small Jars. If you wish to use your sous vide machine to make yogurt, soufflés, crème brûlée, or the best egg bites on the planet, small canning jars will come in handy. You can easily find them on Amazon. In order to use small jars for sous vide, you need to twist the lids until "fingertip tight," meaning just barely closed and still possible to open with your fingertips. To close the jars well, place the lid on the jar, then twist the band to tighten using just your fingertips. When you begin to feel resistance, twist once in the opposite direction, then once more in the original direction to tighten.

Sous Vide Silicone Lid. When you use a stockpot as the cooking vessel to sous vide in, you can't use the pot lid to prevent water from evaporating. You can certainly use plastic wrap, but a sous vide silicone lid is more convenient and does a better job. These cost around $10.

WHAT ABOUT ALL THAT PLASTIC?

Yes, it is safe to cook in plastic bags. Nearly all sous vide bags and name-brand storage bags, like Ziploc, are BPA-free and made from the safest plastics. When choosing your bags for sous vide, it's safer to go for name-brands and avoid products using plasticizing additives such as BPA and phthalates. Under high heat and acidic conditions, these additives will release harmful chemicals into your food.

Concerned about our environment? Use reusable sous vide bags. See "Nice-to-Have Gear" on page 6 for recommendations.

SOUS VIDE BAG 101

Choosing the right bag, placing your food in it properly, and sealing it correctly is an essential process for safety and quality.

CHOOSING A BAG

Most of the recipes in this book work with both zip-top and sous vide bags (also known as vacuum-sealed bags). When this is the case (which is to say, in most of the recipes), I refer to the bags as "cooking bags," giving you the option of using whatever you have handy. In the recipes that require using one or the other, I specify which sort of bag and sealing method to use. Here are some general rules of thumb regarding bags.

ZIP-TOP BAGS ARE GOOD FOR . . .

- Any sort of dense food, particularly ones that come in smaller pieces, like steak, fish, pork chops, tenderloins, chicken breasts, burgers, etc.

- Grains and sides, like polenta and millet.

- Foods that cook for a shorter amount of time (less than 6 hours).

- Foods that cook at temperatures below 158°F. The seams of a zip-top bag sometimes fail when exposed to high temperatures, causing your food to leak into the water in the sous vide bath. Nobody wants that.

- Cooking food with a lot of liquid, like a meat with marinade or a stew. Vacuum-sealing a bag with a lot of moisture can be tricky, making zip-top bags the easier alternative.

SOUS VIDE BAGS ARE GOOD FOR . . .

- Cooking at temperatures above 158°F or for longer than 6 hours, because these bags are sturdier.

- Vegetables. Vacuum sealing vegetables is the only way to guarantee the best results, because when cooking at high temperatures (which is required for most vegetables), the air in your zip-top bag can expand and steam out, affecting the overall cooking of your vegetables. Vacuum sealing removes the air, preventing floating or overheating and resulting in the best vegetables you'll ever have.

- Meal prepping. When the bags are properly vacuum-sealed, sous vide cooking pasteurizes vegetables and meat, so you can store them in the fridge for weeks at a time or freeze them for months without freezer burn.

- Large cuts of meat. Using a hand-held vacuum sealer, an oversize bag, and a large container allows you to cook brisket, whole turkeys, and other centerpiece dishes.

A few more things to note: You don't necessarily need a vacuum sealer to use a sous vide bag. Simply remove the air with the water displacement method on page 10, drape the opening of the bag over the side of your cooking vessel, and clip it there or secure it with the lid. Also, the rules I just shared are not hard and fast. For example, you can double up on zip-top bags if you are cooking above 158°F or for a longer amount of time, as a type of insurance.

HOW TO PLACE YOUR FOOD IN A BAG

This isn't rocket science, but a few tips will make the process easier, cleaner, and safer.

1. **Fold the top of your bag before adding food.** Always fold at least one-third of the top of the bag outward over itself to form a hem. This will prevent any seasonings or marinade from interfering with the seal or providing vectors for contamination.

2. **Add prepared food to the bag.** Keep food in a single layer where possible. When cooking delicate proteins, leave space between pieces to prevent fillets from sticking to each other or simply use multiple bags. Don't overcrowd the bag.

3. **Add oil when cooking protein.** Add oil when cooking delicate proteins or small pieces of food to prevent food from getting stuck in the seams of the bag.

4. **Add herbs and aromatics.** For delicate proteins, especially fish, place herbs and aromatics on the skin side so they don't "stamp" your food after cooking.

SEALING THE BAG

Ready to seal your bag? There are different ways to remove air from a bag and seal it for sous vide. Removing all the air from a cooking bag before dropping it into the water bath prevents the bag from floating. If the bag is floating, the food is not completely submerged, which prevents it from cooking evenly.

WITHOUT A VACUUM SEALER OR HAND PUMP

If you don't have a vacuum sealer or hand pump, the water displacement method is an easy and effective way to remove most of the air from your zip-top or sous vide bag.

1. After placing your seasoned food in the bag, zip up 80 percent of the top of the bag, leaving the corner unzipped.

2. Fill up a pot or a container with enough water to fully submerge the bag of food (you can use the same water you're going to cook in before you heat it, or submerge the bag after the water bath is heated if you are cooking at a low temperature). Slowly push the bag into the water, gently squeezing out any air surrounding the food, especially the air bubbles trapped around the food. The pressure of the water will force the air out of the bag as you progressively submerge the bag.

3. Once the water level is just below the zip-line, fully seal the bag.

WITH A HAND PUMP

When you use a hand pump to vacuum seal your reusable sous vide bags, make sure to avoid getting anything on the air valve. You can easily do this by folding the top of the bag all the way down below the air valve before placing your food in. Then unfold and zip up the bag with a clipping seal. Place the pump right on the air valve and suction the air out. Now it's ready for a swim in the water bath.

WITH A VACUUM SEALER

Using a vacuum sealer makes it super easy to batch cook and keeps your food safe and sanitary.

Check your vacuum-sealing machine manufacturer's instructions, but generally, it entails placing the open edge of your food-filled bag into the machine, closing and locking the lid, and pressing the "vacuum" button. This also heat-seals the edge of the bag.

COOKING AND SEARING

The actual cooking is the best part of the whole process: Drop the food in the pre-heated water bath and walk away! But before you do:

- Wait for the water to come to the temperature you want your food to cook at before placing the food in the water bath.

- Secure your bag by clipping it on the side of your pot or sous vide container.

- If your bag floats, use a sous vide rack or weigh it down with a mug, water glass, or a heavy ceramic plate or bowl. Fill these containers with water from the water bath so they sink.

- For long cooking sessions, cover your cooking vessel to avoid water evaporating. You can use plastic wrap, a sous vide silicone lid, or top off your water bath with ping pong balls, which act as an insulator, trapping moisture and heat in the cooking vessel.

The final step of the sous vide cooking process is usually searing, especially for meat. There are various ways to sear a piece of meat: in a hot skillet, under a broiler, on a grill, or using a hand torch. When pan searing in particular (but also with the other methods), keep in mind the following.

1. **Pat your food dry with paper towels as much as possible.** If there's water on it, your food will steam, not sear.

2. **Heat up your pan so it is extremely hot.** If a drop of water sizzles, jumps around, and disappears, your pan is ready.

3. **Add oil.** Use avocado or vegetable oil to coat your pan.

4. **Sear on each side.** If your pan is hot enough, 45 to 90 seconds per side should work.

5. **Don't overcrowd the pan.** Searing will release more juices. Leave enough room between pieces to allow the juice to evaporate.

When searing your meat under a broiler, adjust the top oven rack to 4 to 6 inches below the heat source, set it to HIGH, and let it preheat for a few minutes. You'll need to keep an eye on your food because this method can cook your protein *very* quickly.

If you fancy using a hand torch, make sure to use a dark blue flame to sear your food. Yellow flame carries not fully combusted hydrocarbons from the fuel, which can end up on your food, creating an "off" taste.

MAKING SOUS VIDE WORK FOR YOU

One of the greatest things about sous vide, aside from consistently fantastic results, is that you can make it work around your schedule.

PREP IN ADVANCE

The majority of the hands-on time when it comes to sous vide cooking is spent cutting/trimming, seasoning, and bagging the food. Once you finish prepping the food bags, you don't necessarily have to sous vide right away. Once the food is sealed in a bag, it can be refrigerated for up to 24 hours or frozen until you are ready to cook.

For example, you can prepare a whole prime rib the night before and leave it in the fridge. Drop the bag directly in the preheated water bath the next morning and let it cook for 8 hours. It will be ready by the time you come home from work. All you need to do is sear it before serving. Or bag and label some seasoned chicken breasts with different flavors (salt and pepper, lemon pepper, Cajun, etc.), then freeze them for later. When ready to cook, you can defrost them in the fridge before you sous vide or drop the frozen bag directly in the preheated water bath. Just add a minimum of 30 minutes onto the cooking time if cooking directly from the freezer.

If you're seasoning meat ahead of time, go easy on the salt, because too much salt will cure your meat—unless that's the result you're looking for, in which case, go for it! Also, do not add lemon or lime slices in the bag because the acid from the citrus will "cook" your meat or fish in your fridge or freezer.

COOK IN ADVANCE

You can also sous vide your food, chill the leftovers, store them in the fridge or freezer, then reheat them when you are ready to enjoy them. I have included tips throughout the recipes for how and when to do this. Note that sous vide food needs to be rapidly chilled in an ice bath before refrigerating, which will stave off the harmful bacteria that thrive between 40°F to 140°F.

Once your food is thoroughly chilled, you can store it in the fridge for up to 2 days in its cooking bag (or longer, if you have unopened, vacuum-sealed bags). If you don't plan on consuming it within 48 hours, freeze it.

The easiest and most precise way to reheat pre-cooked sous vide food is to use your sous vide machine, but it does take a while. Set the temperature at or

1 to 2 degrees below the original cooking temperature, so it won't get overcooked, and reheat it for the original cook time.

The reheating time for frozen foods depends on the size and shape of the dish. For smaller frozen portions, generally speaking, add 15 minutes to 30 minutes more to the reheating time.

Of course, you could also just nuke your frozen food, pop it in a saucepan, or heat in the oven, but you won't get the same perfect degree of doneness—it's up to you.

ROUND OUT YOUR MEAL

Maximize your sous vide machine with these ideas.

- **Stagger cooking your meat and vegetables.** You don't want to cook meat and vegetables at the same temperature, but what you can do is to cook vegetables at a high temperature first, then reset your sous vide to a lower temperature for your meat. In order to bring down the temperature faster, scoop out a few cups of water and add several cups of ice to the water bath. While your meat cooks, you can return the cooked vegetables to the water to reheat before serving.

- **Cook an entire meal at the same temperature.** There are instances where this works. For instance, you can sous vide eggs and hollandaise sauce at the same temperature for about the same amount of time. While you wait, butter up some English muffins and you've got some Stupidly Simple Eggs Benedict (page 18).

- **Plan to group like foods.** Prepare several bags of different types of vegetables that you'll use for days and cook them all at once at 183°F for 45 minutes to 1 hour. All red meat (beef and lamb) and even duck breast can cook together (in separate bags) at the same temperature, around 136°F. White meat chicken, turkey, and pork can all cook at 140°F to 146°F for 2 to 2½ hours. Mix and match the proteins and veggies and you've got a delicious variety of meals for days to come.

FREQUENTLY ASKED QUESTIONS

Q: My zip-top bag broke in the water bath! What now?
A: Take it out of the water bath and place it in a second zip-top bag. If the water bath is heavily affected by the leak, rinse your cooking vessel and bring a new water bath to the desired temperature. Gently place the double-bagged food back in the bath using the water displacement method.

Q: Should I do anything with the cooking liquid in the bag after cooking?
A: The cooking liquid in the bag after sous vide cooking is liquid gold, in my opinion, because it contains pure juice from the food. It's both nutritious and flavorful. You can use it for a pan sauce, cook vegetables with it, or add it to soups.

Q: Can I add alcohol to flavor food in my sous vide bag?
A: Alcohol is not optimal in sous vide bags with food because it does not evaporate like it would in other methods of cooking, so the flavors do not blend as well. Cook any alcohol that you intend to use with sous vide food before or after the sous vide process.

Q: Is cooking sous vide healthy? Why?
A: Nothing is lost in the sous vide process, which is your gain. Sous vide foods retain more nutrients, vitamins, and minerals than foods cooked using traditional methods because those methods use higher temperatures that can damage nutrients.

Q: I am concerned about sous vide cooking raw garlic. Is it safe?
A: The risk of getting botulism when adding raw garlic in your sous vide bag is very small, as long as you follow the best practices mentioned in "How to Sous Vide Safely" (page 3). Still, because sous vide uses low temperatures, raw garlic does not actually get cooked through, so it could leave a harsh, acrid flavor in your food. If you don't want to risk it, try these alternatives: Use garlic powder, cook garlic before adding it to the bag, add garlic to the post–sous vide searing process, or use garlic in the toppings or in a sauce instead.

ABOUT THE RECIPES

The book is intended to cover almost anything you'd want to make with a sous vide machine, ranging from your morning bacon to an evening cocktail, and it takes flavor inspiration from America to the farthest reaches of the globe. But I am not into sous vide just for the sake of sous vide—the recipes included in this book are foods that the sous vide does best, with the exception of the last chapter, which includes rubs and sauces that make your sous vide goodies even more delicious.

All ingredients used in the recipes are very accessible. You should be able to find them in any well-stocked grocery store. Most of the recipes provide a cooking-time range for flexibility (though if a recipe doesn't have a range, you should pull the food out right at that time, such as with eggs).

I mentioned this earlier, but most of these recipes will work with either kind of bag, either a zip-top or a vacuum-sealed bag. On rare occasions, you might have to use one type or another. In these recipes, I specify a type of bag and a sealing method.

Once you've tried all the recipes in this book, there are cooking charts (page 236) that will allow you to start creating your own restaurant-quality gourmet food at home. Because once you start sous viding, you won't be able to stop!

Stupidly Simple Eggs Benedict, page 18

CHAPTER 2

EGGS AND DAIRY

STUPIDLY SIMPLE EGGS BENEDICT

SERVES 6 | **PREP TIME:** 10 minutes | **COOK TIME:** 1 to 2 hours | **FINISHING TIME:** 20 minutes | **SOUS VIDE TEMPERATURE:** 147°F | **FAMILY FRIENDLY, PARTY READY**

Most of us find ourselves longing for that weekend brunch classic eggs Benedict by Wednesday. Sous vide makes this typically fussy recipe a no-brainer. You need a two-hour head start, but there's little to do while the soft-cooked eggs and smooth, lemony sauce are simmering to perfection in your sous vide.

1 recipe Classic Hollandaise Sauce (page 23)	6 English muffins, split, toasted, and buttered	12 ounces ham, thinly sliced, or as needed
12 large eggs	Butter, for serving	Minced fresh dill, for serving

1. Preheat the water bath to 147°F.

2. Prepare the hollandaise sauce. You can cook the sauce simultaneously with the eggs.

3. Lower the eggs in their shells gently into the water bath. (You may put all eggs into a zip-top bag first, so it's easy to pull them out of the water bath once they are done.) They can cook for the same amount of time and at the same temperature as the sauce, at 147°F for 1 to 2 hours.

4. Lay the English muffins, buttered and toasted sides up, on a baking sheet. On top of each, form a nest with the thinly sliced ham. Keep the muffins and ham warm in a 200°F oven.

5. About 15 minutes before serving, remove the hollandaise sauce from the water bath. Transfer the sauce to a blender or food processor and blend at medium speed until it's velvety smooth.

6. Plate all the muffin halves, two on each plate.

7. Pull the eggs from the sous vide and place them in a bowl; rest a slotted spoon in another bowl nearby. Carefully crack each egg over the slotted spoon, allowing any runny egg white to drain into the bowl. Place each egg on an English muffin.

8. Pour the hollandaise from the blender onto each muffin. Go slowly so you have enough for all six servings. Garnish with minced dill and serve.

CHANGE IT UP: What's that? Your vegetarian, paleo, kosher, or halal brunch-mates require some substitutions? Not a problem! Replace the ham with avocado, smoked salmon, or even crabmeat. How about bagels or sliced ciabatta (or sautéed spinach) in lieu of the English muffins? If there's no dill on hand, top your masterpiece with chives or paprika.

CHILAQUILES EGGS BENEDICT

SERVES 4 to 6 | **PREP TIME:** 30 minutes | **COOK TIME:** 1 to 2 hours | **FINISHING TIME:** 20 minutes |
SOUS VIDE TEMPERATURE: 147°F | **FAMILY FRIENDLY, PARTY READY**

I've taken the classic eggs Benedict recipe and given it a massive, Mexican-inspired kick in the English muffins. The chilaquiles base could be a meal in itself, but top it with poached eggs, barbacoa beef, and chile hollandaise from your sous vide, and you've got a ready-made party. For a meat-free version, skip the beef. This recipe is rich, so you might be able to serve more people depending on how hungry your guests are.

1 recipe Green Chile
  Hollandaise Sauce
  (page 24)
8 large eggs
2 (14.5-ounce) cans
  fire-roasted diced
  tomatoes with green chiles

Nonstick cooking spray, for
  greasing the pan
24 (6-inch) corn tortillas
2 cups Mexican
  four-cheese blend
4 cups Beef Barbacoa
  (page 174), **warmed**

Freshly ground black pepper
Chopped parsley or cilantro,
  for serving
Pico de gallo, for serving

1. Preheat the water bath to 147°F.

2. Prepare the hollandaise sauce. You can cook the sauce simultaneously with the eggs.

3. While the hollandaise is cooking, lower the eggs in their shells gently into the water bath. (You can put the eggs into a zip-top bag first, so it's easy to pull them out of the water bath once they are done.) They can cook for the same amount of time (1 to 2 hours) and at the same temperature as the hollandaise.

4. To make the chilaquiles base, preheat the oven to 400°F.

5. In a food processor, pulse the diced tomatoes a few times until the tomatoes are slightly pureed but still a bit chunky.

6. Spray a rimmed 18-by-13-inch baking sheet with nonstick cooking spray and line it with 6 corn tortillas, overlapping them slightly so there are no gaps.

7. Spread ¼ cup tomatoes on the tortillas and add ½ cup cheese. Repeat, layering the tortillas, tomatoes, and cheese four times.

8. Bake for 10 minutes, or until the cheese has completely melted. Let cool slightly.

9. Cut the chilaquiles base into eight 4-inch squares with a knife. Prepare four serving plates and place one to two pieces of the base on each plate.

10. To assemble, top each base with ½ cup warmed beef barbacoa, forming a nest for the eggs.

11. Pull the eggs from the sous vide and place them in a bowl; rest a slotted spoon in another bowl nearby. Carefully crack each egg over the slotted spoon, allowing any still-runny egg white to drain into the bowl. Place one egg on each waiting nest of beef.

12. Remove the bag containing the hollandaise from the sous vide; remove and discard the serrano chile. Transfer the sauce to a blender or food processor and blend at medium speed until it's smooth.

13. Drizzle the hollandaise over the eggs.

14. Season each serving with freshly ground black pepper and chopped fresh parsley or cilantro. Serve with your favorite pico de gallo.

EGGS FLORENTINE

SERVES 4 | **PREP TIME:** 15 minutes | **COOK TIME:** 1 to 2 hours | **FINISHING TIME:** 20 minutes | **SOUS VIDE TEMPERATURE:** 147°F | **FAMILY FRIENDLY, PARTY READY**

In the 16th century, Catherine de Medici brought her love of spinach from Florence, Italy, to France, and since then, any dish served à la Florentine will feature spinach in the ingredient list. This is a brunch classic, a close cousin to eggs Benedict but with a bed of iron-rich greenery where the ham or Canadian bacon would be.

1 recipe Classic Hollandaise Sauce (page 23)

8 large eggs

1 tablespoon butter, plus more for serving

1 cup thinly sliced button mushrooms

½ pound (4 cups) baby spinach

Kosher salt

4 English muffins, split, toasted, and buttered

Freshly ground black pepper

Chopped chives, for garnish

1. Preheat the water bath to 147°F.

2. Prepare the hollandaise sauce. You can make the sauce simultaneously with the eggs.

3. Once you start the hollandaise cooking, lower 8 eggs in their shells gently into the water bath. They can cook for the same amount of time (1 to 2 hours) and at the same temperature as the sauce.

4. In a skillet over medium heat, melt 1 tablespoon butter and sauté the sliced mushrooms until lightly browned, about 5 minutes. Add the spinach and season with salt. Cook, stirring, for 1 to 2 minutes. Remove the skillet from the heat.

5. About 15 minutes before serving, remove the hollandaise sauce from the water bath. Transfer the sauce to a blender or food processor and blend at medium speed until it's smooth.

6. Plate the muffin halves, two on each plate. Form a nest of sautéed spinach and mushrooms on each half, with an indentation in the center to hold the egg.

7. Pull the eggs from the sous vide and place them in a bowl; rest a slotted spoon in another bowl nearby. Carefully crack each egg over the slotted spoon, allowing any still-runny egg white to drain into the bowl. Place an egg on each waiting nest of spinach.

8. Pour the hollandaise over each muffin. Season with salt and pepper to taste and garnish with chives.

CLASSIC HOLLANDAISE SAUCE

MAKES about 1 cup (Serves 4 to 6) | **PREP TIME:** 5 minutes | **COOK TIME:** 1 to 2 hours |
FINISHING TIME: 5 minutes | **SOUS VIDE TEMPERATURE:** 147°F | **FAMILY FRIENDLY, PARTY READY, QUICK PREP**

This buttery, lemony concoction is one of the five essential sauces in French cuisine, but you don't need to enroll in culinary school to master it, especially when you have a sous vide machine in your kitchen. This simple recipe will reliably produce hollandaise that the fussiest Parisian saucier chef would be proud of.

10 tablespoons unsalted butter	4 tablespoons water	½ teaspoon kosher salt
3 large egg yolks	1 tablespoon freshly squeezed lemon juice	⅛ teaspoon cayenne pepper (optional)

1. Preheat the water bath to 147°F.

2. In a zip-top bag, combine the butter, egg yolks, water, lemon juice, salt, and cayenne (if using). Lower the bag into the water bath, using the water displacement method to seal it. Don't worry about mixing the ingredients at this stage, as that will come later.

3. Let the hollandaise cook at 147°F for 1 to 2 hours. The longer it cooks, the thicker it will get.

4. Remove the hollandaise sauce from the water bath. If it looks separated and oily at this point, don't panic. Transfer it to a blender or food processor and blend at medium speed until it's silky smooth.

CHANGE IT UP: Hollandaise is, of course, the crowning glory of eggs Benedict, but don't stop there! Drizzle it over steamed asparagus or broccoli, poached fish, roasted potatoes, crepes, or grilled seafood. For some variety, you might replace the lemon juice with lime juice and zest or, if you're feeling really posh, 8 saffron threads steeped in 2 tablespoons orange juice.

GREEN CHILE HOLLANDAISE SAUCE

MAKES about 1 cup (Serves 4 to 6) | **PREP TIME:** 5 minutes | **COOK TIME:** 1 to 2 hours | **FINISHING TIME:** 5 minutes | **SOUS VIDE TEMPERATURE:** 147°F | **FAMILY FRIENDLY, PARTY READY, QUICK PREP**

What happens when you introduce one of Mexico's most popular chiles to a classic French sauce? Fusion cuisine at its finest. Adding a single serrano pepper to the standard hollandaise recipe gives the creamy, lemony sauce an eye-opening kick. This sauce is the ideal topping for Chilaquiles Eggs Benedict (page 20).

10 tablespoons unsalted butter

3 large egg yolks

4 tablespoons water

1 tablespoon freshly squeezed lemon juice

½ teaspoon kosher salt

1 or 2 fresh serrano or jalapeño peppers, top trimmed

1. Preheat the water bath to 147°F.

2. In a zip-top bag, combine the butter, egg yolks, water, lemon juice, salt, and the chile pepper. Lower the bag into the bath using the water displacement method. You don't need to mix the ingredients at this point.

3. Let the hollandaise cook at 147°F for 1 to 2 hours. (The longer it cooks, the thicker it will be.)

4. Remove the sauce from the water bath. Fish out the pepper and discard it. Transfer the sauce to a blender or food processor and blend at medium speed until it's velvety smooth.

CHANGE IT UP: If you don't have fresh peppers on hand, no worries! You can use 1 to 2 tablespoons canned green chiles. In this case, blend the chiles with the sauce in the final step.

TUNA DEVILED EGGS

MAKES 24 deviled eggs | **PREP TIME:** 5 minutes | **COOK TIME:** 20 minutes | **FINISHING TIME:** 1 hour 30 minutes | **SOUS VIDE TEMPERATURE:** 194°F | **FAMILY FRIENDLY, PARTY READY**

These Tuna Deviled Eggs feature the creamy yolks from sous vide eggs. Originating in ancient Rome, these eggs got their name from their devilishly hot additions. Garnished with smoked paprika and fresh dill, they make a deliciously fun appetizer.

12 large eggs	1 (7-ounce) can solid white	Kosher salt
½ cup mayonnaise	albacore tuna, drained	Freshly ground black pepper
1 tablespoon Dijon mustard	4 scallions, green parts only,	Smoked paprika, for garnish
1 tablespoon horseradish	finely chopped	Fresh dill, for garnish

1. Preheat the water bath to 194°F.

2. Once the water is ready, gently and slowly lower the eggs into the water bath. Set a timer for 20 minutes.

3. In a large bowl, prepare an ice bath with a 50/50 mixture of cold water and ice cubes. When the timer goes off, immediately transfer the cooked eggs to the ice bath and allow them to chill thoroughly, about 30 minutes.

4. Remove one egg from the ice bath and crack the shell against your work surface. Roll it gently back and forth a couple times to crack the whole shell. Drop the egg carefully back into the water, and let it sit for a few seconds. Pick it up, and gently remove the shell. Repeat with the remaining eggs.

5. Carefully cut through the middle vertically, creating two equal halves (24 halves total).

6. Transfer the egg yolks to a medium mixing bowl. Set the egg whites aside. Mash the egg yolks with the back of a spoon until smooth.

7. Add the mayonnaise, Dijon mustard, and horseradish. Mix until smooth. Stir in the tuna and scallions. Break the tuna into small pieces while mixing. Season with salt and pepper to taste. (You can also use a food processor to produce a smooth texture. I like a bit of chunkiness in my filling.)

8. Transfer the mixture to a piping bag or a zip-top bag (cut off one corner of the bag) and pipe the mixture into the egg white halves. Chill for 30 minutes.

9. Sprinkle the eggs with paprika and garnish with dill to serve.

GUACAMOLE DEVILED EGGS WITH BACON

MAKES: 24 deviled eggs | **PREP TIME:** 5 minutes | **COOK TIME:** 20 minutes | **FINISHING TIME:** 50 minutes | **SOUS VIDE TEMPERATURE:** 194°F | **FAMILY FRIENDLY, PARTY READY**

Avocado is everywhere these days, so this deviled egg recipe is right on trend. Mashed avocado, chiles, scallions, and cilantro make for a creamy, verdant topping for your perfectly hard-boiled sous vide eggs. (It's also a healthy change from the usual mayo-mustard formula.) Dr. Seuss would give this green egg his stamp of approval.

12 large eggs

2 large ripe avocados

2 tablespoons freshly squeezed lime juice or lemon juice

1 teaspoon kosher salt

2 tablespoons sour cream (optional)

2 tablespoons fresh cilantro, chopped, plus a few leaves for garnish

1 serrano pepper or habañero pepper, seeded and finely minced

2 tablespoons chopped chives

1½ cups crisply cooked diced bacon (such as Perfect Bacon, page 134), crumbled

1. Preheat the water bath to 194°F.

2. Once the water is ready, slowly lower the eggs in their shells into the water bath. (You can put the eggs into a zip-top bag first, so it's easy to pull them out of the water bath once they are done.) Set the timer for 20 minutes. In a large bowl, prepare an ice-water bath with a 50/50 mixture of cold water and ice cubes.

3. When the timer goes off, immediately transfer the cooked eggs to the ice-water bath and allow them to chill thoroughly, about 30 minutes.

4. Remove one egg from the ice bath and crack the shell against your work surface. Roll it gently back and forth a couple times to crack the whole shell. Drop the egg carefully back into the water, and let it sit for a few seconds. Pick it up, and gently remove the shell. Repeat with the remaining eggs.

5. Carefully cut through the middle vertically, creating two equal halves (24 halves total). Place the halves on a serving platter and scoop out the cooked yolks.

6. Halve the avocados, remove the pits, and scoop the flesh into a large mixing bowl. Mash it with a fork. Add 6 to 8 of the cooked egg yolks to the avocado. You can keep the remaining yolks for another use. Stir in the lime juice, salt, and sour cream (if using). Add the cilantro, chile pepper, and chives and mix until well combined.

7. Once the filling is ready, transfer it to a piping bag or a zip-top bag (cut off one corner of the bag) and pipe the mixture into the egg white halves. Transfer the eggs to the fridge to chill.

8. Top each egg with a sprinkle of crispy bacon bits and garnish with a sprig of fresh cilantro.

MAKE-AHEAD MAGIC: Storing hard-boiled eggs for a few days is no problem, but guacamole has an unfortunate tendency to turn brown when exposed to air. Here's the answer: Prepare the deviled eggs following steps 1 through 6 of the recipe. Place the filling into a sous vide bag and vacuum seal it, or use a freezer bag and squeeze the air out as much as possible. You can refrigerate the filling for a couple of days without it going brown. When it's time to serve, cut a corner from the sous vide bag and squeeze the guacamole into the waiting egg white halves. If you don't plan to serve them straightaway, cover the serving dish snugly with plastic wrap.

SIMPLE EGG SALAD

SERVES 4 | **PREP TIME:** 10 minutes | **COOK TIME:** 20 minutes | **FINISHING TIME:** 40 minutes | **SOUS VIDE TEMPERATURE:** 194°F | **FAMILY FRIENDLY**

Consistent results are one of sous vide's biggest advantages and hard-boiled eggs are a great example, coming out with creamy yolks, tender-but-firm whites, and no discoloration every single time. Fresh herbs bring this egg salad to life; check out the tips for variations galore.

8 large eggs

¼ cup mayonnaise

1 teaspoon Dijon mustard

¼ cup chopped fresh dill

2 tablespoons minced fresh chives

½ teaspoon kosher salt

¼ teaspoon freshly ground black pepper

1. Preheat the water bath to 194°F.

2. Slowly lower the eggs in their shells into the preheated water bath and set a timer for 20 minutes. (You can put the eggs into a zip-top bag first, so it's easy to pull them out of the water bath once they are done.) In a large bowl, prepare an ice-water bath with a 50/50 mixture of cold water and ice cubes.

3. When the timer goes off, immediately transfer the eggs to the ice-water bath and allow them to chill thoroughly, about 30 minutes.

4. Remove one egg from the ice bath and crack the shell against your work surface. Roll it gently back and forth a couple times to crack the whole shell. Drop the egg carefully back into the water, and let it sit for a few seconds. Pick it up, and gently remove the shell. Transfer to a clean plate or bowl. Repeat with the remaining eggs, then chop them.

5. In a mixing bowl, combine the chopped eggs, mayonnaise, mustard, dill, chives, salt, and pepper. Mix well and serve on bread or atop lettuce for a salad.

CHANGE IT UP: These are only a few of the extras that can give a basic egg salad a whole new lease on life: bacon bits, chopped olives or pickles, capers, celery, grated carrot, diced chicken or ham, tuna, or salsa. You might use hummus, plain yogurt, or pesto, either in place of or in addition to the mayo.

DID YOU KNOW? Waiting until your water bath is at full temperature before you lower the eggs into it is the best way to ensure that the eggs will peel easily and cleanly.

CLASSIC COBB SALAD

SERVES 4 to 6 | **PREP TIME:** 30 minutes | **COOK TIME:** 20 minutes | **FINISHING TIME:** 45 minutes | **SOUS VIDE TEMPERATURE:** 194°F | **FAMILY FRIENDLY**

Don't let the lengthy ingredient list of this Hollywood classic scare you off; you likely have everything you need in your kitchen already. And if not, this recipe was born for substitutions. It's essentially one big bowl of colors, textures, and flavors, satisfying and nutritious enough for a whole meal.

4 large eggs

8 slices thick-cut bacon, chopped (such as Perfect Bacon, page 134)

¼ cup apple cider vinegar

2 tablespoons minced shallot (about ½ shallot)

1 tablespoon Dijon mustard

½ teaspoon kosher salt, plus more for seasoning

¼ cup extra-virgin olive oil

Freshly ground black pepper

1½ cups cooked, diced chicken (rotisserie chicken or Perfect Poached Whole Chicken, page 119)

1 large head Bibb lettuce

2 romaine lettuce hearts

2 avocados, peeled, pitted, and diced

2 tomatoes, chopped

4 ounces blue cheese, crumbled

1. Preheat the water bath to 194°F.

2. Once the water is ready, slowly lower the eggs into the water bath. (You can put the eggs into a zip-top bag first, so it's easy to pull them out of the water bath when they are done.) Set the timer for 20 minutes. In a large bowl, prepare an ice-water bath with a 50/50 mixture of cold water and ice cubes. When they're done cooking, transfer the eggs to the ice-water bath and allow them to chill thoroughly, about 30 minutes. Peel the eggs and chop them coarsely.

3. If not using sous vide bacon, cook the bacon in a skillet over medium heat until crisp, then transfer it to paper towels to drain.

4. In a large serving bowl, whisk together the vinegar, shallot, mustard, and ½ teaspoon salt. Whisk in the olive oil in a slow stream, then season the dressing with pepper.

5. In a medium bowl, toss the chicken with 1 tablespoon of the dressing.

6. Tear the Bibb and romaine lettuce leaves and place them in the large serving bowl on top of the dressing. Arrange the bacon, eggs, chicken, avocado, tomatoes, and blue cheese on top of the lettuce. When ready to serve (and after everyone has admired your beautiful salad), toss and season with salt and pepper.

SOUS VIDE EGG BITES, 5 WAYS

MAKES 6 bites | **PREP TIME:** 5 minutes | **COOK TIME:** 25 minutes | **FINISHING TIME:** 10 minutes | **SOUS VIDE TEMPERATURE:** 185°F | **FAMILY FRIENDLY, QUICK PREP**

Heeding customer pleas for a no-carb, keto-friendly breakfast option, Starbucks debuted the Sous Vide Egg Bites, which were a mega-hit, in 2017. Not everyone has a Starbucks nearby, though, or wants to spend nearly $5 on breakfast every day. In just a few minutes on a Sunday, you can create a week's worth of these egg bites, with the exact same texture and whatever ingredients tickle your fancy and at a fraction of the cost. Reheat them gently in the microwave or in a water bath before serving.

FOR ESSENTIAL BITES:

6 large eggs (or 12 large egg whites)

1¼ cups ricotta cheese (such as Sous Vide Ricotta, page 37) or heavy (whipping) cream (ricotta gives a fluffier texture, cream gives a richer texture, or use a combination to achieve the texture you want)

½ teaspoon kosher salt

FOR MONTEREY JAZZ BITES:

6 large eggs (or 12 large egg whites)

½ teaspoon kosher salt

½ cup diced roasted red peppers

½ cup finely chopped spinach

½ cup shredded Monterey Jack cheese

FOR GRUYÈRE AND BACON BITES:

6 large eggs (or 12 large egg whites)

½ teaspoon kosher salt

½ cup cooked, chopped bacon or turkey bacon

½ cup shredded Gruyère cheese

FOR MEDITERRANEAN BITES:

6 large eggs (or 12 large egg whites)

½ teaspoon kosher salt

¼ cup crumbled feta cheese

¼ cup diced sun-dried tomatoes

1 tablespoon chopped fresh basil (or 1 teaspoon dried basil)

FOR CHEDDAR-BROCCOLI BITES:

6 large eggs (or 12 large egg whites)

½ teaspoon kosher salt

½ cup shredded cheddar cheese

¼ cup cooked, chopped broccoli

1. Preheat the water bath to 185°F.

2. Make the egg base by blending the eggs and salt together in a blender or in a bowl with an immersion blender, until smooth (for the Essential Bites, add the ricotta and/or cream at this time).

3. Divide the fillings among six 4-ounce Mason jars and pour the egg mixture over the top, filling them to the bottom notch of the jar opening. Give each a gentle stir and close the jars fingertip-tight.

4. Submerge the jars in the water bath and set the timer for 25 minutes.

5. Once the timer goes off, use tongs to remove the jars from the water bath and let them cool at room temperature for 10 minutes. You may then use a knife to remove the egg cups from the jars or serve them directly in the jars.

MAKE-AHEAD MAGIC: The sous vide process in this recipe pasteurizes these egg bites, so they'll last at least 1 week in the fridge. Grab one on your way out the door in the morning or make a batch or three in advance for your weekend brunch.

SHAKSHUKA WITH SOUS VIDE-POACHED EGGS

SERVES 4 to 6 | **PREP TIME:** 30 minutes | **COOK TIME:** 1 hour | **FINISHING TIME:** 30 minutes | **SOUS VIDE TEMPERATURE:** 147°F | **FAMILY FRIENDLY**

With poached eggs nestled into a bed of spicy, slightly charred vegetables, shakshuka comes all the way from North Africa to your breakfast, lunch, or dinner table. Cooking shakshuka the traditional way may result in overcooked, rubbery eggs or undercooked and runny ones. Sous vide to the rescue: Make your sauce in advance, sous vide the eggs, and enjoy with your guests.

6 large eggs

3 tablespoons extra-virgin olive oil

1 medium onion, sliced

1 large red bell pepper, seeded and thinly sliced

1 fresh chile pepper, such as serrano or jalapeño, seeded and thinly sliced

2 or 3 garlic cloves, thinly sliced

1½ tablespoons smoked or sweet paprika

2 teaspoons ground cumin

1 (28-ounce) can whole peeled tomatoes

Kosher salt

Freshly ground black pepper

⅓ cup minced cilantro, parsley, or a mix, divided

Sliced, oil-cured black olives, for topping (optional)

Feta cheese, for topping (optional)

Artichoke hearts, for topping (optional)

Crusty bread, for serving

1. Preheat the water bath to 147°F. Gently place the eggs in their shells into the water and set the timer for 1 hour. (You can put the eggs into a zip-top bag first, so it's easy to pull them out of the water bath once they are done.)

2. About 30 minutes before the eggs are done, preheat the oven to 425°F.

3. On the stovetop, heat the olive oil in a large, deep, ovenproof skillet over medium-high heat. Add the onion, bell pepper, and chile pepper and spread evenly. Cook, without stirring, until the vegetables on the bottom are deeply browned and beginning to char in spots, about 6 minutes. Stir and allow to char for another 6 minutes. Continue to cook until vegetables are fully softened and slightly charred, another 4 minutes. Add the garlic and cook, stirring, until softened and fragrant, about 30 seconds. Add the paprika and cumin and cook, stirring, until fragrant, about 30 seconds. Immediately add the tomatoes, crushing them with your fingers, and stir to combine. Reduce the heat to barely simmering and simmer for 10 minutes, then season to taste with salt and black pepper. Stir in half of the cilantro.

4. Place the skillet in the oven and bake for 5 minutes.

5. Remove the skillet from the oven and, using a large spoon, make a well near the edge and break a sous vide egg directly into it. The eggs will be like poached eggs, just opaque whites with runny yolks. Spoon a little sauce over the edges of the egg white to partially submerge and contain it, leaving the yolk exposed. Repeat with the remaining eggs, working around the skillet as you go. If you would like the eggs a bit more solid, return the pan to the oven for another 5 minutes.

6. Just before serving, sprinkle with the remaining cilantro and any of the optional toppings. Serve with crusty bread for scooping and dipping.

CHANGE IT UP: Say cheese! Feta, mozzarella, and Parmesan are all great additions. Take a look at your spice rack, too: Caraway and nutmeg will add different highlights to the sauce.

KIMCHI FRIED RICE WITH SOUS VIDE EGGS

SERVES 4 | **PREP TIME:** 5 minutes | **COOK TIME:** 35 minutes | **FINISHING TIME:** 5 minutes |
SOUS VIDE TEMPERATURE: 162°F | **QUICK PREP**

At food stalls all over eastern Asia, plates of fried rice are scooped from smoking woks and then topped with fried eggs. I've tweaked my version to include salty, spicy kimchi and sous vide soft-boiled eggs. You can be stir-frying while the eggs are cooking to that perfect consistency.

4 large eggs

4 tablespoons butter

1 cup diced onions

Kosher salt

2 cups coarsely chopped kimchi, juice squeezed out and reserved

1 cup sliced cremini mushrooms

4 cups cooked rice, chilled

2 tablespoons soy sauce

1 tablespoon sesame oil

Sesame seeds, for garnish

Chopped scallions, for garnish

1. Preheat the water bath to 162°F.

2. Carefully lower the eggs into the bath and set the timer for 35 minutes. (You can put the eggs into a zip-top bag first, so it's easy to pull them out of the water bath once they are done.)

3. In a large sauté pan or cast-iron skillet over medium heat, melt the butter. Add the onions and season with salt. Cook for 2 minutes, stirring often, until the onions are fragrant.

4. Add the kimchi, kimchi juice to taste (I usually like about 6 tablespoons), and mushrooms. Let the vegetables cook until bubbly, about 3 minutes.

5. Stir in the cooked rice. Cook over medium heat until the rice has absorbed the sauce, stirring often, about 5 minutes.

6. Add the soy sauce and sesame oil and reduce the heat to medium-low. Let the rice continue to cook for another 2 minutes undisturbed, until lightly brown.

7. At this point, your sous vide eggs should be done. Divide the kimchi fried rice among 4 plates, and top each serving with a sous vide soft-boiled egg; garnish each plate with sesame seeds and chopped scallions.

CHANGE IT UP: If you're tempted to add some meat to this recipe, go for it! Diced cooked ham, chicken, and turkey are great options. Just add the meat with the rice in step 4.

SOUS VIDE YOGURT

MAKES 3 cups | **PREP TIME:** 20 minutes | **COOK TIME:** 5 to 12 hours | **FINISHING TIME:** 5 minutes |
SOUS VIDE TEMPERATURE: 110°F | **FAMILY FRIENDLY**

Making fresh, creamy yogurt at home is surprisingly easy, especially when you use your sous vide.
Two ingredients, a couple of steps, and you have jars of tangy, creamy, probiotic-rich goodness
in your refrigerator, just waiting to be made into smoothies, salad dressings, and dips, or simply
spooned over fresh fruit and muesli.

1 quart whole milk,
   either cow or goat milk,
   preferably organic

3 tablespoons full-fat yogurt
   with live cultures, or
3 tablespoons powdered
   yogurt culture

1. Preheat the water bath to 110°F.

2. In a saucepan over low heat, warm the milk to 180°F, stirring occasionally to prevent
   scalding.

3. Cool the milk: Either transfer it to a bowl submerged in an ice bath, or allow it to cool
   at room temperature until it reaches 110°F or so. Don't let it fall below 100°F.

4. Mix the yogurt thoroughly into the cooled milk.

5. Pour the mixture into a 1-quart Mason jar or several smaller ones; screw the lid(s)
   on fingertip-tight.

6. Submerge the jar(s) in the water bath and set the timer for 5 hours. You can leave
   the jar(s) in the water bath for up to 12 hours.

7. When finished, allow the yogurt to cool at room temperature, then refrigerate.

8. If you prefer a thicker yogurt, you can strain it. Place the yogurt into a coffee filter
   or cheesecloth over a container, allowing the liquid to drip through the filter. Strain
   it at room temperature for a couple of hours or overnight, until it reaches your
   preferred consistency.

MAKE-AHEAD MAGIC: Your homemade yogurt will last about 1 month in the refrigerator. You'll be tempted to eat every last bit of it, but remember to save 3 tablespoons
to culture your next batch.

SOUS VIDE RICOTTA

MAKES 3½ cups | **PREP TIME:** 5 minutes | **COOK TIME:** 45 minutes | **FINISHING TIME:** 1 hour 30 minutes | **SOUS VIDE TEMPERATURE:** 175°F | **FAMILY FRIENDLY**

When you have homemade ricotta on hand, you'll want to put it in . . . well, everything. Try it served with figs or prosciutto, tucked into lasagna, inside a cannoli, or drizzled with honey for dessert. This is no aged cheese, though; it's best eaten on the day it's made. Fortunately, it's so delicious you won't have trouble gobbling it up.

1 gallon whole milk (not UHT or ultra-pasteurized milk)

Kosher salt

1 cup white vinegar

1. Preheat the water bath to 175°F.

2. Pour the milk through a funnel into a 2-gallon zip-top bag and stir in a pinch of salt (or divide it evenly between two 1-gallon bags).

3. Slowly lower the bag(s) into the water bath and seal using the water displacement method. Set the timer for 30 minutes.

4. Gently open the bag(s) and stir in the vinegar (dividing between the bags, if necessary). Reseal the bag(s) in the same way and cook for another 15 minutes.

5. Line a sieve with cheesecloth and set it over a bowl.

6. Use a slotted spoon to collect the curds that have formed in the bag and transfer them to the sieve.

7. Leave the cheese to drain for 1 hour, then tie up the cheesecloth and squeeze out the remaining liquid. Leave for another 30 to 45 minutes to finish draining.

8. Ricotta is best eaten fresh, but it will keep in the refrigerator for up to 1 week.

CHANGE IT UP: Stir some chopped fresh herbs—such as parsley, basil, thyme, or chives—into the ricotta when it's finished draining.

Feta-Beet Salad with Scallions, page 46

CHAPTER 3

VEGETABLES AND SIDES

SIMPLE POLENTA

SERVES 4 | **PREP TIME:** 5 minutes | **COOK TIME:** 2 hours to 2 hours 30 minutes | **FINISHING TIME:** 5 minutes | **SOUS VIDE TEMPERATURE:** 190°F | **FAMILY FRIENDLY, QUICK PREP**

When you're craving a break from rice and potatoes, try this northern Italian dish made with coarsely ground cornmeal; it's naturally gluten-free and has that definite comfort-food vibe. Although the traditional stovetop cooking method requires constant stirring, this sous vide version is hands-off and worry-free. For a richer polenta, increase the milk-to-water ratio.

1 cup polenta (not instant)	2 cups water	Kosher salt
6 tablespoons butter, melted	8 ounces grated	Freshly ground black pepper
2 cups whole milk	Parmesan cheese	

1. Preheat the water bath to 190°F.

2. In a large bowl, stir together the polenta, butter, milk, water, and Parmesan until well combined. Transfer the mixture into double-bagged gallon-size zip-top bags; slowly lower the bags into the water bath and seal using the water displacement method. You might need to weigh it down to keep the bag submerged during cooking. Cook for 2 hours to 2 hours 30 minutes.

3. Just before serving, remove the bag from the water bath and pour into a large bowl. Give the polenta a good stir and season it with salt and pepper to taste.

CHANGE IT UP: Replace the 2 cups water with chicken stock or bone broth to add nutrients and flavor. Stirring slivered fresh basil leaves into the finished polenta is another way to add some pizzazz.

MAKE-AHEAD MAGIC: If you'd like to prepare the polenta a day or two before serving it, pour the finished polenta into a greased loaf pan, refrigerate until firm, and slice. Reheat by frying the slices in butter on a hot skillet or drizzling them with olive oil and grilling them for a wonderfully crispy finish.

ESSENTIAL MILLET

SERVES 4 | **PREP TIME:** 5 minutes | **COOK TIME:** 30 minutes | **FINISHING TIME:** 5 to 10 minutes |
SOUS VIDE TEMPERATURE: 200°F | **FAMILY FRIENDLY, QUICK PREP**

Although it looks like a seed, millet is a cereal grain native to large swaths of Africa and Asia. There are several varieties with colors including white, yellow, and red. In terms of texture, think couscous but with a slightly nuttier flavor. Gluten-free and rich in calcium, iron, and protein, millet is a versatile alternative to rice and cooks up in a flash in the sous vide.

| 1 cup millet | 1 tablespoon | ¼ teaspoon kosher salt |
| 2 cups water | unsalted butter | |

1. Preheat the water bath to 200°F.

2. Combine the millet, water, butter, and salt in a double-bagged zip-top bag.

3. Slowly lower the bags into the water bath and seal using the water displacement method. You might need to weigh the bag down to keep it submerged during cooking. Set the timer for 30 minutes.

4. When the timer goes off, remove the millet from the water bath. Open a small corner of the bag to let air in, and massage it slightly to fluff up the millet.

5. Let the millet rest for 5 to 10 minutes before serving.

CHANGE IT UP: To amp up the flavor and nutrients, replace the water with vegetable, chicken, or bone broth. If you're aiming for a porridge-like consistency, increase the cooking liquid to 3 cups.

CLASSIC SOUS VIDE RICE

SERVES 4 | **PREP TIME:** 2 minutes | **COOK TIME:** 30 minutes | **FINISHING TIME:** 5 to 10 minutes |
SOUS VIDE TEMPERATURE: 200°F | **FAMILY FRIENDLY, QUICK PREP**

Cooking rice on the stovetop can be an unpredictable exercise; the amount of water must account for evaporation, which can vary depending on the pot, altitude, and cooking temperature. Miscalculate and the rice will be undercooked, mushy, or fused to the bottom of the pot. Not so with sous vide! There's no evaporation, so consistent measurements provide consistent results. If you don't have a rice cooker, put your sous vide to work.

2 cups basmati or jasmine rice (or any long-grain white rice of your choice)	2½ cups water	1 teaspoon sesame oil (optional)

1. Preheat the water bath to 200°F.

2. In a double-bagged gallon-size zip-top bag, combine the rice, water, and oil (if using).

3. Slowly lower the bags into the water bath and seal using the water displacement method. Set the timer for 30 minutes. Leaving the rice in the water for an extra 30 minutes or so after the timer goes off is not a problem. It won't overcook, because there's no excess liquid.

4. When it's done (you'll notice that the bag floats to the top), remove the bag from the water, open a small corner to let air in, and massage it slightly to fluff up the rice.

5. Set the bag aside and let the rice rest for 5 to 10 minutes before serving.

CHANGE IT UP: Replace the water with chicken stock or bone broth to add nutrients and flavor.

MEXICAN STREET CORN

MAKES 4 ears | **PREP TIME:** 5 minutes | **COOK TIME:** 30 minutes | **FINISHING TIME:** 5 minutes |
SOUS VIDE TEMPERATURE: 183°F | **FAMILY FRIENDLY, QUICK PREP**

If you don't have an *elote* vendor on your street—and unless you live in Mexico, you probably
don't—rest easy. You can make your own Mexican Street Corn at home. If your taste buds yearn
for a garlicky twist, be sure to try the aioli variation.

4 ears corn, husks and
  silk removed
Kosher salt
Freshly ground black pepper
2 tablespoons butter
½ cup crumbled Cotija
  cheese, divided

¼ cup mayonnaise
¼ cup sour cream
¼ cup minced fresh
  cilantro, plus more
  for garnish

2 teaspoons lime zest
½ teaspoon ancho
  chili powder
Lime wedges, for serving

1. Preheat the water bath to 183°F.

2. Sprinkle the ears of corn with salt and pepper to taste. Place them in a single layer in
   a cooking bag (if using a zip-top bag, double it up) and add the butter. Vacuum-seal
   the bag or seal it using the water displacement method and place the bag into the
   water bath. You might need to weigh it down to keep it submerged during cooking.
   Set a timer for 30 minutes.

3. Meanwhile, in a small bowl, stir together ⅓ cup Cotija cheese, the mayonnaise, sour
   cream, cilantro, lime zest, and chili powder.

4. The corn will be ready in 30 minutes but can safely remain in the bath for 1 hour.
   After removing the corn from the bag, immediately brush each ear liberally with
   the cheese mixture and transfer to a platter. Garnish each ear with a sprinkle of the
   remaining cheese and more cilantro, then serve with lime wedges.

CHANGE IT UP: For a garlicky, cheesy twist, brush the cooked corn with Aioli (page 234),
sprinkle with paprika and Parmesan cheese, and top it off with some chopped parsley.

HERB BUTTER CORN ON THE COB

MAKES 4 ears | **PREP TIME:** 5 minutes | **COOK TIME:** 30 minutes | **FINISHING TIME:** 5 minutes | **SOUS VIDE TEMPERATURE:** 183°F | **FAMILY FRIENDLY, QUICK PREP**

For 800 kernels of deliciousness, try sous viding your corn on the cob. The sous vide traps the corn's juices, ensuring that it arrives on the plate extra moist and with more intense flavor. Place some of your favorite aromatic fresh herbs into the bag to season the butter.

4 ears corn, husks and
  silk removed
Kosher salt
2 tablespoons butter, sliced,
  plus more for serving

1 fresh herb sprig, such as
  cilantro, thyme, chives, or
  rosemary, plus extra leaves
  for garnish

2 garlic cloves (optional)
Flaky sea salt, for
  serving (optional)

1. Preheat the water bath to 183°F.

2. Sprinkle the ears of corn with kosher salt to taste. Arrange them in a single layer in a cooking bag (if using a zip-top bag, double it up); add the butter, fresh herbs, and garlic (if using). Vacuum-seal the bag or seal using the water displacement method and place the bag into the water bath. You might need to weigh it down to keep the corn submerged during cooking.

3. The corn will be done in 30 minutes but can safely stay in the bath for up to 1 hour. Have some extra butter on the table at serving time.

4. If you'd like some added smoky flavor, give the corn a few minutes on a hot grill, rotating to sear the ears on all sides. Sprinkle with leaves of fresh herbs and flaky sea salt, if desired.

FETA-BEET SALAD WITH SCALLIONS

SERVES 4 | **PREP TIME:** 10 minutes | **COOK TIME:** 3 hours | **FINISHING TIME:** 5 minutes |
SOUS VIDE TEMPERATURE: 185°F | **FAMILY FRIENDLY, QUICK PREP**

This salad is a visually dazzling, ruby-and-emerald affair (don't take my word for it—check out the picture on page 38). The star, of course, is the beets, which emerge from the sous vide buttery in texture and bursting with flavor—and most important, with all their many nutrients, specifically antioxidants, intact. The salty feta on top creates a lovely contrast.

2 pounds (6 medium) beets, any color, peeled and cut into ¼-inch-thick slices

Extra-virgin olive oil, for drizzling

Kosher salt

Freshly ground black pepper

2 or 3 slices citrus peel (optional)

1 or 2 fresh thyme sprigs (optional)

2 cups arugula and/or spinach leaves

1 cup crumbled feta cheese

2 scallions, chopped

1. Preheat the water bath to 185°F.

2. Place the beet slices in a cooking bag (if using a zip-top bag, double it up), drizzle them with olive oil, and season them with salt and pepper to taste. Add the citrus peel and thyme (if using). Vacuum-seal the bag or seal using the water displacement method and place the bag into the water bath. Set the timer for 3 hours. You might need to weigh the bag down to keep it submerged during cooking.

3. When ready to serve the salad, arrange the greens on a large serving plate. Spread the beet slices over the top and sprinkle with the feta and scallions.

MAKE-AHEAD MAGIC: This salad is no less fabulous served cold. If the beets have cooked in a vacuum-sealed bag, they'll be fully pasteurized. Transfer the bag into an ice bath to chill thoroughly and then store them in the fridge for up to 10 days, or freeze them.

SPICED HONEY BUTTER CARROTS

SERVES 6 | **PREP TIME:** 10 minutes | **COOK TIME:** 1 hour | **FINISHING TIME:** 10 minutes |
SOUS VIDE TEMPERATURE: 183°F | **FAMILY FRIENDLY**

Sweeten up your veggie intake with this delectable carrot side dish. Retaining all of the nutrients of the carrots but infusing them with a "candied" flavor makes these root veggies true crowd-pleasers. Try this recipe once and you'll never go back to traditionally cooked carrots.

2 pounds carrots, any
    color, peeled and cut into
    lengthwise slices
2 to 3 tablespoons unsalted
    butter, divided
2 to 3 tablespoons
    honey, divided

Kosher salt
2 to 6 fresh thyme sprigs,
    plus more for garnish
Smoked paprika, for
    sprinkling (optional)

Ground cumin, for
    sprinkling (optional)
Freshly ground
    black pepper, for
    sprinkling (optional)

1. Preheat the water bath to 183°F.

2. Use two or three large cooking bags (if using zip-top bags, double them up); evenly divide the carrots between the bags. If using rainbow carrots, separate them by color.

3. Add 1 tablespoon butter, 1 tablespoon honey, and a pinch of salt to each bag. Drop in 1 or 2 thyme sprigs. Vacuum-seal the bags or seal using the water displacement method.

4. Lower the bags into the heated water bath and set the timer for 1 hour. You might need to weigh the bags down to keep them submerged during cooking.

5. When the timer goes off, remove the cooking bags from the water bath and transfer the carrots onto a serving plate, reserving the cooking liquid.

6. Pour the cooking liquid into a small saucepan and bring it to a boil. Reduce the heat to medium and let the sauce reduce by half. Season with more salt, if desired. Once the liquid has thickened, drizzle the shiny glaze over the carrots.

7. For finishing, if you choose, sprinkle the carrots with smoked paprika, ground cumin, pepper, more salt, and thyme leaves.

BUTTERNUT SQUASH AND BRUSSELS SPROUTS SALAD

SERVES 4 | **PREP TIME:** 5 minutes | **COOK TIME:** 30 minutes | **FINISHING TIME:** 5 minutes |
SOUS VIDE TEMPERATURE: 194°F | **FAMILY FRIENDLY, QUICK PREP**

Crunchy, tender, and slightly sweet, this butternut squash salad is the perfect antidote to boring weekday lunches. The butternut squash provides a subtle sweetness, and extra punches of flavor come from the pears, honey, balsamic vinegar, and Italian seasoning. This salad is a nutritional powerhouse, but the luscious colors put it squarely in the eye-candy category as well.

1 medium butternut squash, peeled, halved lengthwise, seeds removed, and cut into ¾-inch-thick slices

3 tablespoons extra-virgin olive oil

Kosher salt

Freshly ground black pepper

½ cup balsamic vinegar

3 tablespoons honey

1 teaspoon Italian seasoning

1 pound fresh Brussels sprouts, trimmed and thinly sliced crosswise

1 large red pear, sliced

1. Preheat the water bath to 194°F.

2. In one or two cooking bags (if using zip-top bags, double them up), arrange the squash pieces in an even layer. Add the oil, salt, and pepper. Vacuum-seal the bag(s) or seal them using the water displacement method.

3. When the water bath is ready, drop the bag(s) in and cook for 30 minutes. You might need to weigh the bag(s) down to keep them submerged during cooking.

4. In the meantime, in a small saucepan, combine the vinegar, honey, and Italian seasoning and warm over medium-low heat. Simmer for 5 to 6 minutes, or until the mixture reduces by two-thirds and thickens.

5. In a microwave-safe bowl, put the Brussels sprouts, cover them, and microwave on high heat for 4 minutes. Drain well.

6. To serve, divide the Brussels sprouts evenly among four serving plates, then add pear slices and sous vide butternut squash to each plate. Drizzle with the balsamic sauce and season with more salt and pepper to taste.

MAKE-AHEAD MAGIC: If you've vacuum-sealed sous vide bags (rather than using the zip-top bags), you can cook the squash several days ahead and refrigerate it until you're ready to make the salad.

PARMESAN AND BALSAMIC BRUSSELS SPROUTS

SERVES 4 | **PREP TIME:** 10 minutes | **COOK TIME:** 40 minutes | **FINISHING TIME:** 10 minutes | **SOUS VIDE TEMPERATURE:** 183°F | **FAMILY FRIENDLY**

Cooking Brussels sprouts in high heat caramelizes them, creating crispness and a sweet, nutty flavor. But just placing them under your broiler will result in the inner part of the sprouts being undercooked. The solution? A 40-minute dip in the sous vide bath, followed by a brief stint under the broiler to sear the outer leaves. Add a touch of Parmesan and balsamic vinegar, and you're good to go.

2 pounds Brussels sprouts, stems trimmed, halved	¼ teaspoon kosher salt	Freshly grated Parmesan cheese, for serving
2 tablespoons extra-virgin olive oil	Balsamic vinegar, for serving	

1. Preheat the water bath to 183°F.

2. In a cooking bag (if using a zip-top bag, double it up), combine the Brussels sprouts, olive oil, and salt.

3. Vacuum-seal the bag, or seal it using the water displacement method. Place the bag in the water bath and set the timer for 40 minutes. You may need to weigh the bag down to keep the Brussels sprouts submerged during cooking.

4. When the timer goes off, preheat the broiler to high. Remove the bag from the water and transfer the Brussels sprouts to a foil-lined baking sheet. Pat them dry with paper towels.

5. Broil the Brussels sprouts, stirring occasionally, until they are browned and slightly charred, about 5 minutes.

6. Drizzle balsamic vinegar over the sprouts and sprinkle them with Parmesan cheese before serving.

DID YOU KNOW? Although records suggest that people in the European lowlands were eating this vegetable in the 13th century, these miniature cabbages weren't known as Brussels sprouts until the 1700s. Whether they originated in Brussels remains a mystery.

ASPARAGUS MIMOSA

SERVES 4 | **PREP TIME:** 5 minutes | **COOK TIME:** 15 minutes | **FINISHING TIME:** 5 minutes |
SOUS VIDE TEMPERATURE: 183°F | **FAMILY FRIENDLY, QUICK PREP**

Nothing celebrates the end of winter like fresh asparagus. After the briefest dip in the sous vide, these stalks are vibrant green, crisp, and naturally sweet. This classic favorite offers a big platter of springtime with a fluffy protein boost. Of course, omit the egg if you want a simpler side dish.

2 pounds asparagus, trimmed, stalks peeled, if desired

Extra-virgin olive oil for drizzling (optional)
1 large hard-boiled egg
(see Egg Chart, page 236)

¼ cup Lemon Vinaigrette
(page 226)

1. Preheat the water bath to 183°F.

2. In a cooking bag (if using a zip-top bag, double it up), spread the asparagus out in a single layer. Drizzle with olive oil (if using). Vacuum-seal the bag or seal it using the water displacement method, and set the timer for 15 minutes. You might need to weigh the bag down to keep it submerged during cooking.

3. Into a bowl, grate the egg by pressing it through a fine-mesh sieve.

4. Remove the asparagus from the water bath. If you'd like to serve this dish cold, chill the bag in an ice-water bath.

5. Place the asparagus on a platter. Spoon the vinaigrette over it and top it with the grated egg.

CHANGE IT UP: Substitute a sunny yellow Classic Hollandaise Sauce (page 23) for the vinaigrette and sprinkle the grated egg over that for the mimosa effect.

DID YOU KNOW? The vivid yellow flower of the acacia shrub, the mimosa, loaned its name not only to the classic orange juice and champagne cocktail but also to this recipe, where the cheerful grated egg "blossoms" are scattered across the bed of asparagus.

GARLIC-HERB MASHED POTATOES

SERVES 4 to 6 | **PREP TIME:** 10 minutes | **COOK TIME:** 1 hour 30 minutes to 2 hours | **FINISHING TIME:** 10 minutes | **SOUS VIDE TEMPERATURE:** 183°F | **FAMILY FRIENDLY**

Especially at the holidays, the oven and the stovetop are at maximum use, with a turkey or a ham here, sauces and vegetables there. . . . Amid all the bustle, your sous vide machine can sit off to the side on the countertop, quietly and reliably preparing this classic comfort food at its best.

1½ pounds russet potatoes, peeled and cut into chunks

¼ teaspoon garlic powder

¼ teaspoon onion powder

¼ teaspoon Herbes de Provence

Kosher salt

Freshly ground black pepper

2 tablespoons butter or extra-virgin olive oil

¼ cup cream or vegetable broth (optional)

1. Preheat the water bath to 183°F.

2. In a cooking bag (if using a zip-top bag, double it up), combine the potatoes, garlic powder, onion powder, and Herbes de Provence and season all with salt and pepper. Shake the bag for the seasonings to distribute evenly. Arrange the potatoes in a single layer and add the butter. Vacuum-seal the bag or seal it using the water displacement method.

3. Submerge the bag in the water and cook for 1 hour 30 minutes to 2 hours, until the potatoes are tender. You might need to weigh the bag down to keep it submerged during cooking.

4. Open the bag and drain any liquid; pour the potatoes into a food processor bowl or a blender and puree until smooth, adding a little cream or broth at a time as needed to reach your preferred consistency. Taste for seasonings and add more if desired. (No food processor? No problem. Use a potato masher or ricer.)

5. Transfer the potatoes to a serving bowl and enjoy.

CHANGE IT UP: Skip the russets and use sweet potatoes instead for a tasty, colorful alternative.

MAKE-AHEAD MAGIC: If you're not serving these right away, put the mashed potatoes into a large zip-top bag. Remove as much air as possible and submerge the bag in an ice-water bath for at least 20 minutes. They can last in the refrigerator for 3 to 4 days. When you're ready, reheat them in a water bath to serving temperature.

CRISPY SMASHED POTATOES

SERVES 4 | **PREP TIME:** 5 minutes | **COOK TIME:** 1 hour | **FINISHING TIME:** 20 minutes |
SOUS VIDE TEMPERATURE: 190°F | **FAMILY FRIENDLY, PARTY READY**

Sure, you could serve French fries at your next fete, but who wants the mess? These potatoes are broiled until crisp, making them an irresistible, gluten-free finger food that will begin their disappearing act the moment you set them out.

2 pounds small-to-medium
  red or yellow potatoes
3 tablespoons
  unsalted butter
2 teaspoons kosher salt
1 teaspoon freshly ground
  black pepper

¼ teaspoon garlic powder
¼ teaspoon onion powder
2 tablespoons chopped fresh
  parsley, chives, and/or
  scallions, for topping

Chipotle-Pecan
  Pesto (page 231) or
  Aioli (page 234), for
  serving (optional)

1. Preheat the water bath to 190°F.

2. Place the potatoes in one or more cooking bags (if using zip-top bags, double them up). Add the butter, salt, pepper, garlic powder, and onion powder. Vacuum-seal the bag(s) or seal them using the water displacement method. Lower them into the sous vide. You might need to weigh the bags down to keep them submerged during cooking. Set the timer for 1 hour.

3. When the potatoes are done, remove them from the bag(s) and place them on a foil-lined baking sheet. Pat them dry with paper towels. Preheat the broiler to high.

4. Using a potato masher or a flat-bottomed vessel (such as a jar or glass), smash the potatoes into flat rounds about ¼-inch- to ½-inch-thick. Thinner rounds will come out of the oven crispier.

5. Broil the potatoes until golden and crisp, about 5 minutes. Flip them and broil the other side, another 5 minutes. Top with fresh herbs and serve with pesto or aioli to dip.

FINGERLING POTATOES WITH ROASTED GARLIC

SERVES 4 | **PREP TIME:** 5 minutes | **COOK TIME:** 1 hour, 15 minutes | **FINISHING TIME:** 5 minutes |
SOUS VIDE TEMPERATURE: 194°F | **FAMILY FRIENDLY, QUICK PREP**

There's something endearing about miniature things, and potatoes are no exception. Let these fingerlings spend an hour in the sous vide bath with garlic and herb–infused olive oil, and they'll go from looking cute to tasting tremendous. In the unlikely event that you have leftovers, think potato salad.

½ cup extra-virgin olive oil	24 fingerling or	Freshly ground black pepper
6 garlic cloves	new potatoes	Blue Cheese Sauce (page 233),
3 or 4 fresh thyme sprigs	Kosher salt	for dipping (optional)

1. Preheat the water bath to 194°F.

2. In a saucepan over medium-high heat, combine and cook the oil and garlic cloves, spooning oil onto the cloves from time to time, until the garlic browns, 10 to 12 minutes. Add the thyme, then transfer everything to a small dish and allow it to cool for 15 minutes.

3. Place the unpeeled potatoes in a cooking bag (if using a zip-top bag, double it up) and season with salt to taste. Pour the garlic-thyme oil and garlic cloves over the potatoes. Vacuum-seal the bag or seal it using the water displacement method and place it into the water. You might need to weigh the bag down to keep it submerged during cooking. Set the timer for 1 hour.

4. When the timer goes off, transfer the potatoes into a serving bowl and season them with black pepper. Serve with blue cheese sauce for dipping (if using).

CHANGE IT UP: Feel free to experiment with different herbs: Sprigs of fresh dill or rosemary would be delicious.

DID YOU KNOW? Fingerlings are a small potato variety. They're harvested when fully mature; they're elongated in shape and roughly the length of a finger, thus the name. New potatoes, by contrast, are harvested when immature—wee, round baby potatoes, in other words. Both new and fingerling potatoes have thin, tender skin, so there's no need to peel them.

GREEK-STYLE POTATOES

SERVES 4 | **PREP TIME:** 5 minutes | **COOK TIME:** 1 hour | **FINISHING TIME:** 10 minutes |
SOUS VIDE TEMPERATURE: 194°F | **FAMILY FRIENDLY, QUICK PREP**

These potato wedges are packed with so many Mediterranean flavors—lemon, garlic, and oregano—you'll feel transported without the plane ride. Don't wait for a Greek-themed meal to prepare them, because they're a perfect pairing for any menu.

2½ pounds russet potatoes (or other starchy potato, like Yukon Gold), peeled and cut into thick wedges

1½ cups chicken broth or vegetable stock

½ cup extra-virgin olive oil

⅓ cup freshly squeezed lemon juice (from 2 to 3 large lemons)

5 garlic cloves, minced

1 tablespoon dried oregano

2 teaspoons kosher salt

Lemon wedges, for garnish (optional)

Chopped fresh parsley or oregano, for garnish (optional)

1. Preheat the water bath to 194°F.

2. In a cooking bag (if using a zip-top bag, double it up), combine the potatoes, broth, olive oil, lemon juice, garlic, oregano, and salt. Vacuum-seal the bag or seal it using the water displacement method. Place the bag into the water bath. You might need to weigh the bag down to keep it submerged during cooking. Set the timer for 1 hour.

3. If you choose to crisp the potatoes a bit, transfer the potato wedges to a foil-lined baking tray using a slotted spoon (reserve the cooking liquid). Pat them dry with paper towels. Place the tray under the broiler for 5 to 10 minutes on high, turning the potatoes occasionally to brown on all sides.

4. Transfer the potatoes to a serving dish and top with the reserved liquid from the sous vide bag. Garnish with lemon wedges, parsley, or oregano, if desired.

DID YOU KNOW? Recipes often call for particular types of potatoes. What's the difference? Waxy potatoes (new and fingerling potatoes, for example) have higher moisture content and hold their shape after cooking. Starchy potatoes like russets, Idahos, and Yukon Golds are lower in moisture and super-absorbent, which makes them ideal for a recipe like this one, where they sponge up all the flavors during cooking.

FIVE-SPICE SWEET POTATOES

SERVES 4 | **PREP TIME:** 20 minutes | **COOK TIME:** 30 minutes | **FINISHING TIME:** 5 minutes |
SOUS VIDE TEMPERATURE: 194°F | **FAMILY FRIENDLY**

For many of us, sweet potatoes only appear on the table at the holidays (think Grandma's casserole with the little marshmallows). That's a shame, really, because this nutritious, fiber-rich
superfood is a versatile year-round trouper. Sous vide promises fork-tender slices, and the
Chinese five-spice powder gives them some zing.

2 tablespoons extra-virgin olive oil	4 medium sweet potatoes, peeled, halved, and cut into half-moon slices	2½ teaspoons Chinese five-spice powder
3 garlic cloves	Kosher salt	3 to 4 tablespoons chopped scallions or chives, for garnish
	Freshly ground black pepper	

1. Preheat the water bath to 194°F.

2. In a small saucepan over medium-high heat, warm the oil and garlic cloves, spooning oil over the cloves from time to time, until the garlic browns slightly, 10 to
   12 minutes. Transfer the oil and garlic to a small dish and allow them to cool for
   15 minutes.

3. In a cooking bag (if using a zip-top bag, double it up), arrange the sweet potato
   slices in a single layer. Season with salt and pepper and add the Chinese five-spice
   powder. Add the oil and roasted garlic to the bag. Vacuum-seal the bag or seal it
   using the water displacement method.

4. Place the bag into the water bath and set the timer for 30 minutes. You might need
   to weigh the bag down to keep it submerged during cooking.

5. When finished, garnish with scallions or chives and serve.

DID YOU KNOW? Sweet potato flesh can be white, yellow, orange, or purple. What a
terrific way to add color to your plate! Also, the nutrient content differs for each, so the
advice to "eat the rainbow" certainly applies here.

POTATO AND SWEET POTATO SALAD

SERVES 4 or 5 | **PREP TIME:** 10 minutes | **COOK TIME:** 1 hour | **FINISHING TIME:** 10 minutes |
SOUS VIDE TEMPERATURE: 194°F | **FAMILY FRIENDLY, PARTY READY**

The weather's great and your friends are coming over for a cookout. Potato salad is all but obligatory, but that doesn't mean it needs to be boring. Add some sunny color and nutty flavor with sweet potatoes and bathe it in a spicy mustard vinaigrette to heat up this summer standby.

1 pound (3 or 4 medium) red potatoes, cut into 1-inch cubes	Extra-virgin olive oil, for drizzling	1½ teaspoons spicy brown mustard
½ teaspoon kosher salt, plus more for seasoning	½ pound (1 medium) sweet potatoes, peeled and cut into 1-inch cubes	¼ cup mayonnaise
¼ teaspoon freshly ground black pepper, plus more for seasoning	2 tablespoons red wine vinegar	2 tablespoons milk
		1 celery stalk, chopped
		½ small red onion, chopped
		3 tablespoons minced fresh parsley

1. Preheat the water bath to 194°F.

2. Place the red potatoes in one cooking bag (if using a zip-top bag, double it up). Season with salt and pepper and drizzle with olive oil. Vacuum-seal the bag or seal it using the water displacement method and place it into the water bath. You might need to weigh the bag down to keep it submerged during cooking. Set the timer for 30 minutes.

3. Place the sweet potatoes in another bag. Season them with salt and pepper and drizzle with olive oil. Vacuum-seal the bag or seal it using the water displacement method and set it aside.

4. When the timer goes off, leave the red potatoes in the bath, add the sweet potatoes, and set the timer for another 30 minutes.

5. Meanwhile, make the salad dressing. In a small mixing bowl, whisk together the vinegar, mustard, ½ teaspoon salt, and ¼ teaspoon pepper.

6. When the potatoes are finished, transfer them to a serving bowl; stir in the vinegar mixture and let them cool slightly. In your mixing bowl, mix together the mayonnaise, milk, celery, onion, and parsley. Stir the mayonnaise dressing gently into the potato mixture. Serve immediately or refrigerate and serve cold.

CAULIFLOWER STEAK WITH SOY-GINGER SAUCE

SERVES 3 or 4 | **PREP TIME:** 5 minutes | **COOK TIME:** 1 hour | **FINISHING TIME:** 20 minutes | **SOUS VIDE TEMPERATURE:** 183°F | **FAMILY FRIENDLY**

Anyone who thinks vegans are limited to munching on celery sticks ought to give this recipe a go. Hearty slabs of cauliflower are cooked so perfectly, it will never cross your mind to ask, "Where's the beef?" The soy-ginger sauce on the side takes it entirely to the next level.

1 large head cauliflower

Extra-virgin olive oil, for drizzling

Kosher salt

2 teaspoons sesame oil

1 tablespoon minced or grated fresh ginger

2 teaspoons (2 medium cloves) minced garlic

¼ cup water

2 tablespoons low-sodium or regular soy sauce

1 tablespoon red wine vinegar

1 teaspoon brown sugar

1 scallion, green parts only, chopped

2 to 3 tablespoons avocado or vegetable oil, for searing

1. Preheat the water bath to 183°F.

2. Trim the leaves and the stem at the base of the cauliflower, but leave the central stem, as this is what holds the steaks together. Slice the head into 1-inch steaks. You should get three or four steaks from one large head of cauliflower.

3. In one or more cooking bags (if using zip-top bags, double them up), lay the steaks in a single layer (not stacked), then drizzle them with olive oil and season them with salt. Vacuum-seal the bag(s) or seal them using the water displacement method and lower the cauliflower into the water bath. You might need to weigh the bag(s) down to keep them submerged during cooking. Set the timer for 1 hour.

4. Meanwhile, in a small skillet over medium-high heat, warm the sesame oil. Add the ginger and garlic and cook until fragrant, 1 to 2 minutes. Reduce the heat to medium-low and stir in the water, soy sauce, vinegar, and sugar. Simmer until the sauce is thickened, 4 to 6 minutes. Transfer the sauce to a small bowl and add the scallions. Set aside.

5. When the timer goes off, remove the cauliflower from the water. Open the sous vide bag and slide the cauliflower steaks onto a large plate. Pat dry with paper towels.

6. Heat the avocado oil in a cast-iron skillet over high heat. Add the steaks and sear, one at a time, for 1 to 2 minutes on each side, until browned. Repeat with the remaining steaks.

7. Serve with the soy-ginger sauce on the side.

BEST CABBAGE WEDGES

SERVES 4 | **PREP TIME:** 5 minutes | **COOK TIME:** 4 hours | **FINISHING TIME:** 10 minutes |
SOUS VIDE TEMPERATURE: 183°F | **FAMILY FRIENDLY, QUICK PREP**

Big wedges of the wrinkly-leafed Savoy cabbage are a treat for the eyes; this recipe is a gorgeous way to prepare this often-underappreciated vegetable. Cabbage is also packed with nutrients, like fiber and powerful antioxidants. It's a member of the same family as broccoli, even though it shares more of a family resemblance with lettuce.

1 medium head Savoy cabbage, cut into four wedges, leaving the core intact

2 tablespoons unsalted butter, divided

½ teaspoon kosher salt

1. Preheat the water bath to 183°F.

2. In a cooking bag (if using a zip-top bag, double it up), combine the cabbage with 1 tablespoon butter and the salt. Vacuum-seal the bag or seal it using the water displacement method and place it in the water bath. You might need to weigh the bag down to keep it submerged during cooking. Set the timer for 4 hours. When the timer goes off, remove the bag from the water bath. Remove the cabbage from the bag and pat it dry with paper towels.

3. In a skillet over medium heat, melt the remaining 1 tablespoon butter. Once the butter is melted, add the cabbage and sear until golden brown on both cut sides, 5 to 7 minutes total.

CHANGE IT UP: Serve the cabbage with Spicy Cilantro-Lime Sauce (page 228) or tangy Chimichurri (page 229) for some tasty drizzling.

ONE-BAG VEGETABLE CURRY

SERVES 6 | **PREP TIME:** 20 minutes | **COOK TIME:** 1 hour | **FINISHING TIME:** 5 minutes |
SOUS VIDE TEMPERATURE: 183°F | **FAMILY FRIENDLY, PARTY READY**

Whether you're making a family dinner or cooking for a party, putting this scrumptious red curry into the sous vide bath for an hour frees you (and your wok) up to prepare other dishes. Better yet, the vegetables will come out just right, not boiled to chunks of mush. Serve with rice or your preferred grain.

3 tablespoons coconut oil

1 medium onion,
  coarsely chopped

1 tablespoon minced ginger

1 tablespoon minced garlic

¼ teaspoon red
  pepper flakes

Kosher salt

¼ cup white wine

3 tablespoons Thai red
  curry paste

1 teaspoon turmeric

1 teaspoon ground cumin

½ cup coconut milk

1 head cauliflower, cut
  into florets

1 sweet potato, peeled and
  diced (about 2 cups)

3 carrots, sliced

Fresh cilantro, chopped,
  for garnish

Cooked rice, for serving

1. Preheat the water bath to 183°F.

2. In a large wok or skillet over medium heat, warm the coconut oil for 1 to 2 minutes, until hot. Keep the heat at medium or the oil will burn.

3. Add the onion, ginger, garlic, red pepper flakes, and a pinch of salt. Cook, stirring often, for 5 minutes.

4. Add the wine and continue cooking for another 5 minutes, stirring occasionally, until the alcohol has evaporated.

5. Add the Thai red curry paste, turmeric, cumin, and coconut milk and stir until blended.

6. In a cooking bag (if using a zip-top bag, double it up), combine the cauliflower, sweet potato, and carrots. Pour the sauce over the vegetables. Vacuum-seal the bag or seal it using the water displacement method. Place the bag into the water bath and set the timer for 1 hour.

7. When finished, transfer the curry to a serving bowl and garnish with fresh cilantro. Serve over rice.

SPICY HONEY-GLAZED PARSNIPS

SERVES 4 | **PREP TIME:** 5 minutes | **COOK TIME:** 30 minutes | **FINISHING TIME:** 5 minutes |
SOUS VIDE TEMPERATURE: 194°F | **FAMILY FRIENDLY, QUICK PREP**

Some people compare parsnips to their cousin root vegetables, carrots and potatoes, but that's really doing the parsnip an injustice. Earthier than potatoes and edgier than carrots, these guys are wintertime gems, especially with this sweet-and-spicy glaze. Winter just got a whole lot more bearable.

4 or 5 large parsnips, peeled, halved lengthwise, and cut into ½-inch pieces	Kosher salt	2 tablespoons unsalted butter
Extra-virgin olive oil, for drizzling	1 thyme sprig	1 tablespoon apple cider vinegar
	2 dried chiles de árbol, crushed, or ¾ teaspoon red pepper flakes	1 tablespoon honey

1. Preheat the water bath to 194°F.

2. Place the parsnips in a cooking bag in a single layer (if using a zip-top bag, double it up). Drizzle them with olive oil, season them with salt, and add the sprig of thyme. Vacuum-seal the bag or seal it using the water displacement method and place it in the water bath. You might need to weigh the bag down to keep it submerged during cooking. Set the timer for 30 minutes.

3. About 5 minutes before the parsnips are done, in a medium saucepan over medium heat, heat the chiles de árbol, butter, apple cider vinegar, and honey, stirring occasionally, until the butter is melted and the sauce is well blended.

4. To serve, transfer the cooked parsnips to a serving dish, drizzle the glaze over them, and stir to coat.

FENNEL WITH PARMESAN

SERVES 4 | **PREP TIME:** 5 minutes | **COOK TIME:** 2 hours | **FINISHING TIME:** 5 minutes |
SOUS VIDE TEMPERATURE: 176°F | **FAMILY FRIENDLY, QUICK PREP**

Although both are known for a black licorice flavor, fennel is unrelated to anise; it's actually a member of the carrot family. The white fennel bulb has a lovely crunch when added raw to salads, but its flavor mellows and its texture turns silky when cooked sous vide. Lemon juice and freshly grated Parmesan provide a tasty little punch of contrast.

2 large fennel bulbs, trimmed and halved lengthwise

½ teaspoon kosher salt

Extra-virgin olive oil, for drizzling

Juice of ½ lemon

¼ cup freshly grated Parmesan, more if desired

Freshly ground black pepper

Fresh herbs, such as dill, for garnish (optional)

1. Preheat the water bath to 176°F.

2. In a cooking bag (if using a zip-top bag, double it up), place the fennel halves side by side. Season them generously with the salt, then drizzle them with the oil. Vacuum-seal the bag or seal it using the water displacement method and place it in the water bath. You might need to weigh the bag down to keep it submerged during cooking. Set the timer for 2 hours.

3. When the timer goes off, remove the fennel from the water bath and transfer it to a serving plate. Slice the fennel halves into quarters. Drizzle them with the lemon juice. Sprinkle the fennel with freshly grated Parmesan, black pepper, and fresh herbs (if using). Serve right away or chill to use later in a cold salad.

DID YOU KNOW? Fennel has a long history; the ancient Greeks and Romans embraced it as a food, insect repellent, and medicine, and soldiers believed fennel tea provided courage before battle. See if you face life a bit more bravely after trying this recipe!

SOUS VIDE KALE

SERVES 4 | **PREP TIME:** 2 minutes | **COOK TIME:** 7 minutes | **FINISHING TIME:** 3 minutes | **SOUS VIDE TEMPERATURE:** 194°F | **QUICK PREP**

There are several varieties of kale: The leaves can be green or purple, curly or flat. No matter which type you buy, kale is one of the most nutrient-dense foods on the planet. When it's over-cooked, though, those nutrients go right down the drain, along with its vivid color and hearty texture. Just 7 minutes in the sous vide and you'll achieve greens that win the superfood medal of honor.

1 bunch kale, stem ends trimmed	Extra-virgin olive oil, for drizzling Kosher salt	Apple cider vinegar, for drizzling (optional)

1. Preheat the water bath to 194°F.

2. Drizzle the kale leaves with olive oil. Place the whole kale leaves in a sous vide bag, spreading them out as much as possible. Vacuum-seal the bag and place it into the water bath. Weigh the bag down to keep it submerged during cooking. Set the timer for 7 minutes.

3. When it's done, remove the kale from the bag and slice it. Season it with salt and serve drizzled with apple cider vinegar (if using).

DID YOU KNOW? Ancient Greeks touted boiled kale leaves as a cure for drunkenness. While modern-day nutritionists sing its praises, they don't seem to uphold that claim.

CHANGE IT UP: Serving the lemony Classic Hollandaise Sauce (page 23) over this kale is bliss.

CREAMY MUSHROOM SOUP

SERVES: 4 | **PREP TIME:** 15 minutes | **COOK TIME:** 1 hour | **FINISHING TIME:** 5 minutes |
SOUS VIDE TEMPERATURE: 190°F | **FAMILY FRIENDLY**

This recipe brings one word to mind—and no, it's not casserole! It's *rich*. The assorted mushrooms lend the soup a rich, earthy flavor and the cream gives it a rich (but not heavy) texture. Served with a loaf of crusty bread, this soup makes an elegant, satisfying dinner on a cold or rainy night.

1 pound assorted wild
   mushrooms, such as
   oyster, chanterelle, morel,
   cremini, and/or shiitake,
   stems removed
½ cup heavy (whipping)
   cream, plus more
   as needed
1 shallot, thinly sliced

3 tablespoons
   unsalted butter
2 tablespoons sherry
1 tablespoon minced
   fresh thyme
2 teaspoons kosher salt,
   plus more for seasoning
1 garlic clove, minced

1 teaspoon freshly ground
   black pepper, plus more
   for seasoning
Splash vegetable or chicken
   broth, as needed (optional)
Fresh thyme springs,
   for garnish
Extra-virgin olive oil, for
   drizzling (optional)

1. Preheat the water bath to 190°F.

2. In a large cooking bag (if using a zip-top bag, double it up), combine the mushrooms, cream, shallot, butter, sherry, thyme, salt, garlic, and pepper. Vacuum-seal the bag or seal it using the water displacement method and submerge it in the preheated water bath. You might need to weigh the bag down to keep it submerged during cooking. Set the timer for 1 hour.

3. When the timer goes off, remove the bag from the water bath. Transfer everything to a blender and puree until smooth, about 1 minute. Add additional cream or broth to reach your desired consistency.

4. Season the soup to taste with more salt and pepper. Garnish with fresh thyme and drizzle with olive oil, if desired.

MAKE-AHEAD MAGIC: If you've vacuum-sealed the ingredients, the soup will come out of the sous vide pasteurized. You can cool it in an ice-water bath, then freeze it for up to 6 months. When ready to use, just thaw, blend, and reheat.

CAULIFLOWER PUREE

SERVES 4 | **PREP TIME:** 5 minutes | **COOK TIME:** 45 minutes | **FINISHING TIME:** 10 minutes | **SOUS VIDE TEMPERATURE:** 185°F | **FAMILY FRIENDLY, PARTY READY, QUICK PREP**

Cauliflower puree is a velvety, tasty alternative to mashed potatoes, especially attractive to those who are aiming for fewer carbs and less starch on their plates. Even veggie-phobic kids will go for this stuff—just don't tell them what's in it. It's an ideal side for salmon or lamb shanks.

1 head cauliflower, trimmed and sliced ¼-inch thick

1 cup chicken stock

3 tablespoons unsalted butter

½ cup freshly grated Parmesan cheese

Kosher salt

1. Preheat the water bath to 185°F.

2. In a large cooking bag (if using a zip-top bag, double it up), combine the cauliflower, chicken stock, and butter. Vacuum-seal the bag or seal it using the water displacement method and place it in the water bath. You might need to weigh the bag down to keep it submerged during cooking. Set the timer for 45 minutes.

3. When the timer goes off, remove the bag from the water bath. Strain the contents of the bag through a fine-mesh strainer set over a large bowl. Reserve the cooking liquid.

4. Transfer the strained cauliflower to a blender and add the Parmesan cheese. Puree until smooth, adding the reserved cooking liquid as needed to thin the puree to your desired consistency. It should be slightly looser than mashed potatoes. Season to taste with salt, reheat if necessary, and serve.

CHANGE IT UP: Do a quick inventory of your fresh herbs. A teaspoon of chopped parsley, tarragon, thyme, rosemary, sage, or chives will give this puree a whole new dimension.

MAKE-AHEAD MAGIC: When chilled, this puree makes a terrific dip. It will keep in the refrigerator for 3 to 4 days.

Classic Salmon, page 68

FISH AND SHELLFISH

CLASSIC SALMON

SERVES 4 | **PREP TIME:** 15 minutes | **COOK TIME:** 40 minutes | **FINISHING TIME:** 5 minutes |
SOUS VIDE TEMPERATURE: 122°F | **FAMILY FRIENDLY**

This is an ultra-simple salmon preparation, but it's far from ordinary tasting. A few minutes with a dry brine mixture give a special boost to the salmon's texture and flavor; the sugar also aids browning. Lemon and dill are a crowning touch. Serve it hot or cold, perhaps with a yogurt-dill sauce.

4 (4- to 6-ounce) skin-on
  salmon fillets
4 tablespoons kosher salt
1 tablespoon brown sugar

Freshly ground black pepper
2 tablespoons extra-virgin
  olive oil
2 or 3 dill sprigs

Lemon zest, for sprinkling
1 to 2 tablespoons avocado
  or vegetable oil, for searing

1. Preheat the water bath to 122°F.

2. Score the skin by cutting a few shallow parallel slices into the skin of the salmon; this will get it nice and crispy when searing.

3. Flip the fillets over and cover them generously with salt and brown sugar. Let the fillets rest in the fridge for 10 minutes and then rinse them with cold water.

4. Pat the fillets dry and season them with black pepper.

5. Place the fish into a cooking bag (or multiple bags, if necessary) and drizzle it with the olive oil. Ensure that the fillets are well coated. Place the dill sprigs on the skin side of the fillets and sprinkle with lemon zest to taste. Vacuum-seal the bag or seal it using the water displacement method and place it into the water bath. You might need to weigh the bag down to keep it submerged during cooking. Set the timer for 40 minutes.

6. Remove the salmon from the cooking bag. Heat a cast-iron or nonstick skillet over high heat, pour in the avocado or vegetable oil, and sear the fish, skin-side down, for 30 seconds to 1 minute, until the skin is crispy.

MAKE-AHEAD MAGIC: Pack up any leftover cooked salmon fillets with some tabbouleh or other grain salad and you've got a takeaway lunch that will leave your coworkers envious.

COCONUT POACHED SALMON

SERVES 4 | **PREP TIME:** 10 minutes | **COOK TIME:** 20 to 30 minutes | **FINISHING TIME:** 10 minutes | **SOUS VIDE TEMPERATURE:** 124°F | **FAMILY FRIENDLY**

In this recipe, salmon leaves its cold northern waters to swim in coconut milk with warm, aromatic seasonings, coming to rest atop that most southern of American staples: grits. It may sound like a strange mash-up, but it works. Serve with a crisp, colorful Asian vegetable mix.

4 (4- to 6-ounce) skinless salmon fillets

1 teaspoon kosher salt, divided

Freshly ground black pepper

1 tablespoon extra-virgin olive oil

1 teaspoon grated fresh ginger

1 leek, white and light green parts only, thinly sliced

1 (13.5-ounce) can coconut milk

½ teaspoon red pepper flakes

3½ cups unsalted vegetable broth, divided

⅓ cup finely chopped yellow onion, divided

¾ cup quick-cooking grits

¼ cup grated Parmesan cheese

1. Preheat the water bath to 124°F.

2. Rinse the salmon and pat dry. Put each piece of salmon into its own cooking bag. Sprinkle the fillets with ¾ teaspoon salt and the black pepper to taste and drizzle with olive oil.

3. Divide the ginger, leek, coconut milk, and red pepper flakes evenly among the four bags. Add 2 tablespoons vegetable broth and 1 tablespoon yellow onion to each bag. Vacuum-seal the bag(s) or seal them using the water displacement method. Submerge the bags in the water bath. You might need to weigh them down to keep them submerged during cooking. Set the timer for 20 to 30 minutes.

4. Meanwhile, in a medium saucepan, bring 3 cups vegetable broth, the remaining yellow onion, and ¼ teaspoon salt to a boil. Add the grits, bring to a boil again, and simmer for 5 to 7 minutes, stirring until the grits reach your desired consistency. Stir in the Parmesan cheese.

5. Divide the grits evenly among four serving plates. When the salmon is done, remove the fillets from the bags and place them on top of the grits, drizzling the coconut milk mixture from the bags over the top.

CHANGE IT UP: Simple Polenta (page 40) and Essential Millet (page 41) make great substitutes for the grits in this recipe.

MACKEREL WITH SPICY CILANTRO-LIME SAUCE

SERVES 4 | **PREP TIME:** 5 minutes | **COOK TIME:** 20 minutes | **FINISHING TIME:** 5 minutes |
SOUS VIDE TEMPERATURE: 122°F | **QUICK PREP**

Poor, maligned mackerel. It's a lean, firm-fleshed fish, loaded with omega-3 fatty acids, but it's gotten a bad rap for its powerful (some say fishy) flavor. This is not entirely deserved, as mackerel can have a rich, creamy taste. The secret is in the freshness. Start with newly caught mackerel (or buy some that was promptly frozen). A short spell in the sous vide, topped with cilantro-lime sauce, and you'll be singing mackerel's praises. Serve on a bed of watercress.

1 pound mackerel fillets, defrosted if frozen 1 teaspoon kosher salt	Freshly ground black pepper 1 tablespoon extra-virgin olive oil	Spicy Cilantro-Lime Sauce (page 228), **for serving**

1. Preheat the water bath to 122°F.

2. Rinse the mackerel fillets under cold water and pat them dry. Season them generously on both sides with the salt and pepper.

3. In a cooking bag, place the fillets in a single layer. Vacuum-seal the bag or seal it using the water displacement method and place it into the water bath. You might need to weigh the bag down to keep it submerged during cooking. Set the timer for 20 minutes.

4. When the timer goes off, remove the mackerel from the bag and pat it dry thoroughly.

5. In a cast-iron or nonstick skillet, heat the olive oil. When it's hot, place the fillets, skin-sides down, in the skillet and sear until skin is crispy and brown, 30 seconds to 1 minute.

6. Serve drizzled with the cilantro-lime sauce.

DID YOU KNOW? Sure, freshness is important for all seafood, but perhaps even more so for mackerel, because the longer it's out of the water, the stronger its flavor. When buying fresh mackerel, look for fish that was caught within 24 hours. The flesh should be very firm to the touch, the eye bright. If you pick up a whole mackerel by the head, the body should not droop. If you're using frozen mackerel, use it within a day or two of thawing.

CHEESY HALIBUT TACOS WITH VEGETABLES

MAKES 10 tacos | **PREP TIME:** 5 minutes | **COOK TIME:** 45 minutes | **FINISHING TIME:** 5 minutes |
SOUS VIDE TEMPERATURE: 131°F | **FAMILY FRIENDLY, QUICK PREP**

The flavor of this nutrient-dense fish is so mild that it is the perfect base for multi-ingredient tacos. Quick enough for a weeknight dinner, these piquant tacos are winners.

1 large (1-pound)
  halibut fillet
2 tablespoons extra-virgin
  olive oil
1 teaspoon kosher salt,
  divided, plus more
  for seasoning
Freshly ground black pepper

2 tablespoons butter
½ cup sliced onion
2 Roma tomatoes, diced
2 medium zucchini, diced
1 (15-ounce) can black
  beans, drained and rinsed
⅓ cup chopped cilantro, plus
  more for garnish

10 corn or flour tortillas
2 cups shredded Oaxaca
  cheese (or mozzarella)
Bottled salsa verde,
  for serving
2 limes, cut into wedges,
  for serving

1. Preheat the water bath to 131°F.

2. Place the halibut fillet into a cooking bag. Drizzle it with the olive oil, sprinkle it with ½ teaspoon salt, and add pepper to taste. Vacuum-seal the bag or seal it using the water displacement method and place the bag into the water bath. Set the timer for 45 minutes. (Add another 15 minutes if the fillet is more than 1 inch thick.)

3. Meanwhile, in a sauté pan, melt the butter over high heat. Add the onion and sauté for 1 minute, or until fragrant. Add the tomatoes, zucchini, and beans. Stir for 2 minutes, or until zucchini is tender.

4. Reduce the heat to medium. Add the remaining ½ teaspoon salt and stir. Cover and cook for 3 minutes. Stir in the cilantro and remove from the heat. Taste and add more salt, if desired.

5. Place the tortillas in a large, nonstick skillet over high heat and add some shredded cheese in the center of each. Let the tortillas cook until the cheese starts to melt. Fold each tortilla and heat each side for a few more seconds. Stack the tortillas and wrap in a kitchen towel to keep warm.

6. Cut the fish into bite-size chunks. Open a tortilla. Pile the bean mixture and the fish on top of the cheese in the center. Garnish with cilantro, then drizzle with salsa verde. Serve with lime wedges.

SESAME-CRUSTED TUNA STEAKS

SERVES 4 | **PREP TIME:** 40 minutes | **COOK TIME:** 30 to 60 minutes | **FINISHING TIME:** 10 minutes |
SOUS VIDE TEMPERATURE: 110°F | **FAMILY FRIENDLY**

This recipe produces a rich, meaty, deep-red tuna steak with a crisp, seared coating of black and
white sesame seeds. The black seeds impart a sharper, nuttier flavor, while the white seeds add a
sweeter one.

4 (4- to 6-ounce) tuna steaks,
  1 to 2 inches thick
1 teaspoon kosher salt
Freshly ground black pepper
2 tablespoons extra-virgin
  olive oil

2 to 4 fresh thyme or dill
  sprigs (optional)
1 strip citrus peel, such as
  lemon or lime (optional)

¼ cup black sesame seeds
¼ cup white sesame seeds
2 teaspoons avocado or
  vegetable oil

1. In a zip-top bag, place the tuna steaks in a single layer. Use multiple bags if necessary. Season with the salt and pepper on both sides; drizzle with the olive oil, and add the thyme, dill (if using), and citrus peel (if using).

2. Seal the bag and allow the tuna to rest in the refrigerator for 30 minutes or up to overnight. This step, known as dry-brining, produces a firmer, more buttery texture.

3. Preheat the water bath to 110°F for a rare steak. For extra-rare tuna, choose 105°F, and for well-done, select 130°F.

4. Open the bag(s), slowly lower them into the water bath, and seal them using the water displacement method. You might need to weigh them down to keep them submerged during cooking. Set the timer, depending upon the thickness of your tuna steaks: For 1- to 1½-inch-thick steaks, 30 to 45 minutes will do. Thicker steaks will need 45 to 60 minutes.

5. Once the timer goes off, remove the bag from the water bath and gently slide the tuna steaks onto paper towels; pat them dry. Discard the aromatics, if used.

6. On a plate, mix the black and white sesame seeds. Coat the tuna steaks on both sides, pressing the fish firmly into the seeds.

7. In a heavy skillet, heat the avocado oil over medium-high heat. Sear both sides of the tuna steaks, turning the steaks gently, until the sesame seeds become fragrant, 30 to 45 seconds on each side. Serve.

OLIVE OIL-POACHED TUNA

SERVES 4 | **PREP TIME:** 45 minutes | **COOK TIME:** 30 minutes | **FINISHING TIME:** 3 to 10 minutes |
SOUS VIDE TEMPERATURE: 113°F | **FAMILY FRIENDLY**

If the mention of albacore brings canned tuna to mind, it's time to remedy that. These hefty slices of tuna spend 30 minutes in a salt-and-sugar brine, which keeps them wonderfully firm while they bask in lemon-infused olive oil in the sous vide. This technique is also great for salmon and trout.

½ cup kosher salt

½ cup sugar

6 cups room-temperature water

1 pound tuna steaks

¼ cup extra-virgin olive oil

1 strip lemon peel

1. In a container that will fit in your refrigerator, combine the salt and sugar with the water, stirring until they are dissolved.

2. Place the tuna steaks in the brine. Refrigerate them for 30 minutes, stirring occasionally and ensuring that the fish is evenly soaked.

3. Preheat the water bath to 113°F.

4. Remove the tuna steaks from the brine and pat them dry with paper towels.

5. Place the tuna, olive oil, and lemon peel in a zip-top bag. Slowly lower the bag into the water bath and seal it using the water displacement method. You might need to weigh the bag down to keep it submerged during cooking. Set the timer for 30 minutes.

6. When it's done, remove the tuna from the bag and serve hot. Alternatively, prepare an ice-water bath in a large bowl with a 50/50 mixture of cold water and ice cubes. Place the cooking bag in the bath for 10 minutes to chill the tuna steaks before serving them cold.

DID YOU KNOW? Many of us are paying more attention to sustainably, ethically sourced seafood these days. The Monterey Bay Aquarium has an excellent website (and a companion app that you can use at the fish market) called Seafood Watch, with "recommendations [to] help you choose seafood that's fished or farmed in ways that have less impact on the environment." Look for it at SeafoodWatch.org.

KERALAN-STYLE SCALLOP CURRY

SERVES 4 | **PREP TIME:** 5 minutes | **COOK TIME:** 30 minutes | **FINISHING TIME:** 5 minutes |
SOUS VIDE TEMPERATURE: 123°F | **QUICK PREP**

Kerala, a state in southwestern India, has a long coastline and, with it, a long tradition of seafood curries. This one is redolent of coconut and fragrant spices with tender scallops as the protein. You can whip up the curry sauce while the scallops are cooking. Serve with fluffy white rice.

1½ pounds (about 45)
   sea scallops
1 teaspoon kosher salt
Freshly ground black pepper
3 tablespoons extra-virgin
   olive oil, divided
1 onion, very finely chopped
2 green chiles, halved,
   seeded, and thinly sliced

4 garlic cloves, minced
1 (1-inch) piece fresh ginger,
   peeled and grated
½ teaspoon mustard powder
¼ teaspoon ground cumin
Zest of 2 limes
4 bay leaves
1 tablespoon curry powder

½ teaspoon ground turmeric
1 (13.5-ounce) can
   coconut milk
12 cherry tomatoes, halved
Freshly squeezed lime juice,
   for serving
Fresh cilantro, chopped,
   for serving

1. Preheat the water bath to 123°F.

2. Season the scallops with the salt and pepper. In a sous vide bag, arrange them in a single layer with a bit of space between them. Add 1 tablespoon olive oil, then vacuum-seal the bag, maintaining the space between the scallops. Use multiple bags if necessary.

3. Place the bag in the heated water. You might need to weigh it down to keep it submerged during cooking. Set the timer for 30 minutes.

4. Meanwhile, in a medium saucepan over medium heat, heat 1 tablespoon olive oil. Add the onion, chiles, garlic, ginger, mustard powder, ground cumin, lime zest, and bay leaves. Cook until the onion softens and begins to brown. Add the curry powder and turmeric, cook for a minute, then add the coconut milk. Bring to a simmer and add the cherry tomatoes. Cook for 15 minutes, or until the sauce thickens.

5. When the sous vide timer goes off, remove the scallops and pat them dry with paper towels. In a sauté pan, heat the remaining 1 tablespoon of olive oil over medium-high heat. Sear the scallops for about 20 seconds on each side, then add them to the curry sauce.

6. Add lime juice to taste, and top with chopped fresh cilantro.

CHANGE IT UP: For a milder curry, reduce or eliminate the green chiles from the sauce.

SCALLOPS WITH LEMON-BUTTER SAUCE

SERVES 4 | **PREP TIME:** 5 minutes | **COOK TIME:** 30 minutes | **FINISHING TIME:** 15 minutes | **SOUS VIDE TEMPERATURE:** 123°F | **FAMILY FRIENDLY**

You order the scallops at a gourmet seafood restaurant, and they arrive looking marvelous and so artfully served . . . all three of them. May I suggest an alternative? Make them at home for tender, tasty, *generous* servings at a fraction of the price. Who says you can't enjoy fine dining on a Tuesday night?

1½ pounds (about 45) sea scallops	2 tablespoons extra-virgin olive oil	1 tablespoon freshly squeezed lemon juice
1 teaspoon kosher salt, plus more for seasoning (optional)	3 tablespoons unsalted butter, divided	Fresh parsley, chopped, for garnish
Freshly ground black pepper	3 garlic cloves, minced	Lemon wedges, for serving
	¼ cup dry white wine	

1. Preheat the water bath to 123°F.

2. Season the scallops with 1 teaspoon salt and pepper. In a sous vide bag, arrange them in a single layer with a bit of space between them. Add the olive oil, then vacuum-seal the bag, maintaining the space between the scallops. Use multiple bags if necessary.

3. Place the bag(s) in the heated water. You might need to weigh the bag(s) down to keep them submerged during cooking. Set the timer for 30 minutes.

4. When they're finished, remove the scallops and pat them dry with paper towels.

5. In a heavy skillet or saucepan, heat 1 tablespoon butter over medium-high heat. Place the scallops in the pan in a single layer, about 1 inch apart. Allow them to sear, undisturbed, until golden brown, about 20 seconds on each side.

6. Transfer the scallops to a plate and set aside. In the same pan, melt the remaining 2 tablespoons butter, scraping up the browned bits from the pan with a wooden spoon. Stir in the garlic and let it infuse into the butter for about 1 minute. Add the wine and lemon juice. Let the sauce cook until the alcohol has evaporated and the sauce has thickened slightly, about 10 minutes. Taste and add salt, if desired. Turn off the heat.

7. Return the scallops to the pan to warm them up. Sprinkle them with chopped parsley and serve with lemon wedges.

CAJUN SHRIMP TACOS

MAKES 12 tacos | **PREP TIME:** 10 minutes | **COOK TIME:** 10 minutes | **FINISHING TIME:** 10 minutes |
SOUS VIDE TEMPERATURE: 158°F | **FAMILY FRIENDLY**

Fusion cuisine, when it works, combines ingredients from various cultures to bring out the best in each of them. Pile big, tender Cajun shrimp and a bright mango-avocado salsa onto Mexican tortillas, then top it all off with some Greek feta cheese. And it'll all be on the table in just 30 minutes.

FOR THE CAJUN SHRIMP:

2 teaspoons chili powder

1 teaspoon kosher salt

1 teaspoon dried oregano

½ teaspoon ground cumin

½ teaspoon freshly ground
black pepper

½ teaspoon garlic powder

2 pounds (52 to 60)
large shrimp, peeled
and deveined

2 tablespoons extra-virgin
olive oil

FOR THE MANGO-AVOCADO SALSA:

¼ cup diced red onion

1 jalapeño pepper, seeded
and minced

1 small bunch cilantro,
chopped (about 1 cup)

3 Hass avocados, diced

1 ripe mango, peeled and
diced (about 1 cup)

Juice of 1 lime

Kosher salt

Freshly ground black pepper

FOR ASSEMBLING THE TACOS:

12 corn or flour
tortillas, warmed

¾ cup crumbled feta cheese

Lime wedges, for
serving (optional)

1. Preheat the water bath to 158°F.

2. **Make the shrimp:** In a small bowl, mix together the chili powder, salt, oregano, cumin, pepper, and garlic powder thoroughly. In a large bowl, combine the shrimp and the spice mix, stirring to coat evenly. In multiple sous vide bags, arrange the shrimp in a single layer. Drizzle them lightly with olive oil and vacuum-seal the bags.

3. When the water reaches the right temperature, place the bags into the sous vide bath. You might need to weigh them down to keep them submerged during cooking. Set the timer for 10 minutes.

4. **Make the mango-avocado salsa:** In a medium bowl, combine the red onion, jalapeño, cilantro, avocado, mango, and lime juice. Season the salsa with salt and black pepper and stir to mix well.

5. **Assemble the tacos:** Place 5 or so shrimp on each tortilla, spoon the mango-avocado salsa over the top, and garnish with 1 tablespoon crumbled feta cheese. Serve with lime wedges, if desired.

SHRIMP COCKTAIL

SERVES 6 to 8 | **PREP TIME:** 20 minutes | **COOK TIME:** 10 minutes | **FINISHING TIME:** 10 minutes |
SOUS VIDE TEMPERATURE: 158°F | **PARTY READY**

What a classic! The fresh, zingy tomato-and-horseradish sauce is the perfect foil for the sweet, succulent shrimp. The trick, of course, is getting the shrimp just right; overcooking turns them to rubber or chalk. Follow these steps and yours will be restaurant-ready.

2 tablespoons kosher salt

1 tablespoon sugar

2 pounds (32 to 40) extra-large shrimp, peeled and deveined

Extra-virgin olive oil, for drizzling

1 strip lemon peel, per bag

½ cup ketchup

2 tablespoons horseradish

1 tablespoon freshly squeezed lemon juice

1 teaspoon hot sauce

1 teaspoon Worcestershire sauce

Lemon wedges, for garnish

Italian parsley sprigs, for garnish

1. Preheat the water bath to 158°F.

2. In a bowl, mix together the salt and sugar, then sprinkle the mixture over the shrimp. Let them sit for 15 minutes. This dry brine will ensure that the shrimp retain a firm, fresh texture.

3. Rinse the shrimp and place them in one or more sous vide bags in a single layer. Drizzle them lightly with olive oil and add a strip of lemon peel to each bag. Vacuum-seal the bag(s) and place them in the water bath. You might need to weigh them down to keep them submerged during cooking. Set the timer for 10 minutes.

4. Meanwhile, in a medium mixing bowl, mix the ketchup, horseradish, lemon juice, hot sauce, and Worcestershire thoroughly to combine.

5. In a large bowl, prepare an ice-water bath with a 50/50 mixture of cold water and ice cubes. Remove the sous vide bag(s) from the water and place them immediately into the ice-water bath to stop the cooking. Replenish the ice as needed for 10 minutes or so to chill the shrimp.

6. Place the sauce in a small serving bowl in the center of a platter. Arrange the shrimp around the bowl. Alternatively, spoon the sauce into attractive cocktail glasses and drape the cooked shrimp around the rims. Garnish with lemon wedges and Italian parsley, if desired.

SHRIMP CEVICHE

SERVES 6 | **PREP TIME:** 10 minutes, plus up to 6 hours to marinate | **COOK TIME:** 15 minutes |
FINISHING TIME: 4 hours | **SOUS VIDE TEMPERATURE:** 130°F | **PARTY READY**

Ceviche, said to have originated in Peru a couple of millennia ago, is typically prepared with raw seafood that cures in citrus juice. I found that giving the shrimp a few minutes in the sous vide gives them a lovely texture, while eliminating any food safety concerns. Otherwise, this is a ceviche you might find in a Lima eatery, just perfect for a summer party.

1 to 1½ pounds (16 to 24) extra-large shrimp, peeled and deveined

½ cup freshly squeezed lime juice (from 4 or 5 limes)

1 cup freshly squeezed lemon juice (from 5 or 6 large lemons)

Juice of 1 orange

1 large tomato, diced

½ red onion, diced

½ serrano or jalapeño pepper, minced

2 tablespoons fresh cilantro, chopped

1 large cucumber, peeled and diced

1 large avocado, diced

1. Preheat the water bath to 130°F.

2. In a sous vide bag, place the shrimp in a single layer; vacuum-seal the bag and place it in the water bath. You might need to weigh it down to keep it submerged during cooking. Set the timer for 15 minutes. In a large bowl, prepare an ice-water bath with a 50/50 mixture of cold water and ice cubes.

3. Remove the bag and place it in the ice-water bath to chill for 5 minutes.

4. Cut the shrimp into 1-inch pieces. In a large bowl, combine the shrimp with the lime, lemon, and orange juices and let it marinate in the fridge for 15 minutes to 4 hours.

5. Add the tomato, red onion, serrano pepper, and cilantro and marinate for 2 more hours in the fridge.

6. Stir in the cucumber and avocado just before serving.

OCTOPUS WITH CHIMICHURRI

SERVES 4 | **PREP TIME:** 10 minutes | **COOK TIME:** 5 hours | **FINISHING TIME:** 30 minutes |
SOUS VIDE TEMPERATURE: 175°F

The most common complaint about octopus is the texture. It can be oh-so-chewy when it's cooked poorly. But fear not! If you can let your sous vide take over for a few hours, it will produce consistently tender octopus, all ready for a quick sear to blacken the edges. Chimichurri adds a tangy splash of green.

1 whole octopus (about 2½ pounds), well rinsed

3 tablespoons extra-virgin olive oil, divided

1 teaspoon kosher salt

Freshly ground black pepper

1 fresh rosemary sprig

Chimichurri (page 229), for serving

1. Preheat the water bath to 175°F.

2. Bring a large pot of water to a boil on the stovetop. Using tongs, submerge the octopus in the water for about 30 seconds, just until the tentacles hold a nice curl. In a large bowl, prepare an ice-water bath with a 50/50 mixture of cold water and ice cubes. Remove the octopus to the ice-water bath. (Blanching the octopus in this way clarifies the skin.)

3. Divide the octopus into four portions. If the head is still on, remove the hard beak from its center (where the tentacles begin) and the eyes, which are near the bottom of the head.

4. Place the octopus in a cooking bag (if using a zip-top bag, double it up); drizzle with about 1½ tablespoons olive oil and season with salt and black pepper. Add the rosemary. Vacuum-seal the bag or seal it using the water displacement method and place the bag into the water bath. Set the timer for 5 hours.

5. When the timer goes off, lift the bag out of the water. Place the cooking bag in the ice-water bath for 15 to 20 minutes, then remove the octopus and pat it dry. Heat a grill for searing.

6. Drizzle the octopus lightly with the remaining 1½ tablespoons olive oil and sear on a hot grill until nicely charred. If you prefer to sear under the broiler, place the octopus on a greased baking sheet under the broiler until crisp, 1 to 2 minutes on each side.

7. Slice the octopus into 2-inch pieces, plate it, and drizzle it with chimichurri.

OCTOPUS TAPAS

SERVES 4 | **PREP TIME:** 30 minutes | **COOK TIME:** 5 hours | **FINISHING TIME:** 3 to 8 hours |
SOUS VIDE TEMPERATURE: 175°F | **PARTY READY**

Galicia, in Spain's northwestern corner, is renowned for its *pulpo*, or octopus, and the recipes invariably feature local olive oil and smoked paprika. Your octopus will be bathed in a piquant marinade. A quick sear before serving will crisp it up, and all that's left to do is pour a glass of chilled Spanish white wine.

2 tablespoons extra-virgin olive oil, divided

2 yellow onions, coarsely chopped

6 garlic cloves, peeled and crushed

2 large bay leaves

3 teaspoons smoked paprika

3 teaspoons kosher salt, plus more for seasoning

1 cup white wine

1 whole octopus (about 2½ pounds), well rinsed

2 tablespoons freshly squeezed lemon juice

2 tablespoons finely chopped Italian parsley, plus a few leaves for garnish

1 generous pinch cayenne pepper

1. Preheat the water bath to 175°F.

2. In a saucepan over medium-high heat, warm 1 tablespoon olive oil. Add the onions, garlic, bay leaves, paprika, and salt. Cook, stirring, until the onions begin to soften, about 5 minutes. Add the white wine and bring to a boil; reduce the heat and simmer until the liquid has reduced, about 15 minutes. Remove from the heat and set aside.

3. Bring a large pot of water to a boil on the stovetop. With tongs, submerge the octopus in the water for about 30 seconds, just until the tentacles hold a nice curl. In a large bowl, prepare an ice-water bath with a 50/50 mixture of cold water and ice cubes. Remove the octopus to the ice-water bath for 5 minutes to chill, then pat it dry.

4. Divide the octopus into four portions. If the head is still on, remove the hard beak from its center (where the tentacles begin) and the eyes, which are near the bottom of the head.

5. Place the octopus pieces in a sous vide bag and pour the marinade over them. Ensure the octopus is evenly coated and in a single layer. Vacuum-seal the bag and place it into the water bath. Set the timer for 5 hours.

6. When it's done, remove the bag to an ice-water bath to cool for 1 hour, then refrigerate it for at least 2 hours or up to overnight.

7. Remove the pieces of octopus from the bag, leaving as much of the cooking liquid in the bag as possible. Transfer the liquid with its seasonings to a saucepan. Bring it to a rapid boil, then remove it from the heat. Pour the cooking liquid through a fine-mesh strainer to remove any solids. Transfer ⅔ cup of the cooking liquid to a mixing bowl and let it cool for 10 minutes. Stir in the remaining 1 tablespoon olive oil, the lemon juice, parsley, and cayenne pepper. Season with additional salt, if desired.

8. Pat the octopus pieces dry with a paper towel. Heat a broiler to high or fire up the outdoor grill and sear the octopus until the flesh is just beginning to char: in the broiler for 1 to 2 minutes on each side, and on the grill, about 3 minutes per side.

9. Slice the octopus into thick, diagonal pieces. Place on serving dishes and ladle the serving sauce over the top. Garnish with parsley leaves.

DID YOU KNOW? Perhaps the Spaniards' favorite accompaniment to *pulpo Gallego* is roasted or boiled potatoes, which they use to mop up the sauce. Fingerling Potatoes with Roasted Garlic (page 54) would fit the bill.

MAKE-AHEAD MAGIC: This recipe works brilliantly for a party; cook the octopus the day before, marinate it overnight, and then finish the sauce and sear the octopus before your guests arrive.

LOBSTER TAILS

SERVES 4 | **PREP TIME:** 15 minutes | **COOK TIME:** 45 minutes | **FINISHING TIME:** 5 minutes | **SOUS VIDE TEMPERATURE:** 140°F | **FAMILY FRIENDLY**

For many of us, lobster tails are the greatest luxury to come out of the ocean. Like so many other types of seafood, however, they are easily overcooked, and lobster with a rubbery consistency is an expensive mistake. Never fear. With just a tiny bit of prep work, this sous vide recipe will deliver tender, buttery lobster tails in very short order.

4 fresh lobster tails, still in the shells	4 tablespoons unsalted butter, cut into small pieces	2 tablespoons chopped parsley, for garnish (optional)
½ teaspoon kosher salt	4 lemon slices, for garnish (optional)	
Freshly ground black pepper		
1 garlic clove, minced		

1. Preheat the water bath to 140°F.

2. Using sharp kitchen shears, cut down the middle of the top of each shell, stopping just short of the tail fins.

3. Gently separate the shell. Using a spoon, carefully lift the meat up and out of the shell, leaving it attached at the tail flippers. Season the lobster meat with salt, pepper, and minced garlic.

4. Dot the top of the opened shell with pieces of butter, then gently lower the meat back into the shell.

5. Place the four lobster tails into a cooking bag. Vacuum-seal the bag or seal it using the water displacement method and place the bag into the water bath. Set the timer for 45 minutes.

6. When the timer goes off, remove the lobster tails and serve them garnished with lemon slices and parsley (if using).

CHANGE IT UP: If you're working with frozen lobster tails that are still in the shell, place them into a zip-top bag and submerge them in a bowl of room-temperature water for 15 to 20 minutes. This will thaw them enough to allow you to cut the top of the shell. Then cook as directed. These lobster tails could be the surf half of an extravagant surf and turf. How about a Classic Rib Eye (page 176) to accompany them?

TERIYAKI COD WITH VEGETABLE STIR-FRY

SERVES 4 | **PREP TIME:** 10 minutes | **COOK TIME:** 40 minutes | **FINISHING TIME:** 20 minutes |
SOUS VIDE TEMPERATURE: 113°F | **FAMILY FRIENDLY**

Cod is such a versatile fish: snowy white in color, mild in flavor, loaded with nutrients, and it has less mercury than other seafood. This recipe decks cod out with Japanese-inspired flavors. Enjoy it atop a bed of vivid, tender-crisp veggies.

2 tablespoons teriyaki sauce	Zest and juice of 2 limes	1 pound (4 to 5 cups) mixed
2 tablespoons Thai sweet	4 (6-ounce) skin-on	frozen stir-fry vegetables
chili sauce	cod fillets	1 tablespoon avocado or
2 tablespoons coconut	2 tablespoons sesame seeds	vegetable oil, for searing
oil, melted	2 tablespoons soy sauce	

1. Preheat the water bath to 113°F.

2. In a large bowl, mix the teriyaki sauce, sweet chili sauce, coconut oil, and the lime zest and juice. Put the cod in the marinade and turn it to coat evenly.

3. Transfer the cod and marinade to a zip-top bag. Slowly lower the bag into the water bath and seal it using the water displacement method. You might need to weigh the bag down to keep it submerged during cooking. Set the sous vide timer for 40 minutes.

4. In a dry skillet, toast the sesame seeds over medium-high heat, stirring them with a wooden spoon, until they turn golden and slightly fragrant.

5. When the timer goes off, remove the cod from the bag, pat it dry, and set it aside; reserve the marinade. In a sauté pan over medium-high heat, combine the marinade and the soy sauce. Add a splash of water, if needed, to thin the sauce. Sauté the vegetables in the sauce until tender-crisp, about 3 minutes. Remove the pan from the heat and cover it.

6. In a large cast-iron skillet over high heat, warm the avocado oil. Once it is really hot, sear the cod, skin-side down, for 30 seconds to 1 minute, until the skin is brown and crispy.

7. Plate the vegetables and lay the cod fillets on top. Sprinkle each serving generously with the toasted sesame seeds.

DID YOU KNOW? For years, both Atlantic and Pacific cod were among the most over-fished species. Thankfully, cod farming is slowly gaining traction in the United States.

CHIPOTLE-HONEY TILAPIA

SERVES 4 | **PREP TIME:** 10 minutes | **COOK TIME:** 30 minutes | **FINISHING TIME:** 5 minutes | **SOUS VIDE TEMPERATURE:** 134°F | **FAMILY FRIENDLY, QUICK PREP**

This recipe packs a complex array of flavors into a remarkably simple sauce. The chipotle chiles bring smoke and heat to the party, the adobo adds tang, and the honey provides the earthy sweetness that holds it all together. It's a lot of *wow!* in a short time.

¼ cup chipotle chiles in adobo sauce (or less, for a milder flavor)

2 tablespoons honey

2 scallions, white and green parts, coarsely chopped

2 tablespoons extra-virgin olive oil

1 teaspoon kosher salt

Freshly ground black pepper

4 (6- to 8-ounce) tilapia fillets

Coleslaw, for serving

Lemon wedges, for serving

1. Preheat the water bath to 134°F.

2. In a food processor, combine the chipotle chiles, honey, scallions, olive oil, salt, and a dash of pepper and pulse until blended.

3. Place the tilapia fillets in a cooking bag, making sure they are spread out in one layer. Use multiple bags, if necessary. Add the chipotle-honey sauce to the bag and ensure that the fillets are evenly coated. Vacuum-seal the bag(s) or seal them using the water displacement method and place them into the water bath. You might need to weigh them down to keep them submerged during cooking. Set the timer for 30 minutes.

4. When finished, transfer the fillets to serving plates with a drizzle of the sauce on top. Serve with coleslaw and lemon wedges.

SHRIMP AND GRITS

SERVES 4 | **PREP TIME:** 10 minutes | **COOK TIME:** 30 minutes | **FINISHING TIME:** 5 minutes |
SOUS VIDE TEMPERATURE: 130°F | **FAMILY FRIENDLY, QUICK PREP**

A big heap of shrimp, sautéed with bacon and served over grits, is a satisfying staple at restaurants all along the Gulf Coast. This variation marries light pink, moist, tender shrimp with pan-fried bacon and seasonings. This dish comes together fast and will build a big fan base, guaranteed.

1 pound shrimp of any size, peeled and deveined

Extra virgin olive oil, for drizzling

4 cups chicken broth or bone broth

1 cup corn grits

3 tablespoons butter

1 cup grated Parmesan cheese

Kosher salt

Freshly ground black pepper

6 slices bacon, chopped

4 teaspoons freshly squeezed lemon juice

2 tablespoons chopped parsley, plus a few leaves for garnish

1 cup thinly sliced scallions

1 large garlic clove, minced

1. Preheat the water bath to 130°F.

2. In a sous vide bag, place the shrimp in a single layer. Drizzle them with olive oil and vacuum-seal the bag. Use multiple bags, if necessary. Place the bag(s) in the water bath. You might need to weigh them down to keep them submerged during cooking. Set the timer for 30 minutes.

3. In a saucepan on the stovetop, bring the chicken or bone broth to a boil. Add the grits and simmer until the liquid is absorbed, about 20 minutes. Stir in the butter and Parmesan and season with salt and pepper.

4. Five minutes before the shrimp is done, in a skillet over medium heat, cook the bacon. Once the bacon fat starts to render, add the lemon juice, parsley, scallions, and garlic. Sauté for 3 minutes.

5. When the sous vide timer goes off, remove the shrimp from the water, open the bag, and add the shrimp and the cooking juice directly to the skillet, mixing well.

6. Serve the grits and spoon the shrimp and bacon mixture over them. Garnish with parsley leaves.

CHANGE IT UP: Skip the grits and serve the shrimp with Simple Polenta (page 40) or Essential Millet (page 41).

MEDITERRANEAN WHOLE RED SNAPPER

SERVES 4 | **PREP TIME:** 15 minutes | **COOK TIME:** 1 hour | **FINISHING TIME:** 5 minutes |
SOUS VIDE TEMPERATURE: 140°F | **FAMILY FRIENDLY**

Have you ever looked at a whole fish at the market, felt intimidated, and turned to the fillets? Your sous vide can get you past that apprehension. Let's start with a red snapper, enhancing this sweet, mild, nutty fish with a warm, rich spice mix. Surround it with colorful sautéed vegetables.

2 (1- to 1½-pound) whole red snappers, cleaned and gutted

10 garlic cloves, minced

Kosher salt

2 teaspoons ground cumin

2 teaspoons ground coriander

1 teaspoon freshly ground black pepper

1 teaspoon lemon zest

½ cup chopped fresh parsley

3 tablespoons extra-virgin olive oil, divided

1 medium red onion, sliced

3 bell peppers, different colors, cut into rounds

1 large tomato, sliced

1 to 2 tablespoons avocado or vegetable oil, for searing

2 lemons, cut into wedges, for serving

1. Preheat the water bath to 140°F.

2. Make 2 or 3 parallel shallow slits on each side of the fish. Mix the minced garlic with a pinch of salt and place some of the garlic-salt mixture into the slits; spread the remainder evenly throughout the gut cavities.

3. In a small bowl, combine the cumin, coriander, salt, black pepper, and lemon zest. Use about three-quarters of this mixture to season the fish both inside and out, pressing some into the slits on the sides.

4. Pack each gut cavity with the chopped parsley.

5. Place the snappers into a cooking bag; drizzle them with 2 tablespoons olive oil. Vacuum-seal the bag or seal it using the water displacement method and place it into the water bath. You might need to weigh the bag down to keep it submerged during cooking. Set the timer for 1 hour.

6. About 10 minutes before the sous vide timer goes off, in a sauté pan, heat the remaining 1 tablespoon olive oil over medium heat. Add the onion, bell peppers, and tomato; stir occasionally until the onion and peppers are tender, 3 to 4 minutes. Sprinkle with the remaining spice mix. Set aside.

7. Remove the fish from the water bath and pat it dry. Using the same skillet over high heat, add the avocado oil and sear each side of the fish for 30 seconds to 1 minute, until the skin is crisp.

8. Fillet the finished snapper into serving portions and plate it with the vegetables and lemon wedges.

CHANGE IT UP: In keeping with the Mediterranean theme, couscous would make a good companion for this dish, as would a serving of Essential Millet (page 41).

SEA BASS IN LEMON SAUCE

SERVES 4 | **PREP TIME:** 10 minutes | **COOK TIME:** 25 minutes | **FINISHING TIME:** 5 minutes |
SOUS VIDE TEMPERATURE: 122°F | **FAMILY FRIENDLY, QUICK PREP**

When you want an elegant seafood dinner but haven't the time or energy to fuss over one, this should be your go-to recipe. Sea bass fillets go into the sous vide in an Asian-inspired marinade and come out firm and moist just 25 minutes later. Quickly crisp the skin, place the fish on a bed of vermicelli, top with a bright and easy lemon sauce, and dig in!

3 tablespoons plus
2 teaspoons extra-virgin
olive oil, divided

2 teaspoons ginger juice, or
½ teaspoon ground ginger

1 tablespoon rice wine

1 tablespoon plus
1 teaspoon soy
sauce, divided

2 teaspoons cornstarch,
plus ½ teaspoon
cornstarch mixed with
½ teaspoon water

4 (4- to 6-ounce) skin-on
sea bass fillets

3 garlic cloves, crushed

¼ cup chicken stock

2 tablespoons freshly
squeezed lemon juice

3 lemon slices

½ teaspoon salt

1 tablespoon finely
chopped scallions

1 teaspoon sugar

8 ounces vermicelli

2 tablespoons sesame oil

1 tablespoon avocado or
vegetable oil, for searing

1. Preheat the water bath to 122°F.

2. In a large mixing bowl, combine 3 tablespoons olive oil, the ginger juice, rice wine, 1 tablespoon light soy sauce, and 2 teaspoons cornstarch and mix well.

3. Place the bass fillets in a cooking bag; use multiple bags, if necessary. Pour the marinade over them and ensure that the fish is evenly coated. Vacuum-seal the bag(s) or seal them using the water displacement method and place them into the water bath. You might need to weigh them down to keep them submerged during cooking. Set the timer for 25 minutes.

4. Meanwhile, in a saucepan, heat the remaining 2 teaspoons olive oil over medium heat. Add the garlic and sauté for 30 seconds. Add the chicken stock, lemon juice, lemon slices, the remaining 1 teaspoon soy sauce, the cornstarch-water slurry, salt, scallions, and sugar and bring to a simmer for 2 to 3 minutes, stirring. Set aside.

5. On another burner, bring a pot of water to a boil and cook the vermicelli according to the package instructions. When they're done, drain the noodles and toss them with the sesame oil.

6. When the sous vide timer goes off, remove the bass from the water bath and pat it dry. If you wish, reserve the cooking liquid for a future fish soup broth. Place the fish, skin-side down, in a very hot skillet lightly oiled with the avocado or vegetable oil, and sear over high heat for 30 seconds to 1 minute, until the skin is crisp and brown.

7. Divide the noodles among four serving plates. Portion the sea bass into 4 servings and place the pieces on top of the noodles. Top with the lemon sauce.

CHANGE IT UP: If the fish market is out of sea bass but has some handsome snapper, striped bass, cod, or grouper, they'll work fine with this recipe, too.

FRIED COD SANDWICHES WITH TARTAR SAUCE

MAKES 4 sandwiches | **PREP TIME:** 20 minutes | **COOK TIME:** 40 minutes | **FINISHING TIME:** 20 minutes | **SOUS VIDE TEMPERATURE:** 113°F | **FAMILY FRIENDLY**

This is the real deal, so much so that you'll feel like you're frequenting the most authentic British fish and chips shop. For this Americanized version, enjoy it with buns instead of the "chips" and serve with your favorite slaw.

4 (4- to 6-ounce) skinless cod fillets

2 tablespoons extra-virgin olive oil

½ cup all-purpose flour

1 cup panko bread crumbs

1 teaspoon kosher salt, divided

1 teaspoon freshly ground black pepper, divided

1 teaspoon onion powder

1 teaspoon paprika

1 teaspoon dried thyme

½ teaspoon cayenne

½ teaspoon garlic powder

2 large eggs

1 cup mayonnaise

6 tablespoons finely minced kosher dill pickles, plus optional pickle slices, for topping

¼ cup minced chives

1 teaspoon dried dill

2 to 4 tablespoons freshly squeezed lemon juice

Vegetable oil, for pan-frying

4 burger buns

Shredded lettuce, for topping (optional)

Tomato, thinly sliced, for topping (optional)

Coleslaw, for serving (optional)

1. Preheat the water bath to 113°F.

2. Place the cod fillets in a cooking bag in a single layer and drizzle them with olive oil. Vacuum-seal the bag or seal it using the water displacement method and place the bag into the water bath. You might need to weigh the bag down to keep it submerged during cooking. Set the timer for 40 minutes.

3. Sift the flour onto one plate and spread it out. On another plate, combine the panko with ½ teaspoon salt, ½ teaspoon pepper, the onion powder, paprika, thyme, cayenne, and garlic powder. In a bowl, whisk the eggs. Set aside.

4. In a large mixing bowl, combine the mayonnaise, pickles, chives, dill, and lemon juice and mix thoroughly.

5. When the timer goes off, remove the cod from the cooking bag and pat it dry. Sprinkle it with the remaining ½ teaspoon salt and ½ teaspoon pepper. Dredge each piece in flour; coat it thoroughly, and shake off the excess. Dip each piece in beaten egg and shake off any excess. Finally, dredge each piece in the panko mixture to coat well, pressing the fillet into the crumbs.

6. Heat a cast-iron skillet over high heat. Add the oil to the pan, up to about ¼ inch high. Fry the breaded fillets on each side for about 1 minute, or until the breading is golden and crisp. Slather the buns with the tartar sauce, add the fish fillets and any optional toppings, and enjoy with a big helping of slaw on the side!

CHANGE IT UP: Chopped capers can replace some or all of the chopped pickle in the tartar sauce.

MAKE-AHEAD MAGIC: By all means, make the tartar sauce and slaw a day or two in advance and refrigerate them until the fillets are ready.

THAI-STYLE SQUID WITH GREEN BEANS AND BASIL

SERVES 4 | **PREP TIME:** 2 hours or overnight | **COOK TIME:** 2 hours | **FINISHING TIME:** 10 minutes |
SOUS VIDE TEMPERATURE: 136°F

Asian squid stir-fries are unforgettable when done well and equally unforgettable, for different reasons, when the squid is tougher than shoe leather. It takes a lot of know-how to get it right: The cooking vessel, temperature, and time are all important factors. Sous vide takes all those variables out of play. You'll add your perfectly, predictably tender squid to the wok only at the last moment. This recipe gives you all the Thai flavor with none of the stress.

5 garlic cloves,
  finely chopped

2 fresh Thai chiles,
  thinly sliced

1 teaspoon brown sugar

1 tablespoon fish sauce

1 tablespoon oyster sauce

1 pound fresh whole squid

2 tablespoons vegetable oil,
  for stir-frying, plus more
  for drizzling

½ cup sliced red onion

1 cup sliced green beans

1½ cups Thai basil leaves

Classic Sous Vide Rice
  (page 42), for serving

1. In a large bowl, mix the garlic, chiles, brown sugar, fish sauce, and oyster sauce. Add the squid, stir, and cover; allow to marinate in the refrigerator for at least 2 hours or up to overnight.

2. When ready, preheat the water bath to 136°F. Transfer the squid from the marinade into a cooking bag, reserving the marinade separately; drizzle the squid with oil. Vacuum-seal the bag or seal it using the water displacement method and place the bag into the water bath. Set the timer for 2 hours.

3. When the timer goes off, remove the squid and cut it into 1-inch slices. Set aside.

4. In a wok or sauté pan, heat the vegetable oil over medium-high heat. Add the onion and sauté for 1 or 2 minutes, until it sweats. Add the green beans and the reserved marinade (including the garlic and chiles); cook, stirring, until the beans are a deep green but still crisp.

5. Add the squid and stir just long enough to reheat it and mix thoroughly. Turn off the heat and stir in the basil leaves. Serve with rice.

CHANGE IT UP: Can you substitute sweet basil for the Thai basil? Well, yes, but it will impart a less intense and less authentic flavor. It's worth a trip to your Asian grocer for the Thai variety if you crave that authentic flavor.

CHILI SOFT-SHELL CRAB

MAKES 4 crabs | **PREP TIME:** 10 minutes | **COOK TIME:** 3 hours to 3 hours 30 minutes |
FINISHING TIME: 5 minutes | **SOUS VIDE TEMPERATURE:** 145°F | **PARTY READY, QUICK PREP**

Singaporeans and Malaysians feud over who invented Chili Crab and who makes it better. Not to brag, but I've bested the whole lot of them with this recipe. (Okay, yes, I'm bragging.) My secret is to pour the traditional sweet, sour, and spicy sauce over soft-shell crabs. After all, why spend time fighting with crab shells when you can simply eat them?

4 soft-shell crabs, either fresh and live or frozen (frozen require 30 extra minutes' cooking time)
1 tablespoon cornstarch
2 tablespoons water

¼ cup vegetable oil
½ cup minced shallots
2 tablespoons grated ginger root
6 medium garlic cloves, minced

4 Thai chiles, minced
2 cups chicken broth
¼ cup tomato paste
½ cup Thai sweet chili sauce
½ cup thinly sliced scallions

1. Preheat the water bath to 145°F.

2. If you've bought live soft-shell crabs from your fish market, you'll need to prepare them before cooking. First, using scissors, snip straight across the front part of the shell just behind the eyes. This kills the crab instantly. Next, lift each half of the top shell and remove the feathery gills. Finally, flip the crab over and pull off the lower hinged plate (the pointed part) at the bottom of the shell.

3. When the water is at temperature, place the crabs into sous vide bags, vacuum-seal them, and put them into the bath. You might need to weigh them down to keep them submerged during cooking. Set the timer for 3 hours (or 3 hours 30 minutes, if the crabs are frozen).

4. About 15 minutes before the crabs are done, in small bowl, mix the cornstarch with the water and set it aside. In a saucepan, heat the vegetable oil over medium heat. Stir in the shallots, ginger, garlic, and chiles. Cook until fragrant, stirring, about 1 minute. Stir in the chicken broth, tomato paste, and chili sauce. Simmer for 1 minute and, if you like, season to taste with salt, sugar, and/or additional chili sauce. Stir in the cornstarch mixture and bring to a boil, stirring until thickened. Remove the sauce from the heat and stir in the scallions.

5. Remove the crabs from the sous vide when they're finished, spoon the chili sauce over them, and serve.

SWORDFISH STEAKS WITH ROMESCO

SERVES 4 | **PREP TIME:** 5 minutes | **COOK TIME:** 30 to 45 minutes | **FINISHING TIME:** 5 minutes |
SOUS VIDE TEMPERATURE: 130°F | **FAMILY FRIENDLY, QUICK PREP**

Swordfish can get tough or, worse, mushy when cooked incorrectly, but there's no risk of that here. Paired with a smoky Romesco sauce and oven-roasted asparagus, this swordfish could become your signature dish.

FOR THE FISH

4 (6-ounce) swordfish steaks

1 teaspoon kosher salt

Freshly ground black pepper

½ teaspoon paprika

¼ teaspoon
ground coriander

2 tablespoons extra-virgin
olive oil

FOR THE ROMESCO SAUCE

1 (16-ounce) jar roasted red
peppers, drained

1 cup unsalted
almonds, toasted

4 Roma tomatoes

2 garlic cloves, chopped

2 tablespoons
flat-leaf parsley

1 tablespoon sherry vinegar
or red wine vinegar

1 teaspoon smoked paprika

½ teaspoon chili powder or
cayenne pepper

¼ to ½ cup extra-virgin olive
oil, as needed

Kosher salt

1. Preheat the water bath to 130°F.

2. Season both sides of the swordfish steaks with salt and pepper. In a small bowl, mix the paprika and coriander together; sprinkle the spice mixture over both sides of the steaks. Place the steaks in a cooking bag in a single layer and drizzle them with the olive oil. Vacuum-seal the bag or seal it using the water displacement method and place the bag into the water bath. Set the timer for 30 to 45 minutes.

3. **Make the Romesco sauce:** Add the red peppers, almonds, tomatoes, garlic, parsley, vinegar, paprika, and chili powder or cayenne to a food processor or blender and puree until everything is finely chopped. With the machine running, drizzle in the olive oil a little at a time until a smooth sauce forms. Taste and add salt or more chili powder as necessary.

4. When the swordfish steaks are done, remove them from the bag and sear each side in a hot, lightly oiled skillet for 1 to 2 minutes, just long enough to brown and crisp the surfaces.

5. Plate the swordfish and top with a spoonful of Romesco sauce. A side of roasted asparagus or Sous Vide Kale (page 63) would complement this fish beautifully.

VINDALOO-SPICED MONKFISH

SERVES 4 | **PREP TIME:** 5 minutes | **COOK TIME:** 20 minutes | **FINISHING TIME:** 10 minutes |
SOUS VIDE TEMPERATURE: 125°F | **QUICK PREP**

Let's not pull any punches here: The monkfish is one ugly creature. Get past its sea-monster looks, though, and you have fillets with the mild flavor of other white fish and texture that's been likened to lobster. Here, you'll rub the fillets with a super-spicy vindaloo seasoning before sending them into the sous vide. A quick sear in butter creates just the right amount of crunch.

2 teaspoons turmeric

2 teaspoons cinnamon

1 teaspoon ground coriander

1 teaspoon ground ginger

1½ teaspoons to 1 tablespoon
  cayenne pepper

1 teaspoon garlic powder

1 teaspoon garam masala

1 teaspoon mustard powder

1 teaspoon paprika

2 pounds monkfish fillets,
  cut into 4 equal portions

2 tablespoons extra-virgin
  olive oil

1 tablespoon butter

1. Preheat the water bath to 125°F.

2. In a dry skillet over medium-high heat, toast the turmeric, cinnamon, coriander, ginger, cayenne, garlic powder, garam masala, mustard powder, and paprika until aromatic. Cover the monkfish fillets thoroughly with the toasted spice mix. Place the fillets in a cooking bag in a single layer and add a light drizzle of olive oil. Vacuum-seal the bag or seal it using the water displacement method and place the bag into the water bath. Set the timer for 20 minutes.

3. When the timer goes off, ensure that the fillets feel firm to the touch before removing them from the water. When it's done, remove the fish from the bag and pat it dry.

4. In a pan, melt the butter over medium-high heat. Sear the monkfish on both sides to form a nice crust, 1 to 2 minutes per side. Consider serving with Herb Butter Corn on the Cob (page 45).

DID YOU KNOW? When the Portuguese arrived in Goa, on the southwestern coast of India, in the 16th century, they brought a traditional garlic-and-wine marinade (*vinha d'alhos*) with them. It didn't take Goan chefs long to improve on the recipe, adding depth and heat, using just about every spice in their kitchens. We've been relishing vindaloo dishes ever since.

Thanksgiving Whole Turkey, page 128

POULTRY

CHICKEN LIVER PÂTÉ

MAKES 7 (4-ounce) Mason jars | **PREP TIME:** 20 minutes | **COOK TIME:** 1 hour 30 minutes |
FINISHING TIME: 3 hours | **SOUS VIDE TEMPERATURE:** 154°F | **PARTY READY**

Pâté is one of those things that most of us associate with posh restaurants and pricey food shops. Let your party guests ooh and ahh; it's not such a feat to whip up a batch in the kitchen, but you don't need to tell them that. It's also great for gifts. Serve with a crusty baguette or soda crackers.

6 tablespoons unsalted butter, divided

⅓ cup minced shallots

1 tablespoon fresh thyme leaves

1 garlic clove, minced

1 teaspoon anchovy paste (optional)

¼ cup Madeira wine

1 pound chicken livers, fat and connective tissues removed

¼ cup heavy (whipping) cream

Kosher salt

1. Preheat the water bath to 154°F.

2. In a medium sauté pan over medium heat, melt 2 tablespoons butter and cook until it is nutty brown and fragrant (taking care not to burn it), 3 to 5 minutes. Add the shallots and sauté for 1 minute. Add the thyme, garlic, and anchovy paste (if using) and sauté for 1 more minute. Add the Madeira and stir for 1 or 2 minutes more, allowing some of the alcohol to boil off.

3. Remove the pan from the heat and allow the mixture to rest for 10 minutes.

4. Strain the mixture through a fine-mesh sieve, pressing down with a cooking spoon to extract as much of the liquid as possible.

5. Pour the strained liquid into a blender or food processor; add the raw chicken livers and cream and season with salt. Blend until just smooth, then add the remaining 4 tablespoons butter slowly, blending to emulsify.

6. Transfer the puree into seven 4-ounce Mason jars. Twist the lids until fingertip-tight.

7. Place the jars in the sous vide and set the timer for 1 hour 30 minutes. In a large bowl, prepare an ice-water bath with a 50/50 mixture of cold water and ice cubes.

8. When the timer goes off, remove the jars and transfer them to the ice-water bath. Keep refilling the bowl with ice until the jars are completely chilled; it may take up to 3 hours.

BUFFALO WINGS

SERVES 6 to 8 | **PREP TIME:** 15 minutes | **COOK TIME:** 1 hour | **FINISHING TIME:** 30 minutes |
SOUS VIDE TEMPERATURE: 165°F | **PARTY READY**

The story goes that Teressa Bellissimo, owner of the Anchor Bar in Buffalo, New York, invented Buffalo wings as a bar snack in 1964. Food historians say the recipe is decades older, appearing first in Chicago's speakeasies during Prohibition. Maybe, but we don't call them Chicago wings.

4 pounds chicken wings

Kosher salt

8 tablespoons
  unsalted butter

1 cup Frank's RedHot
  Original Cayenne
  Pepper Sauce

3 quarts peanut or canola oil

Blue Cheese Sauce
  (page 233), for serving

Celery sticks, for serving

1. Preheat the water bath to 165°F.

2. Cut the wings into drumettes and flats; remove the wing tips and save them for stock or discard them.

3. Season the wings all over with salt. Place in a single layer in a sous vide bag with space between the pieces. Vacuum-seal the bag and place it into the heated water. Set the timer for 1 hour.

4. When the timer goes off, remove the wings from the bag and pat them dry with paper towels; discard the cooking liquid or save it for stock.

5. In a small saucepan, combine the butter and hot sauce and cook over medium-low heat, stirring occasionally, until the butter is melted. Transfer the sauce to a large bowl.

6. Meanwhile, in a Dutch oven or wok, heat the oil to 400°F. Working in small batches, carefully add the wings and cook, flipping them occasionally, while keeping the oil at 375 to 400°F, adjusting the heat as needed, until they are golden brown and crisp, about 3 minutes per batch. Using a slotted spoon, remove the wings to paper towels to drain. When all the wings are done, transfer them to the bowl with the sauce, toss to coat, and serve with the blue cheese sauce and celery.

CHANGE IT UP: Frank's RedHot Original Sauce claims to be "the secret ingredient in the first ever Buffalo wings recipe," but if you can't find it, then sriracha is a good substitute, having similar proportions of chili and vinegar.

THE BEST EVER WINGS

SERVES 4 | **PREP TIME:** 10 minutes | **COOK TIME:** 2 hours | **FINISHING TIME:** 20 minutes |
SOUS VIDE TEMPERATURE: 160°F | **FAMILY FRIENDLY, PARTY READY**

Mention wings nowadays, and one word jumps into most people's minds: Buffalo. Well, we're going to veer off that road to Buffalo with this recipe, and I think you'll find it a delicious change. These wings will get a good rubdown with a mix of smoked paprika, cumin, garlic, and cayenne before they go into the sous vide, creating your family's newest addiction.

1½ teaspoons kosher salt

2 teaspoons smoked paprika

1 teaspoon ground cumin

1 teaspoon cumin seeds, or 1¼ teaspoons ground cumin

1 teaspoon freshly ground black pepper

1 teaspoon garlic powder

1 teaspoon cayenne pepper

3 pounds chicken wings

3 tablespoons butter, melted

1. Preheat the water bath to 160°F.

2. In a bowl, combine the salt, paprika, cumin, cumin seeds, black pepper, garlic powder, and cayenne pepper and mix well.

3. Cut the wings into drumettes and flats; remove the wing tips and save them for stock or discard them.

4. Coat the chicken wings thoroughly with the spice mix. Place them in a single layer in a sous vide bag and vacuum-seal it. Place it into the heated water and set the timer for 2 hours. In a large bowl, prepare an ice-water bath with a 50/50 mixture of cold water and ice cubes.

5. When the timer goes off, remove the bag from the sous vide and place it into the ice-water bath until chilled, 10 to 15 minutes. Place an oven rack near the broiler and preheat the broiler to high.

6. Remove the wings, pat them dry with paper towels, and place them on a baking sheet. Brush them with melted butter and broil them until the skin is crisped up nicely, 2 to 3 minutes. Watch them closely, as they burn quickly.

MAKE-AHEAD MAGIC: If you'd like to cook the wings ahead of time and simply finish them before serving, you can place them on either wire racks or a baking sheet in your fridge for up to 24 hours after you take them out of the cooking bags and pat them dry.

CHINESE-STYLE STICKY AND CRISPY DRUMSTICKS

SERVES 4 | **PREP TIME:** 5 minutes | **COOK TIME:** 2 hours | **FINISHING TIME:** 25 minutes |
SOUS VIDE TEMPERATURE: 155°F | **FAMILY FRIENDLY, PARTY READY**

Set the phone down. You don't need to call for Chinese takeout. These spicy, crispy sous vide drumsticks will answer that craving just fine. And did I mention you need only 5 minutes of prep time? This recipe gives you all the flavors and textures you've come to love from the Chinese place around the corner, no tip required. Double the recipe and rock your next party!

2 pounds
  chicken drumsticks
Kosher salt
Freshly ground black pepper
2 tablespoons sesame oil
2 tablespoons oyster sauce
  or soy sauce

3 tablespoons hoisin sauce
2 tablespoons sriracha
2 garlic cloves, minced
2 teaspoons minced ginger
2 tablespoons honey
1 bird's eye chile,
  chopped (optional)

White sesame seeds,
  for serving
Chopped scallions,
  for serving

1. Preheat the water bath to 155°F.

2. Season the drumsticks with salt and pepper. Arrange in a single layer in a sous vide bag. Vacuum-seal the bag and place it into the heated water. Set the timer for 2 hours.

3. In a large bowl, prepare an ice-water bath with a 50/50 mixture of cold water and ice cubes. When the timer goes off, remove the bag and place it into the ice-water bath, allowing it to chill thoroughly, 10 to 15 minutes.

4. Remove the drumsticks from the bag and pat them dry. Save the cooking juices for a soup stock, if you wish.

5. Add the sesame oil to a skillet and heat it over high heat. Sear the chicken for 1 to 2 minutes on each side, or until the skin is golden brown and crispy. Transfer the drumsticks to a plate and set aside.

6. In the same pan, whisk the oyster sauce, hoisin sauce, sriracha, garlic, ginger, honey and chile pepper (if using) together over medium heat until well combined. Remove from the heat.

7. Place the drumsticks into the skillet with the sauce and stir till they're well-coated. Serve sprinkled with white sesame seeds and chopped scallions.

CARIBBEAN-INSPIRED CHICKEN

SERVES 4 | **PREP TIME:** 10 minutes, plus 2 to 12 hours to marinate | **COOK TIME:** 2 hours |
FINISHING TIME: 25 minutes | **SOUS VIDE TEMPERATURE:** 155°F | **FAMILY FRIENDLY**

A few of the cultural gems that have traveled round the world with the Caribbean diaspora are reggae music, Red Stripe beer, and Creole cuisine. Here, you'll bathe chicken drumsticks in a sweet, spicy, jerk-inspired marinade, and while they're cooking to perfection in the sous vide, you might consider roasting a mix of veggies to accompany it.

1 (0.7-ounce) packet Italian
  salad dressing mix
2 tablespoons brown sugar
2 tablespoons extra-virgin
  olive oil
2 tablespoons soy sauce

1 teaspoon cinnamon
1 tablespoon minced
  fresh thyme leaves, or
  1 teaspoon dried thyme
½ teaspoon chili powder

2 pounds skin-on
  chicken drumsticks
2 tablespoons avocado or
  vegetable oil
Potato bread, for
  serving (optional)

1. In a large bowl, combine the dressing mix, sugar, olive oil, soy sauce, cinnamon, thyme, and chili powder. Stir the marinade until combined well.

2. Rinse the chicken drumsticks, pat them dry with paper towels, and place them in the marinade; turn them to make sure they are well coated. Allow them to marinate in the fridge for 2 to 12 hours.

3. When ready to cook, preheat the water bath to 155°F. Place the drumsticks in a sous vide bag in one layer with some space between them. Vacuum-seal the bag, lower it into the water, and set the timer for 2 hours.

4. In a large bowl, prepare an ice-water bath with a 50/50 mixture of cold water and ice cubes. When the sous vide timer goes off, transfer the bag to the ice-water bath and chill thoroughly. Remove the drumsticks and pat them dry with paper towels. Reserve the cooking juice (see *Change It Up* tip).

5. Heat the avocado oil in a skillet over medium-high heat and sear the drumsticks until the skin is crispy on all sides, 3 to 4 minutes per side. Serve immediately. For a true Jamaican touch, serve with potato bread to mop up the sauce.

CHANGE IT UP: For that roasted veggie mix I suggested, in a baking pan, combine 1 pound red potatoes, quartered; 1 carrot, cut into thick slices; 3 stalks celery, cut into thick slices; and the reserved cooking juice. Season with salt, pepper, and 1 tablespoon minced fresh thyme or 1 teaspoon dried. Roast the vegetables in a 400°F oven for about 30 minutes.

CRISPY CHICKEN THIGHS

SERVES 4 | **PREP TIME:** 10 minutes | **COOK TIME:** 45 minutes | **FINISHING TIME:** 10 minutes |
SOUS VIDE TEMPERATURE: 167°F | **FAMILY FRIENDLY**

Thighs are among the tastiest parts of the chicken; their darker meat has more intense flavor, especially when cooked sous vide. They have more fat than white meat, but bear in mind, it's monounsaturated, or the "good" fat, so enjoy freely.

2 to 3 pounds skin-on, deboned chicken thighs (about 8 thighs)
Kosher salt

Freshly ground black pepper
Extra-virgin olive oil, for drizzling

Thyme or rosemary sprig (optional)
2 to 3 tablespoons avocado or vegetable oil, for searing

1. Preheat the water bath to 167°F.

2. Place the chicken thighs on a work surface, skin facing up, and use a wooden mallet to flatten them evenly and tenderize them.

3. Season the thighs with salt and pepper on both sides.

4. Place them in a sous vide bag and drizzle with olive oil. Add the fresh herbs (if using) and vacuum-seal the bag. Place it into the water bath and set the timer for 45 minutes.

5. When the timer goes off, remove the chicken from the bag (save the cooking juices for future use or for a pan sauce, if you like—see *Change It Up* tip). Pat the thighs dry with paper towels.

6. In a cast-iron skillet, heat the avocado oil over medium-high heat. Place the thighs, skin-side down, in the hot pan and press them down with a spatula until the skin is crispy and golden brown, 4 to 5 minutes. Flip them and cook the other side for another 1 to 2 minutes to ensure that the meat is heated all the way through. Serve, crispy skin facing up.

CHANGE IT UP: If you'd like a simple but lovely pan sauce, when you've removed the chicken thighs from the skillet after searing, add 1 minced shallot or 1 minced garlic clove to the pan. Sauté until fragrant, then pour in 1 cup white wine and the reserved cooking juices from the sous vide bag. Add a pat of butter, some minced fresh herbs (optional), and 1 teaspoon mustard (optional). Stir until the sauce is smooth, season with salt and pepper, and serve.

THAI-INSPIRED CHICKEN THIGHS

SERVES 4 | **PREP TIME:** 10 minutes, plus 30 minutes to 12 hours to marinate | **COOK TIME:** 2 hours |
FINISHING TIME: 15 minutes | **SOUS VIDE TEMPERATURE:** 149°F | **FAMILY FRIENDLY, PARTY READY**

You could fly to Bangkok and buy this dish at everyone's favorite "secret" food stall, or Plan B,
you could create it in your kitchen. Boost the flavor of the sous vide chicken thighs with Thai
aromatics—such as ginger, garlic, basil, cilantro, and sriracha—and serve them on a bed of
sliced tomatoes.

¼ cup coarsely chopped
fresh Thai basil (or
sweet basil, if Thai is
unavailable), divided

¼ cup coarsely chopped
fresh cilantro, divided

1½ tablespoons finely grated
fresh ginger

2 tablespoons brown sugar

3 tablespoons
reduced-sodium soy sauce
or light soy sauce

3 tablespoons extra-virgin
olive oil

1½ tablespoons
minced garlic

1½ tablespoons sriracha

1½ tablespoons fish sauce

4 pounds skin-on, bone-in
chicken thighs (8 thighs)

2 to 3 tablespoons avocado
or vegetable oil, for searing

4 medium tomatoes, sliced

1. In a small bowl, whisk together the basil, cilantro, ginger, brown sugar, soy sauce,
   olive oil, garlic, sriracha, and fish sauce until blended. Cover and refrigerate half of
   the marinade.

2. Pour the remaining half of the marinade in a large zip-top bag; add the chicken
   and shake to coat. Let the chicken marinate in the refrigerator for 30 minutes
   or overnight.

3. Preheat the water bath to 149°F. When the water reaches temperature, take the bag
   out of the fridge, open it, and reseal it using the water displacement method. Place
   the bag into the water and set the timer for 2 hours.

4. When the timer goes off, remove the bag from the water bath. Remove the chicken
   and pat it dry with paper towels; save the cooking juices for soup or an optional pan
   sauce for the chicken thighs (see *Change It Up* tip).

5. In a large cast-iron skillet, heat the avocado oil over high heat. Place the chicken in the hot pan to sear, skin-side down. Press the chicken down slightly to allow good contact between the skin and the pan. Sear for 2 to 3 minutes, or until the skin is crispy.

6. Lay the tomato slices on 4 serving plates. Place the chicken on top and drizzle with the reserved Thai marinade.

CHANGE IT UP: Any dark meat would work as nicely with this bold Thai sauce, so bring on the drumsticks. If you'd like some extra sauce, reserve the chicken juices after cooking, add a pat of butter and simmer it down until it has reduced by half to make a pan sauce.

MAKE-AHEAD MAGIC: If you like, when you remove the chicken from the sous vide (still in its cooking bag), transfer it to an ice-water bath to chill completely, roughly 15 minutes. You can then store the cooked chicken in the fridge for up to 3 days before finishing and serving.

CHICKEN TAGINE

SERVES 4 to 6 | **PREP TIME:** 10 minutes | **COOK TIME:** 45 minutes | **FINISHING TIME:** 40 minutes |
SOUS VIDE TEMPERATURE: 167°F | **FAMILY FRIENDLY, PARTY READY**

Tagine (or tajine) is the name of a type of North African earthenware cooking vessel with a conical lid, and it's also the name for the hearty stews cooked in it. Although the brightly painted clay tagines are gorgeous to look at, we're going to use the greater precision of the sous vide to guarantee tender, juicy chicken thighs. Otherwise, though, this recipe includes an authentic Moroccan spice mixture and the classic tagine vegetables. It's popular to serve tagine with couscous, but if you want to score authenticity points, serve this with a Middle Eastern flatbread (traditionally used in lieu of utensils to scoop up the tagine).

3 to 4 pounds skin-on, deboned chicken thighs (8 to 12 thighs)
Kosher salt
Freshly ground black pepper
3 tablespoons extra-virgin olive oil, divided
Zest and juice of 1 lemon
5 garlic cloves, minced, divided
1 teaspoon paprika

1 teaspoon ground cumin
½ teaspoon ground ginger
½ teaspoon ground coriander
¼ teaspoon cayenne pepper
¼ teaspoon ground cinnamon
1 large yellow onion, halved and cut into ¼-inch-thick slices

2 tablespoons all-purpose flour
1¾ cups chicken broth
2 tablespoons honey
2 or 3 carrots, peeled and cut crosswise into ½-inch-thick slices
½ cup green olives, pitted and halved
2 tablespoons chopped fresh cilantro leaves

1. Preheat the water bath to 167°F.

2. Place the thighs on a work surface with the skin facing up and pound them with a wooden mallet to flatten and tenderize them.

3. Season the thighs with salt and black pepper on both sides. Place them in a sous vide bag (using multiple bags, if needed, to maintain a bit of space between the pieces) and drizzle with 2 tablespoons olive oil. Vacuum-seal the bags. Place them in the water bath and set the timer for 45 minutes.

4. In a bowl, combine 1 teaspoon lemon zest with 1 minced garlic clove; set aside and reserve the remaining zest separately. In a separate bowl, squeeze the juice from the lemon and set it aside.

5. In another bowl, combine the paprika, cumin, ginger, coriander, cayenne pepper, and cinnamon.

6. In a large bowl, prepare an ice-water bath with a 50/50 mixture of cold water and ice cubes. When the sous vide timer goes off, transfer the bag to the ice-water bath to chill completely, 10 to 15 minutes. Remove the chicken from the bag and reserve the cooking juices. Pat the thighs dry with paper towels.

7. In a Dutch oven or large pan, heat the remaining 1 tablespoon olive oil over high heat. Sear the thighs, skin-side down, applying pressure with a spatula until the skin is golden and crispy, 2 to 3 minutes. Transfer the chicken to a plate and let it rest.

8. Reduce the heat to medium and, in the same pan, cook the onion slices for about 5 minutes, until they just start to brown. (Add small amounts of water, as necessary, if the pan gets too dry.)

9. Add the remaining 4 minced garlic cloves and cook for about 30 seconds. Add the spice mix and flour, stirring constantly, until the spices are fragrant.

10. Add the broth, honey, and remaining lemon zest; mix thoroughly and scrape the bottom of the pan to loosen any browned bits.

11. Add the reserved cooking juices and the carrot slices. Bring to a boil, then reduce the heat and cover, allowing the tagine to simmer until the carrots are tender-crisp, 10 to 15 minutes.

12. Place the chicken thighs into the pan and stir in the olives, the lemon zest–garlic mixture, cilantro, and 1 tablespoon lemon juice. Taste the sauce and adjust the seasoning with salt, pepper, and more lemon juice to taste.

MAKE-AHEAD MAGIC: You can prepare the sous vide chicken before you make your tagine. Simply remove the sous vide bag from the ice-water bath and place it in your fridge for up to 3 days. When you're ready, sear the chicken and carry on from there.

HONEY-BALSAMIC CHICKEN LEGS

SERVES 4 | **PREP TIME:** 10 minutes, plus 1 to 12 hours to marinate | **COOK TIME:** 1 hour |
FINISHING TIME: 25 minutes | **SOUS VIDE TEMPERATURE:** 158°F | **FAMILY FRIENDLY**

Chicken legs pair well with colorful sauces like this one: Sweet, sour, infused with garlic and herbs, this is a marinade that turns into a thick, dark sauce at serving time. Your friends will be asking you for this recipe—or asking you to make it again!

3 to 4 pounds bone-in, skin-on chicken drumsticks or thighs

2 garlic cloves

1½ tablespoons fresh rosemary, or 1½ teaspoons dried

1½ tablespoons fresh oregano, or 1½ teaspoons dried

1½ tablespoons fresh thyme, or 1½ teaspoons dried

¼ cup balsamic vinegar

1 teaspoon kosher salt

½ teaspoon freshly ground black pepper

1 tablespoon honey

2 tablespoons avocado or vegetable oil, for searing

1. Rinse the drumsticks and pat them dry. Place them in a large zip-top bag.

2. In a small bowl, whisk the garlic, rosemary, oregano, thyme, vinegar, salt, pepper, and honey together. Pour the marinade over the chicken. Seal the bag and shake well. Let the chicken marinate in the refrigerator for at least 1 hour, or as long as overnight.

3. Preheat the water bath to 158°F. Transfer the drumsticks to a sous vide bag (or multiple bags if necessary), placing them in a single layer; reserve the marinade in a bowl. Vacuum-seal the bag and place it into the water. Set the timer for 1 hour.

4. In a large bowl, prepare an ice-water bath with a 50/50 mixture of cold water and ice cubes. When the timer goes off, transfer the bag to the ice-water bath; let it chill for 10 to 15 minutes.

5. Remove the drumsticks from the sous vide bag and pat them dry. Save the cooking juices for other uses, if you like.

6. Heat the oil in a skillet over high heat. When the pan is hot, sear the drumsticks until the skin is crispy, about 2 minutes on each side. Set the seared drumsticks aside and let them rest.

7. Add the reserved marinade to the same skillet. Bring it to a rapid boil and simmer, stirring, until the sauce has thickened, 2 to 3 minutes. Pour the honey-balsamic sauce over the chicken and serve.

PERFECT CHICKEN BREASTS

SERVES 4 | **PREP TIME:** 5 minutes | **COOK TIME:** 2 hours | **FINISHING TIME:** 10 minutes |
SOUS VIDE TEMPERATURE: 146°F | **FAMILY FRIENDLY, QUICK PREP**

The recipe needs only 15 minutes of hands-on attention and produces flawless chicken breasts, every single time. These chicken breasts are the foundation for out-of-this-world chicken salad, sandwiches, stir-fries, a burrito bowl, or a Classic Cobb Salad (page 29), just for starters.

4 whole boneless, skinless or bone-in, skin-on chicken breasts	Kosher salt Freshly ground black pepper 2 teaspoons smoked paprika	4 thyme sprigs 2 to 3 tablespoons avocado or vegetable oil, for searing

1. Preheat the water bath to 146°F.

2. Season the chicken breasts generously on both sides with salt, pepper, and paprika.

3. Place the chicken in a cooking bag, along with the thyme. Vacuum-seal the bag or seal it using the water displacement method and place the bag into the water bath. Set the timer for 2 hours.

4. When the timer goes off, remove the chicken breasts from the cooking bag and pat them dry with paper towels. Save the cooking juices for soup stock, if you like.

5. In a cast-iron skillet, heat the oil over high heat. Sear the chicken breasts, pressing down with a spatula, for about 45 seconds on one side (the skin side, if the breasts have skin).

6. Transfer the seared chicken breasts to a cutting board and let them rest for 2 to 3 minutes. Slice and serve.

CLASSIC BBQ CHICKEN

SERVES 4 | **PREP TIME:** 5 minutes | **COOK TIME:** 2 hours | **FINISHING TIME:** 15 minutes |
SOUS VIDE TEMPERATURE: 158°F | **FAMILY FRIENDLY, PARTY READY**

Using the sous vide for the lion's share of the cooking results in exquisitely tender meat, and grilling the chicken at the end with BBQ sauce adds the requisite smokiness. The finale will be the juiciest BBQ chicken you've ever had. Just double the recipe if you're hosting the neighborhood cookout. Serving with a bowl of Potato and Sweet Potato Salad (page 57) is an excellent plan.

3 to 4 pounds bone-in, skin-on chicken drumsticks and thighs

Kosher salt
Freshly ground black pepper

1 to 2 cups Honey-Spiced Barbecue Sauce (page 230) **or your favorite store-bought sauce**

1. Preheat the water bath to 158°F.

2. Place the chicken in a sous vide bag in a single layer, using multiple bags, if needed. Season it with salt and pepper and vacuum-seal the bag(s). Submerge them in the heated water and set the timer for 2 hours.

3. When the chicken is finished, remove it from the sous vide bag and pat it dry.

4. To finish, place the chicken parts on a hot grill, skin-side down. Brush with barbecue sauce and let them crisp up for about 5 minutes. Flip them over, brush the top side with barbecue sauce and let them cook another 2 to 3 minutes. Serve with extra barbecue sauce.

MAKE-AHEAD MAGIC: If you'd like to cook the chicken ahead of time, remove the bag from the sous vide when it's done and place it in an ice-water bath to chill thoroughly. Keep the bag in your refrigerator for up to 3 days before you grill the chicken.

CHICKEN ROULADES WITH PROSCIUTTO AND SPINACH

SERVES 4 | **PREP TIME:** 30 minutes | **COOK TIME:** 2 hours | **FINISHING TIME:** 40 minutes | **SOUS VIDE TEMPERATURE:** 149°F | **FAMILY FRIENDLY**

Roulades may look, at first glance, like fussy "restaurant food," but don't be shy. I'll walk you through the steps to load up chicken breasts with prosciutto, cheese, baby spinach, and red onion. As the crowning glory, you'll sear them in bacon grease. Not fussy, simply fabulous.

4 whole boneless, skinless chicken breasts
Kosher salt
Freshly ground black pepper
Garlic powder, for seasoning

12 slices prosciutto
¼ cup finely diced red onion
1 cup baby spinach
4 ounces provolone cheese, cut into sticks

2 to 3 tablespoons avocado or vegetable oil, for searing
Finely chopped parsley, for garnish

1. Preheat the water bath to 149°F.

2. Butterfly each breast, carefully slicing through the meat laterally, leaving it joined at the far side and then opening it like the wings of a butterfly. Place the butterflied chicken between sheets of plastic and flatten each piece with the flat side of a tenderizing mallet or a rolling pin.

3. Place one flattened chicken breast, skinned-side down, on a piece of food-safe plastic wrap. Season the chicken with salt, pepper, and garlic powder. Cover half of the breast with 3 slices prosciutto. Place 1 tablespoon diced onion on top of that, followed by ¼ cup baby spinach and 1 or 2 cheese sticks. Starting with this "loaded" end of the chicken breast, roll it into a tight wrap, and then wrap it snugly in the plastic wrap. The end result should look like a plump, firm sausage encased in chicken breast. Repeat with the remaining chicken breasts.

4. Place the roulades in a large sous vide bag and vacuum-seal it. Lower the bag into the water and set the timer for 2 hours.

5. When the timer goes off, remove the roulades from the sous vide bag and the plastic wrap and pat them dry. In a skillet, heat the oil over high heat and sear the roulades until they are golden and crispy. Serve, sliced or whole, garnished with chopped parsley.

CHANGE IT UP: By all means, adjust the types of meat and cheese inside the roulades. Thinly sliced Danish ham, chorizo, and speck are all good candidates. Mozzarella, Emmental, Gouda, and Jack cheese will all bring distinctive flavors to the party.

CHICKEN TORTILLA SOUP

SERVES 4 | **PREP TIME:** 5 minutes | **COOK TIME:** 1 hour | **FINISHING TIME:** 40 minutes |
SOUS VIDE TEMPERATURE: 150°F | **FAMILY FRIENDLY**

I've always been a fan of keeping shredded chicken in the fridge. It's one of those ultra-versatile staples and it's just the thing for soups like this one. But all tortilla soup fans know that the best part is the toppings. Who can resist the avocado, tortilla chips, and shredded cheese melting over everything?

4 whole boneless, skinless
  chicken breasts
1 tablespoon extra-virgin
  olive oil
Kosher salt
Freshly ground black pepper
2 thyme sprigs
2 cups water
2 tablespoons avocado or
  vegetable oil, for searing
8 to 10 plum tomatoes,
  or 1 (28-ounce) can
  diced tomatoes

1 cup chopped white
  onion, divided
1 cup packed cilantro, plus
  more for topping
3 garlic cloves
1 to 2 cups chicken
  broth, divided
2 cups chopped zucchini
2 cups mixed frozen carrots
  and peas

⅛ teaspoon hot sauce
  (I like ghost pepper
  sauce) (optional)
2 cups tortilla chips,
  crushed, for topping
2 avocados, sliced,
  for topping
1 cup shredded cheddar
  cheese, for topping
Lime or lemon wedges,
  for serving

1. Preheat the water bath to 150°F.

2. Place the chicken breasts in a zip-top bag. Drizzle them with the olive oil and season with salt and pepper. Add the thyme sprigs and water to the bag. Slowly lower the bag into the water bath and seal it using the water displacement method. Set the timer for 1 hour. The chicken breasts can be cooked for up to 3 hours.

3. When the chicken is finished, remove the breasts from the bag. Reserve the broth. Pat the chicken dry with paper towels. In a cast-iron skillet, heat the avocado oil and sear the chicken breasts for about 1 minute on each side, or until browned. Remove the chicken to a plate and set it aside.

4. In a blender or food processor, combine the tomatoes, ½ cup onion, cilantro, and garlic and blend until smooth. Add the chicken broth to the reserved broth from the cooking bag to get a total of 2 cups liquid; add this to the blender and process to mix thoroughly.

5. In a medium saucepan, combine the blended broth, any remaining chicken broth, zucchini, frozen carrots and peas, and remaining ½ cup onion. Bring to a boil and allow the mixture to simmer, covered, until the vegetables are tender, about 15 minutes.

6. Shred the chicken with two forks. Measure out 2 firmly packed cups shredded chicken for the soup. Refrigerate the rest for another use; it'll keep in the refrigerator for up to 3 days.

7. Add the shredded chicken and the hot sauce (if using) to the soup. Stir until well mixed and evenly heated.

8. Divide the soup among 4 bowls and add the tortilla chips, avocado, and cheese. Garnish each bowl with cilantro and serve with lime wedges.

FRIED CHICKEN

SERVES 6 to 8 | **PREP TIME:** 10 minutes | **COOK TIME:** 3 hours | **FINISHING TIME:** 30 minutes |
SOUS VIDE TEMPERATURE: 155°F | **FAMILY FRIENDLY, PARTY READY**

If the thought of making fried chicken at home is enough to send you running to KFC, this recipe will put the brakes on that—the chicken pieces will cook to the ideal temperature in the sous vide, and then you'll simply bread them and fry just long enough to give that coating some major-league crunch. Consider serving this chicken on top of waffles, drizzled with maple syrup.

1 (4-pound) whole chicken, or 4 pounds bone-in, skin-on chicken pieces	2 quarts vegetable oil	3 tablespoons onion powder (optional)
Kosher salt	6 cups all-purpose flour	1 tablespoon garlic powder (optional)
Freshly ground black pepper	3 tablespoons paprika (optional)	2 cups buttermilk

1. Preheat the water bath to 155°F.

2. If you're starting with a whole chicken, divide it into skin-on thighs, drumsticks, and wings and two whole boneless, skin-on breasts. Save the bones for stock, if desired.

3. Season the chicken pieces with salt and pepper.

4. Place the chicken pieces into sous vide bags, putting the dark meat (thighs and drumsticks) into one bag and breasts and wings into another. The dark meat will cook longer. Make sure all the pieces are in a single layer and vacuum-seal the bags. Put the bag with the white meat into the fridge for the time being and place the dark meat in the heated water. Set the timer for 2 hours.

5. When the timer goes off, add the bag containing the chicken breasts and wings to the water bath, leaving the dark meat in the water, and set the timer for 1 more hour.

6. In a large pot or Dutch oven, heat 3 to 4 inches of oil until it reaches about 400°F. At the same time, preheat the oven to its lowest setting to keep the finished chicken pieces warm between frying and serving.

7. While the oil is heating, in one bowl, mix the flour, paprika (if using), onion powder (if using), and garlic powder (if using); season with pepper. Pour the buttermilk into a separate bowl and set both aside.

8. When the sous vide timer goes off, remove the chicken pieces and pat them dry with paper towels. Cut the chicken breasts in half.

9. Dip each chicken piece in buttermilk, then in the flour mixture. If you like a thicker, crunchier coating, dip first in the flour mixture, then in buttermilk, and then once more in the flour.

10. Fry the chicken pieces in batches until the coating is golden and crispy, 2 to 3 minutes per side. Transfer finished chicken batches to the oven to stay warm, then serve.

CHANGE IT UP: Feel free to experiment with the seasonings in the breading mix, adding cayenne pepper for some heat, or dried herbs, ground mustard, or ginger.

HONEY-GARLIC CHICKEN

SERVES 4 | **PREP TIME:** 10 minutes, plus 8 hours to marinate | **COOK TIME:** 2 hours |
FINISHING TIME: 10 minutes | **SOUS VIDE TEMPERATURE:** 146°F | **FAMILY FRIENDLY**

This recipe hinges on the richly flavorsome marinade, which will infuse both the chicken and
the oven-roasted vegetables that will accompany it. With nominal hands-on time, you can put
a wholesome, delicious dinner on the table.

½ cup soy sauce

6 tablespoons honey

½ cup ketchup

2 tablespoons minced garlic
  (about 3 medium cloves)

1 teaspoon dried basil

½ teaspoon dried oregano

¼ teaspoon red
  pepper flakes

¼ teaspoon freshly ground
  black pepper

4 boneless, skinless
  or bone-in, skin-on
  chicken breasts

1 pound red potatoes,
  chopped, unpeeled

4 medium carrots, chopped

2 tablespoons avocado or
  vegetable oil, for searing

Fresh parsley leaves,
  for garnish

1. In a zip-top bag, combine the soy sauce, honey, ketchup, garlic, basil, oregano, red
   pepper flakes, and black pepper. Add the chicken and mix as needed to coat all
   the meat. Put the chicken in the refrigerator to marinate for at least 8 hours or up
   to overnight.

2. Preheat the water bath to 146°F. Transfer the chicken breasts to a sous vide bag;
   reserve the marinade. Ensure that the breasts are in a single layer with a bit of space
   between them. Vacuum-seal the bag and place it into the heated water. Set the timer
   for 2 hours.

3. About 45 minutes before the sous vide is finished, preheat the oven to 400°F. Toss the
   potatoes and carrots in the marinade. Line a baking sheet with foil and spread the
   vegetables and marinade on it. Roast in the oven for 30 minutes, or until the vegetables are fork-tender. Remove them from the oven and set aside.

4. When the timer goes off, remove the chicken breasts from the bag and pat them dry
   with a paper towel.

5. In a cast-iron skillet over high heat, heat the avocado oil. Sear the chicken breasts,
   pressing down with a spatula, for about 45 seconds on one side (the skin side, if the
   breasts have skin).

6. Serve the chicken breasts, either whole or sliced, with the roasted carrots and
   potatoes and garnished with parsley leaves.

PERFECT POACHED WHOLE CHICKEN

SERVES 4 | **PREP TIME:** 25 minutes | **COOK TIME:** 6 hours | **FINISHING TIME:** 20 minutes | **SOUS VIDE TEMPERATURE:** 150°F | **FAMILY FRIENDLY**

There's nothing as homey as serving an entire chicken for dinner. Coated with a dry rub, your chicken will poach in stock with an array of vegetables, emerging from the sous vide evenly cooked and blessedly moist. Five minutes under the broiler to brown the skin, and you have your entire meal on a platter.

2 teaspoons kosher salt

2 teaspoons paprika

1 teaspoon cayenne pepper

1 teaspoon dried thyme

2 teaspoons freshly ground black pepper

½ teaspoon garlic powder

1 (3- to 4-pound) whole chicken

4 cups chicken stock

¾ pound pearl onions or shallots, peeled

¾ pound new potatoes, unpeeled (about 8)

2 garlic cloves

3 medium carrots

4 ounces dried shiitake mushrooms, soaked and drained, liquid reserved

1 tablespoon Dijon mustard

1 thyme sprig

2 bay leaves

1 to 2 tablespoons butter

1 to 2 tablespoons all-purpose flour (optional)

1. Preheat the water bath to 150°F.

2. In a bowl, combine the salt, paprika, cayenne pepper, thyme, black pepper, and garlic powder and mix well. Rub the seasoning mixture over the outside of the chicken and throughout the cavity. Truss the drumsticks together with kitchen twine.

3. Place the chicken into a large zip-top bag. Add the stock, pearl onions, new potatoes, garlic, carrots, mushrooms and their soaking liquid, mustard, thyme, and bay leaves. Slowly lower the bag into the water bath and seal it using the water displacement method. Set the timer for 6 hours.

4. About 15 minutes before the sous vide timer goes off, preheat the broiler to high. Remove the bag from the sous vide. Remove the chicken and pat it dry with paper towels. Pour the cooking liquid through a sieve and reserve the broth. Set the vegetables aside, covered to keep them warm. Place the chicken on a roasting rack, untruss it, and place it under the broiler for 5 minutes to brown the skin.

5. In a saucepan, bring the broth to a boil, reduce the heat, and simmer until it's reduced by half. Add the butter. If you'd like a thicker gravy, add the flour, stirring constantly, until it reaches your preferred consistency. Serve with the chicken and vegetables.

TURMERIC CHICKEN WITH GINGER-CILANTRO SAUCE

SERVES 6 to 8 | **PREP TIME:** 10 minutes, plus 2 to 12 hours to marinate | **COOK TIME:** 3 hours | **FINISHING TIME:** 10 minutes | **SOUS VIDE TEMPERATURE:** 155°F | **FAMILY FRIENDLY, PARTY READY**

For your next family meal or dinner party, treat chicken to a turmeric-ginger rubdown, and you too can jump on the turmeric bandwagon. Touted for its anti-inflammatory, antioxidant goodness, this spice is rumored to help prevent cancer, heart disease, and Alzheimer's. But for our purposes, this recipe just tastes *really* good. Couscous, steamed broccoli, or Best Cabbage Wedges (page 59) would be lovely accompaniments.

1 (4-pound) whole chicken, or 4 pounds skin-on chicken parts

1 tablespoon turmeric

2 tablespoons water

2 teaspoons kosher salt, divided

1 teaspoon ground ginger

1 teaspoon dried thyme

1 cup packed fresh cilantro

⅓ cup peeled and coarsely chopped fresh ginger

5 scallions, green parts only

¼ cup extra-virgin olive oil

1. If you're starting with a whole chicken, divide it into skin-on thighs, drumsticks, wings, and two whole boneless breasts.

2. In a small bowl, mix the turmeric and water and stir until smooth. Spread the turmeric paste onto the chicken pieces, coating them evenly. This will give the meat a rich golden color before the seasoning rub goes on.

3. In another small bowl, combine 1½ teaspoons kosher salt, the ground ginger, and thyme. Rub the seasoning mixture onto the chicken pieces.

4. If you are using a mixture of dark meat pieces (thighs, drumsticks) and white meat (breasts and wings), place them into separate sous vide bags, because the dark meat will cook longer. Vacuum-seal the bags, ensuring that the chicken pieces are in a single layer, and place them into the fridge. Allow the chicken to marinate for at least 2 hours but preferably overnight.

5. Preheat the water bath to 155°F.

6. Place the bag containing the dark meat in the water bath and set the timer for 2 hours. When the timer goes off, add the bag with the white meat to the sous vide and set the timer for 1 more hour.

CONTINUED →

7. In a food processor bowl, combine the fresh cilantro, fresh ginger, and scallions. Process until everything is finely chopped. Transfer the mixture to a medium bowl, add the remaining ½ teaspoon salt and the olive oil, and stir well. Set aside.

8. Place a rack close to the broiler and preheat the broiler to high. When the sous vide timer goes off, remove the chicken pieces and pat them dry. Place them on a baking sheet or roasting pan. Slide the pan under the broiler, a few inches below the element. When the chicken skin has darkened and crisped (5 to 7 minutes, but keep an eye on it), flip the pieces and sear the other side.

9. Serve with the ginger-cilantro sauce.

CAVEMAN-WORTHY TURKEY LEGS

SERVES 4 | **PREP TIME:** 10 minutes, plus 24 hours curing time | **COOK TIME:** 24 hours |
FINISHING TIME: 15 minutes | **SOUS VIDE TEMPERATURE:** 149°F | **FAMILY FRIENDLY**

Do you pine for the enormous smoked turkey legs you get at carnivals and fairs? Okay, so let's do it! The legs will cure for a day in a brine containing Prague Powder #1, a special curing salt that will turn the legs that distinctive smoky pink. For more on this ingredient, check out the *Did You Know?* tip.

2 tablespoons Morton's kosher salt	6 tablespoons dark brown sugar	4 (1-pound) turkey drumsticks
1 teaspoon Prague Powder #1	2 cups distilled water	4 to 8 tablespoons extra-virgin olive oil

1. Dissolve the salt, Prague Powder #1, and the sugar in the distilled water and then divide it. Divide the liquid between two 1-gallon zip-top bags. Add 2 drumsticks to each bag and refrigerate them for about 24 hours. Don't leave it much beyond that, or the turkey can get too salty. While the meat is curing, move the bags around a few times to make sure all the parts are covered with the liquid.

2. Preheat the water bath to 149°F. Remove the drumsticks from the brine, rinse them thoroughly, and pat them dry. Place each one in its own sous vide bag; drizzle them with olive oil (1 to 2 tablespoons per drumstick), and vacuum-seal the bags. Submerge the bags and set the timer for 24 hours. Cover the sous vide with a lid or plastic wrap to prevent the water from evaporating.

3. Remove the drumsticks from the sous vide when they're done and pat them dry. Sear them either on a hot grill or with a kitchen torch until the skin crisps up. Dig in!

DID YOU KNOW? The brine ingredients in this recipe are critical—the chemical qualities of the Morton's kosher salt and Prague Powder #1 are specifically suited to the job. Please don't substitute other brands or products. Luckily, they're easy to buy online. Likewise, the water purity will affect both food safety and flavor, so be sure to use distilled water.

ESSENTIAL TURKEY BREAST

SERVES 4 to 8 | **PREP TIME:** 15 minutes | **COOK TIME:** 8 hours | **FINISHING TIME:** 15 minutes |
SOUS VIDE TEMPERATURE: 131°F | **FAMILY FRIENDLY**

You don't often hear "juicy" and "turkey" in the same sentence, but let's change that. Turkey is a lean meat, not given to succulence of its own accord, but we've got a few tricks up our sleeves. First, we'll sear the meat both before and after cooking to lock in the moisture and flavor. Then we'll task the sous vide with cooking it evenly throughout, without drying out the meat. A pan gravy tops it off.

1 (2- to 4-pound)
turkey breast

Extra-virgin olive oil,
for searing

2 tablespoons kosher salt,
plus more for seasoning

2 teaspoons sugar

1 rosemary sprig

1 thyme sprig

2 or 3 sage leaves

2 tablespoons butter

3 tablespoons
all-purpose flour

2 cups chicken or
turkey stock

Freshly ground black pepper

1. Preheat the water bath to 131°F.

2. Rinse the turkey breast and pat it dry with paper towels.

3. In a cast-iron skillet, heat the olive oil over high heat. When the skillet is very hot, place the breast, skin-side down, in the pan and apply pressure with a spatula. Sear until the skin is golden, about 1 minute.

4. Season the meat on both sides with the 2 tablespoons salt and sugar.

5. Place the turkey breast in a cooking bag, drizzle it with olive oil, and add the rosemary, thyme, and sage. Vacuum-seal the bag or seal it using the water displacement method and place the bag into the water bath. Set the timer for 8 hours. If it's convenient to leave it in the bath for longer, don't worry; it won't overcook!

6. About 20 minutes before serving, remove the turkey breast from the cooking bag and pat it dry. Reserve the cooking juices for the gravy.

7. Reheat the skillet. Add the butter and allow it to melt. Place the breast, skin-side down, in the pan. Using a spoon, scoop up some of the melted butter and drizzle it over the top. Sear for 1 to 2 minutes over high heat, then flip and do the same with the other side. Remove the turkey from the skillet and set it aside, covered, to keep it warm.

8. In the same skillet, over medium heat, sprinkle the flour over the pan and, with a spatula or wooden spoon, blend it with the fat and juices in the pan, scraping up any browned bits. Cook, stirring constantly, for 1 to 2 minutes. Slowly add the cooking juices from the sous vide bag and the stock. Bring the gravy to a boil and stir constantly until it reduces and thickens to your desired consistency, 8 to 10 minutes. Season the gravy with salt and pepper.

9. Slice the turkey and serve it with the gravy.

TURKEY ROULADE

SERVES 4 to 6 | **PREP TIME:** 45 minutes | **COOK TIME:** 3 hours | **FINISHING TIME:** 20 minutes |
SOUS VIDE TEMPERATURE: 145°F | **FAMILY FRIENDLY, PARTY READY**

This eye-catching dish hits the spot when you want an out-of-the-ordinary entrée for Thanksgiving or any other occasion. Serve with cranberry sauce or your favorite chutney.

1 (3-pound) boneless
   turkey breast, both sides
   of one bird, divided into
   2 breast pieces
Kosher salt
4 tablespoons butter

1 cup panko bread crumbs
¼ cup fresh thyme leaves
3 tablespoons sage
2 cups parsley leaves
6 garlic cloves

½ teaspoon red
   pepper flakes
Freshly ground black pepper
Vegetable oil, for
   searing (optional)

1. Preheat the water bath to 145°F.

2. To butterfly the turkey breast pieces, place one hand on the thicker edge of the breast and slice the turkey breast horizontally along the length without cutting all the way through; leave the last ½ inch of the breast intact. Open the turkey breast as you would open a book and press the meat flat onto your work surface.

3. Season the cut side of each breast generously with salt.

4. In a large skillet, melt the butter, add the bread crumbs, and toast them until they are golden brown. Transfer the crumbs to a food processor, then add the thyme, sage, parsley, and garlic and process until finely chopped. Add the red pepper flakes and season the mixture with salt and black pepper. Sprinkle the mixture evenly over the two butterflied turkey breasts.

5. Working with one breast piece at a time, start rolling from the edge toward the center (the "book's binding") and then to the far edge. Roll the meat as tightly as possible and secure each roll with kitchen twine.

6. Place each roulade into one cooking bag. Vacuum-seal the bags or seal them using the water displacement method and place them into the water bath. Set the timer for 3 hours.

7. After 3 hours, remove the roulades from the sous vide. Slip them out of the bags and pat them dry. To crisp the skin, bake in a 475°F oven for 10 minutes, or heat about 1 inch of vegetable oil in a pan and shallow-fry the roulades until they're golden brown on all sides. Let them rest for 5 minutes, then slice and serve.

CALIFORNIA TURKEY BURGERS

SERVES 4 | **PREP TIME:** 10 minutes, plus 4 hours for freezing | **COOK TIME:** 1 hour |
FINISHING TIME: 10 minutes | **SOUS VIDE TEMPERATURE:** 145°F | **FAMILY FRIENDLY**

Turkey burgers have earned a bit of a dubious reputation, but let's change that! The sous vide will keep them juicy and a few seasonings will beef up the flavor (so to speak). Top them with everything you'd expect in a trendy burger bar—avocado, lettuce, sprouts, and mayo.

½ medium onion	¾ teaspoon kosher salt	Romaine lettuce leaves,
1 pound ground turkey	Freshly ground black pepper	for serving
2 tablespoons ketchup	4 hamburger buns	Sprouts of choice, for serving
1 tablespoon	Sliced avocado, for serving	Mayonnaise, for serving
Worcestershire sauce		

1. Grate the onion, using either a Microplane grater or the fine holes of a box grater. You should have about 2 tablespoons grated onion; discard the juice. In a bowl, combine the grated onion, ground turkey, ketchup, Worcestershire sauce, salt, and pepper. Using a fork, mix well. Shape into four ½-inch-thick patties. The mixture will be quite moist.

2. Line a baking sheet with plastic wrap and place the patties on it. Cover them with another sheet of plastic wrap and put them in the freezer until fully frozen, about 4 hours. Freezing helps them keep their shape during sealing and cooking.

3. Preheat the water bath to 145°F.

4. Place each frozen patty in its own cooking bag. Vacuum-seal the bags or seal them using the water displacement method and place the bags into the water bath. Set the timer for 1 hour.

5. Shortly before the timer goes off, heat an outdoor grill or a grill pan. When finished, remove the patties from the bags and pat them dry. Sear them on the grill until they are a deep golden brown on the surface, 1 minute on each side. Toast the hamburger buns on the grill, too, if you like.

6. Place the burgers in the buns and load them up with the avocado, lettuce, sprouts, and mayonnaise.

THANKSGIVING WHOLE TURKEY

SERVES 12 | **PREP TIME:** 20 minutes | **COOK TIME:** 20 to 26 hours | **FINISHING TIME:** 20 minutes |
SOUS VIDE TEMPERATURE: 150°F, then 131°F | **FAMILY FRIENDLY, PARTY READY**

Holiday meals are often one big heap of stress on a platter, but your sous vide can change that, at least where the turkey is concerned. While you're doing other things, the turkey, seasoned with a scrumptious rub, will be quietly cooking to moist, juicy perfection. Consider asking your butcher to divide the turkey into quarters, giving you the bones for stock.

1 (12- to 15-pound) whole
  fresh turkey
2 tablespoons extra-virgin
  olive oil, plus more
  as needed
3 tablespoons brown sugar

2 tablespoons
  smoked paprika
1 tablespoon kosher salt
2 teaspoons ground cumin
2 teaspoons dried oregano
2 teaspoons dried sage

2 teaspoons dry mustard
1 teaspoon dried thyme
1 teaspoon dried cilantro
2 tablespoons butter

1. Preheat the water bath to 150°F.

2. If the butcher didn't do so when you bought the turkey, divide it into four pieces: Two breasts (boneless breast with drumette) and two legs (thigh and drumstick together).

3. Heat a skillet over medium-high heat and add the olive oil. (If you drop a pinch of flour into the pan, it should sizzle.) Working in batches, place each piece of the turkey, skin-side down, in the skillet and apply pressure with a spatula. Shift the turkey parts around to sear as much of the skin as possible, holding them in place with tongs, if necessary.

4. In a bowl, combine the brown sugar, paprika, salt, cumin, oregano, sage, mustard, thyme, and cilantro and mix well. Once they're seared, season all four turkey parts generously. Place the turkey breasts into one cooking bag and the legs into another. Drizzle both with olive oil. Allow the breasts to cool to room temperature and then put them in the refrigerator until it's time to cook them. Vacuum-seal the bag containing the legs, or seal it using the water displacement method, and place the bag into the water bath. (If using a zip-top bag, double it up.) Set the timer for 12 hours. Cover the water vessel with a lid or plastic wrap to prevent evaporation during cooking; check the water level from time to time and top it up, if necessary.

5. When the timer goes off, drop the temperature in the sous vide to 131°F. Vacuum-seal the bag containing the turkey breasts or seal it using the water displacement method. (If using a zip-top bag, double it up.) Place the bag into the water bath, leaving the legs in the water as well. Cover the water bath again and set the timer for another 8 to 14 hours, as suits your schedule. Don't worry about the turkey overcooking.

6. When you're ready, preheat your oven's broiler. Remove the bags from the sous vide. Take the turkey pieces out and pat them dry.

7. Place the turkey legs on a baking sheet or in a broiler pan; place them on the oven's top rack and allow them to broil until the skin is golden brown, 5 to 15 minutes (just keep an eye on them).

8. In a skillet, melt the butter over medium-high heat. Place the turkey breasts in the pan, skin-side down; scoop up some butter with a spoon to baste the exposed side. Sear until the skin is golden, 1 to 2 minutes, then flip and repeat.

9. Serve the pieces whole on a platter or slice and plate.

MAKE-AHEAD MAGIC: If you like, you can cook the turkey up to 3 days ahead of time and just finish it up right before you serve. Once the pieces come out of the sous vide, transfer them to an ice-water bath to chill for 1 hour. They will then keep for up to 3 days in the fridge. On serving day, reheat in the sous vide for 1 hour 30 minutes to 2 hours at 131°F, then finish and serve.

DUCK CONFIT

SERVES 4 | **PREP TIME:** 10 minutes | **COOK TIME:** 16 hours | **FINISHING TIME:** 15 minutes |
SOUS VIDE TEMPERATURE: 158°F | **FAMILY FRIENDLY**

This classic French recipe does require a big chunk of time, but almost all of it is hands-off, just allowing the gloriously seasoned duck legs to bask in the sous vide. Preparing the duck like this makes it especially juicy because it is being infused with its own fat. Transfer it to the broiler for a few minutes, *et voilà*! Crispy, ridiculously tender duck.

3 tablespoons kosher salt

1 teaspoon whole juniper
berries, toasted and
ground in a spice mill

4 bone-in, skin-on duck legs

1 to 2 tablespoons duck fat

4 thyme sprigs

2 lemon slices

2 fresh bay leaves

3 garlic cloves

1. Preheat the water bath to 158°. (This temperature will result in tender, moist duck with medium doneness. For a different texture, please refer to the Poultry cooking chart on page 240.)

2. In a bowl, combine the salt and ground juniper and mix well.

3. You have the option to make a bone-deep cut around each duck drumstick about 1½ inches from the tip. This will make it easier to French the legs (clean the meat away from the bones) when they come out of the sous vide, if you choose to do so.

4. Sprinkle the four legs liberally with the salt and juniper and place them into a sous vide bag in a single layer, using multiple bags if necessary. Add the duck fat, thyme, lemon, bay leaves, and garlic, dividing between the bags as needed. Vacuum-seal the bag(s), place them in the water, and set the timer for 16 hours.

5. When the timer goes off, gently remove the legs from the bag(s). Save the flavorful cooking juice for future use. If you'd like to French the leg bones, pull the meat and skin up and off the bone with a paper towel and scrape away the excess meat with a paring knife, exposing the bone.

6. Preheat the broiler to high. Gently place the legs on a broiler pan and broil until the skin is crispy and browned, 7 to 10 minutes, watching them carefully to be sure they don't burn. Plate and serve.

CHANGE IT UP: Experiment with the seasonings. The salt is essential, but the rest is fair game; orange rind and rosemary are great variations.

PERFECT DUCK BREASTS

SERVES 4 | **PREP TIME:** 5 minutes | **COOK TIME:** 1 hour 30 minutes | **FINISHING TIME:** 5 minutes |
SOUS VIDE TEMPERATURE: 144°F | **FAMILY FRIENDLY, QUICK PREP**

Duck quite possibly takes the Best Flavor award in the poultry category, and it is richer in several essential minerals than turkey and chicken. For some reason, though, we tend to think of it as a dish for special occasions. I hope that after you've tasted these succulent and all-but-effortless duck breasts, that will change.

4 boneless, skin-on duck breasts	6 to 8 thyme sprigs 4 large garlic cloves	Kosher salt Freshly ground black pepper

1. Preheat the water bath to 144°F.

2. Rinse the duck breasts and pat them dry with paper towels. Place them on a cutting board, skin-side up. Using a sharp knife, score the skin with even strokes at 1-inch intervals, taking care not to cut through the meat.

3. Heat a cast-iron skillet over high heat and sear the skin side for 2 to 3 minutes. No need to use oil: The duck breasts will produce enough fat to keep the pan greased.

4. Add the thyme and garlic to the skillet. Flip the breasts and sear the meat side for 1 more minute. Let the fresh thyme and garlic toast in the duck fat at the same time.

5. Turn off the heat and remove the seared duck breasts from the skillet. Season the meat generously with salt and pepper. Place the breasts in a single layer in a cooking bag (or multiple bags, if required). Add the thyme and garlic from the pan. Vacuum-seal the bag(s) or seal them using the water displacement method and place them into the water bath. Set the timer for 1 hour 30 minutes.

6. When the timer goes off, remove the duck breasts from the bag and pat them dry. In the same skillet, sear them on the skin side one more time over high heat, until the skin is a crispy golden brown. Slice the breasts along the scores in the skin and serve. Consider braising some leeks in the skillet, using the cooking juices from the sous vide bag and a splash of white wine.

DID YOU KNOW? Duck fat is an excellent cooking fat. It offers intense flavor, has a high smoke point, and is one of the healthiest animal fats. Once you've seared the duck breasts, pour the fat into a glass container and store it in the refrigerator. It will be a great boost to your Duck Confit (page 130), for example.

Classic BBQ Pork Ribs, page 148

PORK

PERFECT BACON

SERVES 4 | **PREP TIME:** 5 minutes | **COOK TIME:** 24 hours | **FINISHING TIME:** 5 minutes |
SOUS VIDE TEMPERATURE: 147°F | **FAMILY FRIENDLY, QUICK PREP**

Go ahead, ask: Why would you cook bacon for hours in a sous vide, especially if you're going
to sear it in a skillet anyway before serving? Here's the short answer: Sous vide bacon is crispy
around the edges but fabulously moist and tender and chewy on the inside. You may think you
couldn't possibly love bacon any more than you do now . . . but trust me, you will!

1 pound thick-cut bacon	Maple syrup, for brushing	Freshly ground black pepper

1. Preheat the water bath to 147°F.

2. Place the whole slab of bacon into a sous vide bag and vacuum-seal it. When the
   water reaches temperature, put the bag in and set the timer for 24 hours. Cover the
   water vessel with a lid or plastic wrap to prevent evaporation during cooking; check
   the water level from time to time and top it up, if necessary.

3. Remove the bacon from the sous vide bag.

4. In a hot skillet, sear the strips on just one side for 2 minutes. Brush with maple syrup
   and season with pepper, then serve.

DID YOU KNOW? If you're tempted to put the bacon into the sous vide in its original
packaging—hey, it's already wrapped in plastic, right?—just *don't*. Generally speaking,
if packaging is labeled as "microwave-safe" or "boil-safe" it is usually fine to use with
sous vide. Otherwise, play it safe. Take the bacon out of the package.

MAKE-AHEAD MAGIC: Chill the sealed bag thoroughly in an ice-water bath when it
comes out of the sous vide, then the cooked bacon can be stored for up to 2 weeks
in your refrigerator or frozen for months. Just defrost and sear.

MAPLE-MUSTARD PORK BELLY

SERVES 6 | **PREP TIME:** 10 minutes | **COOK TIME:** 24 or 7 hours | **FINISHING TIME:** 5 minutes |
SOUS VIDE TEMPERATURE: 154 or 176°F | **FAMILY FRIENDLY, PARTY READY, QUICK PREP**

Pork belly is essentially uncured bacon—but even better. Cooked well, it's absolutely succulent.
It's an affordable and versatile cut of meat, and with this recipe, we'll give it a taste of Canada
with a sweet and smoky maple cure. Yes, it will need a chunk of time, but almost no effort, and
the results are well worth the wait. It's delicious with cabbage slaw or Garlic-Herb Mashed Potatoes (page 52) and a side of leafy vegetables.

1 (2-pound) skin-on pork belly	1 tablespoon kosher salt	2 teaspoons apple cider vinegar
2 tablespoons maple syrup	2 teaspoons whole-grain mustard	2 fresh rosemary sprigs

1. Preheat the water bath to 154°F for pork that is tender with a hint of snappiness to
   the texture or 176°F for ultra-tender, braise-like meat.

2. Score the pork skin with diagonal lines. In a bowl, combine the maple syrup, salt,
   mustard, and vinegar, and mix well. Place the pork belly in a cooking bag and drizzle
   the maple syrup mixture over it. Add the rosemary sprigs. Vacuum-seal the bag or
   seal it using the water displacement method and place the bag into the water bath.
   (If using a zip-top bag, double it up.) Set the timer for 24 hours if your water is 154°F,
   or 7 hours if your water is 176°F.

3. When the timer goes off, remove the pork belly from the bag. If you would like a
   crispy skin, you can sear it in a hot skillet. Otherwise, it's ready to serve. Cut into
   slices or chunks, as you wish.

KOREAN-STYLE BOSSAM WRAPS

SERVES 6 to 8 | **PREP TIME:** 10 minutes | **COOK TIME:** 7 hours | **FINISHING TIME:** 40 minutes |
SOUS VIDE TEMPERATURE: 176°F | **PARTY READY**

The centerpiece here is the pork belly, which poaches in coffee and spices to emerge juicy, tender, and unbelievably tasty. Following the Korean custom, serve it thinly sliced with a spicy radish salad and salted shrimp, plus softened napa cabbage leaves to wrap it all up. Accompany with a bottle of ice-cold soju and a K-pop playlist (optional). See the *Change It Up* tip for notes on the ingredients.

FOR THE PORK BELLY:

1 (2-pound) skin-on pork belly or pork shoulder

½ medium onion, sliced

3 large scallions, white parts only

3 or 4 garlic cloves, minced

1 (1-inch) piece ginger, peeled and sliced

1 teaspoon whole black peppercorns

1½ tablespoons doenjang (fermented soybean paste)

¼ teaspoon instant coffee or ¼ cup brewed coffee

½ cup plus 1 teaspoon kosher salt, divided

2 bay leaves

4 to 6 cups water, plus 4 cups

1 napa cabbage head, for wrapping

FOR SPICY RADISH SALAD:

1 pound mu (Korean radish)

1 teaspoon kosher salt

2 tablespoons gochugaru (Korean red chili flakes)

2 teaspoons minced garlic

½ teaspoon grated ginger

1 tablespoon fish sauce

1 teaspoon sugar

2 scallions, finely chopped

1 teaspoon sesame seeds (optional)

Saewujeot (salted shrimp), for topping (optional)

Kimchi, for topping (optional)

Sesame oil, for topping (optional)

Gochujang (a sweet, savory, and spicy Korean chili-rice paste), for topping (optional)

1. Preheat the water bath to 176°F.

2. **Make the pork belly:** Place the pork in a cooking bag. Add the onion, scallions, garlic, ginger, peppercorns, doenjang, coffee, 1 teaspoon salt, and bay leaves. Add enough water to the bag to cover the pork completely. Vacuum-seal the bag or seal it using the water displacement method and place the bag into the water bath. (If using a zip-top bag, double it up.) Set the timer for 7 hours.

3. Two to four hours before serving, separate the cabbage leaves. Dissolve ½ cup kosher salt in 4 cups of water and soak the cabbage leaves to soften them. After soaking them for 2 to 4 hours, rinse and drain the cabbage leaves and set them aside for serving.

4. **Make the spicy radish salad:** Clean the radish thoroughly, peeling only if the skin is too blemished. Julienne the radish, place it in a bowl, and sprinkle it with the salt. Let it sit for about 20 minutes. Drain the released liquid, but do not rinse. Add the gochugaru, garlic, ginger, fish sauce, and sugar and mix well. Taste and adjust the salt and fish sauce as desired. Add the scallions and sesame seeds (if using) and toss to mix.

5. When the sous vide timer goes off, remove the pork belly, pat it dry, and slice it thinly. Serve wrapped in cabbage leaves with spicy radish salad and optional toppings, like saewujeot, kimchi, sesame oil, and gochujang.

CHANGE IT UP: Or, more to the point, why *not* change it up? There are some traditional Korean ingredients in this recipe, and while it might be tempting to substitute more familiar things, I wouldn't recommend it. Although mu and daikon are both large white Asian radishes, their flavors are quite distinct. Likewise, gochugaru has a smoky tinge that you won't find in ordinary chili flakes. The same goes for the doenjang, which has a deeper, richer flavor than miso. If at all possible, go for the real Korean stuff, which you can likely find in your local Asian food store. If not, then go ahead and substitute.

DID YOU KNOW? The word *bossam* translates as "wrapped" or "packaged." It's one of several dishes that are served frequently when drinking soju. An idea for your next dinner party, perhaps?

RED BRAISED PORK BELLY

SERVES 4 | **PREP TIME:** 10 minutes | **COOK TIME:** 7 hours | **FINISHING TIME:** 10 minutes |
SOUS VIDE TEMPERATURE: 176°F | **FAMILY FRIENDLY**

This is a classic pork dish in Eastern China, famous for its "red cooking," in which food is heavily imbued with the color of different soy sauces. The marinade features two kinds of soy sauce (which both season and color the pork), Shaoxing cooking wine, and spices. Before serving, you'll reduce the marinade to a gloriously shiny, sticky glaze.

1 (2-pound) skin-on
   pork belly
2 tablespoons light
   soy sauce

3 tablespoons dark soy
   sauce (see *Did you
   know?* tip)
3 tablespoons brown sugar
¼ cup Shaoxing rice wine
2 scallions

1 (½-inch) piece fresh ginger
2 garlic cloves
3 whole star anise
1 to 2 tablespoons
   cornstarch

1. Preheat the water bath to 176°F.

2. Slide the pork belly into a large cooking bag.

3. In a blender or food processor, blend the light and dark soy sauces, brown sugar, rice wine, scallions, ginger, and garlic until smooth. Pour the marinade into the bag and add the star anise. Vacuum-seal the bag or seal it using the water displacement method and place the bag into the water bath. (If using a zip-top bag, double it up.) Set the timer for 7 hours.

4. When the pork is done, remove the bag from the water. Transfer the pork belly onto a cutting board and pour the cooking liquid into a small saucepan. Discard the star anise.

5. Bring the cooking liquid to a boil and simmer until it's reduced by half. If it isn't as thick as you'd like, dissolve the cornstarch in cold water and add it to the sauce, stirring until it reaches the consistency you want.

6. Cut the pork belly into slices, 1-inch bites, or 2-inch pieces, as you like; plate it and pour a generous amount of sauce over it.

CHANGE IT UP: If the thought of pork belly without crispy skin is unthinkable to you, pat the meat dry when it comes out of the sous vide and place it under the broiler, skin-side up, for about 3 minutes. Then go ahead and serve it with the glaze.

DID YOU KNOW? Dark and light soy sauces are very common in Chinese cooking. American supermarkets typically stock light soy sauces (e.g. Kikkoman). You may need to visit your Asian food shop to find the thicker, sweeter dark soy sauce. If you can't find it, you can substitute a mixture of light soy sauce, molasses, and water. For about 1 tablespoon, use 2 teaspoons regular soy sauce mixed with ½ teaspoon molasses and ½ teaspoon water. Add a small pinch of sugar to the mixture and stir until combined.

DID YOU KNOW? Shaoxing cooking wine is a staple in many Chinese dishes. Made from fermented brown glutinous rice, it's intended for cooking, not drinking, and it imparts a distinctive nutty flavor. You could substitute dry sherry, but the real thing is ideal.

SHINJUKU RAMEN

SERVES 4 to 6 | **PREP TIME:** 5 minutes, plus 6 to 24 hours to marinate | **COOK TIME:** 7 hours |
FINISHING TIME: 20 minutes | **SOUS VIDE TEMPERATURE:** 176°F | **FAMILY FRIENDLY**

Bustling Shinjuku is home to more than 200 ramen shops, and competition between them is
fierce. Slurp-worthy is probably my favorite word to describe this traditional-style ramen. I use
packaged ramen noodles but doll them up with tender strips of pork belly, marinated soft-boiled
eggs from the sous vide, nori, and bok choy, all in a porky, mushroom-y broth. Don't let the list of
components for this recipe alarm you—you can do it!

3 tablespoons kosher salt

3 tablespoons sugar

1 (2-pound) skinless
  pork belly

6 large eggs

1 cup mirin, divided

¼ cup regular soy sauce,
  plus more for the broth

¼ cup dark soy sauce (or
  substitute with an equal

amount of regular soy
  sauce plus 1 tablespoon
  brown sugar)

5 or 6 dried
  shiitake mushrooms

6 cups low-sodium beef or
  chicken broth

3 shallots, finely minced

1 bunch (about
  4 ounces) enoki
  mushrooms, trimmed

8 to 12 baby bok choy heads,
  vertically sliced

2 garlic cloves, finely minced

4 to 6 packets dried
  ramen noodles

4 to 6 nori sheets

¼ cup sliced scallions

1. In a small bowl, mix the salt and sugar. Rub it all over the pork belly until it is well
   coated; discard any excess rub.

2. Place the pork belly in a cooking bag. (If using a zip-top bag, double it up.) Vacuum-
   seal the bag or seal it using the water displacement method. Allow it to marinate in
   the fridge for at least 6 hours but no more than 24 hours.

3. Preheat the water bath to 176°F. Place the eggs in the water, in their shells, and
   set the timer for 13 minutes. In a large bowl, prepare an ice-water bath with a
   50/50 mixture of cold water and ice cubes. When the timer goes off, remove the
   eggs from the sous vide and transfer them to the ice-water bath.

4. With the water still at 176°F, place the pork belly in the sous vide and set the timer
   for 7 hours.

5. When the eggs are well chilled, peel them carefully. In a tall, airtight container,
   combine ¾ cup mirin and the soy sauces and mix well; if using sugar, mix until it's
   dissolved. Place the peeled eggs in the container to marinate for 2 to 8 hours; the

CONTINUED →

longer they marinate, the deeper the color and flavors of the marinade will penetrate the eggs. Refrigerate if marinating for more than 2 hours. After marinating, you can place the eggs in an airtight container in your refrigerator, where they will keep for up to 4 days.

6. About 30 minutes before the sous vide timer goes off, put the shiitake mushrooms in a bowl and cover them with boiling water. Allow them to soak for 30 minutes.

7. When the pork is finished, remove the cooking bag from the sous vide. Slide the pork belly out and set it aside. Pour the cooking liquids through a fine-mesh strainer into a soup pot.

8. Remove and discard the tough stems of the mushrooms and slice the caps; add them and their soaking liquid to the soup pot. Add the broth, shallots, enoki mushrooms, baby bok choy, garlic, remaining ¼ cup mirin, and soy sauce to taste. Bring the broth to a boil, and simmer for 5 minutes.

9. Bring a separate pot of water to a boil. Place the dried ramen noodles into the water (discarding any enclosed spice packets) and simmer for 1 minute. Drain.

10. Meanwhile, slice the pork belly and cut the ramen eggs in half.

11. Divide the noodles evenly among the soup bowls. Scoop the bok choy and mushrooms from the broth and divide those among the bowls, then pour the hot ramen broth over them. Add the two halves of an egg and slices of pork to each bowl. Using scissors, cut thin slices of nori over each bowl, sprinkle with scallions, and serve.

CHANGE IT UP: This recipe is super versatile. Change the vegetables to include different greens or shredded carrot. Use different kinds of seaweed such as kombu or wakame. Skip the instant ramen noodles and use fresh. Adjust the broth seasonings with bonito flakes, miso, or ginger.

MAKE-AHEAD MAGIC: The ramen eggs are irresistible all on their own. Make up a large batch and keep them around for snacks and lunches.

ESSENTIAL PORK CHOPS

SERVES 4 | **PREP TIME:** 5 minutes | **COOK TIME:** 1 hour | **FINISHING TIME:** 5 minutes |
SOUS VIDE TEMPERATURE: 140°F | **FAMILY FRIENDLY, QUICK PREP**

These pork chops are basic only in the very best sense of the word—flavorful, uncomplicated, and easy, easy, easy. This makes for a quick, midweek dinner that will excite the family. Fennel with Parmesan (page 62) or Parmesan and Balsamic Brussels Sprouts (page 49) make terrific side dishes.

4 bone-in or boneless
  pork chops
2 tablespoons kosher salt
Freshly ground black pepper

2 tablespoons extra-virgin
  olive oil
2 fresh thyme or rosemary
  sprigs (optional)

1 to 2 tablespoons avocado
  or vegetable oil, for searing

1. Preheat the water bath to 140°F.

2. Season the chops with the salt and pepper. Place them in a zip-top bag (using more bags, if needed, to keep them in a single layer). Add the olive oil and thyme (if using) to the bag and seal it using the water displacement method. Submerge the bag in the heated water and set the timer for 1 hour.

3. When the timer goes off, remove the chops from the bag and pat them dry with paper towels.

4. Heat the avocado or vegetable oil in a skillet over high heat and sear the pork chops on both sides until golden and slightly crisp, about 2 minutes on each side. Serve immediately.

CHANGE IT UP: To jazz up your chops, rub them with some Sassy Pig Rub (page 227) instead of the salt and pepper.

SPICY PEACH PORK CHOPS

SERVES 4 | **PREP TIME:** 15 minutes, plus 2 to 12 hours to marinate | **COOK TIME:** 1 hour |
FINISHING TIME: 20 minutes | **SOUS VIDE TEMPERATURE:** 140°F | **FAMILY FRIENDLY**

Ohhh, the sauce, the sauce! Sweet, spicy, tangy, and salty. The first time I encountered a peach-based sauce for meat I had some serious doubts, but I'm a convert. Marinate some pork chops in this sauce, cook them in the sous vide, thicken the sauce into a rich glaze to drizzle over the fabulously tender meat, and you, too, will be a convert.

1 cup peach preserves or peach jam	2 tablespoons extra-virgin olive oil	3 garlic cloves, minced
2 tablespoons finely chopped scallions, green parts only	1 tablespoon sriracha	4 bone-in or boneless pork chops
	1 tablespoon Dijon mustard	1 to 2 tablespoons avocado or vegetable oil, for searing
	1 tablespoon soy sauce	

1. In a bowl, combine the preserves, scallions, olive oil, sriracha, mustard, soy sauce, and garlic and stir to mix well.

2. Place the pork chops in a cooking bag in a single layer, using multiple bags if necessary. Pour the sauce over them. Vacuum-seal the bag(s) or seal them using the water displacement method. Place the bag(s) in the refrigerator and allow the chops to marinate for 2 to 12 hours.

3. Preheat the water bath to 140°F. Submerge the bag(s) and set the timer for 1 hour.

4. When the timer goes off, remove the cooking bag(s) from the sous vide. Reserving the cooking liquids, remove the pork chops and pat them dry with paper towels.

5. Transfer the cooking liquids to a medium saucepan over medium heat. Simmer them, stirring occasionally, until the liquid has reduced to a thick glaze, about 10 minutes.

6. Meanwhile, in a skillet, heat the avocado oil over high heat, add the chops, and sear on both sides until golden and slightly crisp, about 2 minutes on each side.

7. Plate the pork chops and drizzle them with the spicy peach glaze.

CHEESY BACON PORK CHOPS

SERVES 4 | **PREP TIME:** 5 minutes | **COOK TIME:** 1 hour | **FINISHING TIME:** 10 minutes |
SOUS VIDE TEMPERATURE: 140°F | **FAMILY FRIENDLY, QUICK PREP**

As the end of a long day approaches and you wish some comfort food would simply materialize on your table, just reach for this recipe. Juicy and tender pork chops topped with bacon, cheese, and mayo, with a kick of adobo sauce, can be on the table with about 15 minutes of hands-on time. Doesn't life sound better already?

4 bone-in or boneless
  pork chops
2 teaspoons
  mesquite seasoning
2 tablespoons extra-virgin
  olive oil

1 cup shredded pepper
  Jack cheese
¼ cup sliced scallions, green
  parts only, plus more
  for garnish

¼ cup cooked bacon pieces
  (2 or 3 strips of bacon)
¼ cup mayonnaise
2 teaspoons adobo sauce
  from chipotles in adobo

1. Preheat the water bath to 140°F.

2. Rub the pork chops well with mesquite seasoning and place them in a cooking bag in a single layer, using multiple bags if necessary. Add the olive oil to the bag(s). Vacuum-seal the bag(s) or seal them using the water displacement method and place them into the water bath. Set the timer for 1 hour.

3. While the pork chops are cooking, in a bowl, combine the cheese, scallions, bacon, mayonnaise, and adobo sauce. Preheat the broiler.

4. When the timer goes off, remove the pork chops from the bag(s), place them on a broiler pan, and pat them dry. Spread the cheese mixture evenly over the meat.

5. Broil the coated chops for 2 to 3 minutes, or until browned. Serve, garnished with chopped scallions.

FIVE-SPICE PORK RIBS

SERVES 4 | **PREP TIME:** 20 minutes, plus 4 to 12 hours to marinate | **COOK TIME:** 12 hours |
FINISHING TIME: 15 minutes | **SOUS VIDE TEMPERATURE:** 165°F | **FAMILY FRIENDLY**

Sticky-sweet, garlicky, and tangy, Five-Spice Pork Ribs are five-star. Although they take a fair bit of time, it's almost all hands-off. These ribs will land on your plate coated with a fragrant, caramelized glaze.

2 (3-pound) racks
St. Louis–style ribs

3 tablespoons dark
brown sugar

1 tablespoon kosher salt

1 tablespoon plus
1 teaspoon Chinese
five-spice powder, divided

½ cup hoisin sauce

½ cup soy sauce

3 tablespoons honey

1 (4-inch) piece fresh
ginger, peeled

5 garlic cloves

1. Remove the membrane on the back of the ribs by grasping it with a paper towel and pulling it away in one piece. Cut the ribs into four portions.

2. In a small bowl, mix the brown sugar, salt, and 1 tablespoon Chinese five-spice powder to make a rub. Season the ribs all over with the spice rub, being sure to coat all surfaces and press the rub into the meat.

3. Carefully place each portion of the pork ribs in its own sous vide bag and vacuum-seal the bags. Place the bags in the refrigerator to marinate for 4 to 12 hours.

4. Preheat the water bath to 165°F. Submerge the bags and set the timer for 12 hours. Cover the water vessel with a lid or plastic wrap to prevent evaporation during cooking; check the water level from time to time and top it up, if necessary.

5. When the timer goes off, remove the bags from the sous vide. Take out the ribs and pat them dry.

6. In a small saucepan, whisk the hoisin sauce, soy sauce, honey, and remaining 1 teaspoon Chinese five-spice powder to combine. Finely grate the ginger and garlic into the saucepan. Bring to a simmer over medium heat, whisking often. Cook, stirring, until just thick enough to coat the back of a spoon, 2 to 3 minutes longer.

7. Preheat the broiler. Place the ribs on a foil-lined baking pan and brush half of the sauce over the ribs, turning to coat both sides. With the meat-side facing up, place the ribs on the oven's top rack for 4 to 5 minutes, until the sauce on the ribs is slightly caramelized. Remove them from the oven and brush the remaining sauce over them. If you prefer, you can finish the ribs on your grill, turning and basting them with the sauce until they've got a good sear.

8. Cut the racks into individual ribs and serve.

DID YOU KNOW? The contents and flavor profiles of Chinese five-spice powder may differ a bit from one part of China to another, but most commonly it consists of Sichuan pepper, fennel seeds, cinnamon, star anise, and cloves.

MAKE-AHEAD MAGIC: After the ribs come out of the sous vide, go ahead and chill them in an ice-water bath, then stow them in the refrigerator for up to 5 days.

CLASSIC BBQ PORK RIBS

SERVES 4 | **PREP TIME:** 20 minutes, plus 30 minutes to 12 hours to marinate | **COOK TIME:** 12 hours |
FINISHING TIME: 20 minutes | **SOUS VIDE TEMPERATURE:** 165°F | **FAMILY FRIENDLY, PARTY READY**

Sous vide sure isn't the typical way to make pork ribs, but it allows you to walk away from the kitchen once the timer's set and results in melt-in-your-mouth tender meat. These ribs are packed full of flavor from an amazing dry rub and a homemade barbecue sauce glaze.

5 teaspoons smoked paprika	3 teaspoons kosher salt	2 (3- to 4-pound) whole racks
4 teaspoons garlic powder	2 teaspoons cayenne pepper	spareribs, about 26 ribs
3 teaspoons onion powder	1 teaspoon freshly ground	1 to 2 cups Honey-Spiced
3 teaspoons dried thyme	black pepper	Barbecue Sauce (page 230)
3 teaspoons dried oregano		or bottled sauce

1. In a small bowl, combine the paprika, garlic powder, onion powder, thyme, oregano, salt, cayenne pepper, and black pepper and set aside.

2. Prepare the pork ribs by removing the papery membrane on the back of the ribs. Use a sharp knife to divide the racks into four portions with 5 or 6 ribs each.

3. Rub the dry rub onto both sides of the ribs, coating all surfaces well.

4. Place each section of ribs into its own sous vide bag. Vacuum-seal the bags and place them in the refrigerator to marinate for 30 minutes or overnight.

5. When ready to cook, preheat the water bath to 165°F. Immerse the bags of ribs in the water and set the timer for 12 hours. Cover your cooking vessel with plastic wrap or a lid to prevent the water from evaporating. Check periodically; add water to the vessel, if necessary, to make sure the ribs stay submerged the entire time.

6. When the ribs are cooked, remove them from the water bath and remove them from the sous vide bags. Pat the ribs dry with paper towels.

7. Preheat the broiler to high. Place the ribs on a broiler pan, meat-side up. Place under the broiler for a quick, intense sear, about 3 minutes. Take them out, brush them generously with the BBQ sauce, then put them back under the broiler for another 2 minutes. (If you have a hand torch or a grill, those are fine alternatives to searing under the broiler.)

DID YOU KNOW? Spareribs come from the pig's underside; when the slabs of pork belly are cut away to make bacon, pancetta, and the like, the spareribs retain a fair amount of that fabulous belly meat.

MAKE-AHEAD MAGIC: If you like, do the initial cooking on one day and finish the ribs several days later. Remove the bags of ribs from the sous vide when they're done. Place them, unopened, in an ice-water bath to chill thoroughly. In the vacuum-sealed bags, the ribs will keep for up to 5 days in the fridge.

SALT AND PEPPER BABY BACK RIBS

SERVES 4 to 6 | **PREP TIME:** 10 minutes, plus 1 to 10 hours to marinate | **COOK TIME:** 12 hours | **FINISHING TIME:** 10 minutes | **SOUS VIDE TEMPERATURE:** 165°F | **FAMILY FRIENDLY, PARTY READY**

We so often think of ribs as vehicles for sauces, but that's really doing them a disservice. Lean and tender baby back ribs can do quite nicely on their own with a simple but tasty rub. Serve with a salad or sautéed greens.

3 (1½- to 2-pound) racks baby back ribs

2 tablespoons kosher salt

1 tablespoon freshly ground black pepper

1 tablespoon garlic powder

1 tablespoon brown sugar

1. Remove the papery membrane from the back of the ribs. With a sharp knife, divide each rack of ribs as needed to fit into your sous vide bags.

2. In a small bowl, mix the salt, pepper, garlic powder, and brown sugar. Rub into the ribs, front and back. Really massage it in and use all the rub.

3. Place each portion of the ribs in its own sous vide bag. Vacuum-seal the bag(s) and then place them in the fridge to marinate for at least 1 hour and up to 10 hours.

4. Preheat the water bath to 165°F. When the water reaches temperature, immerse the bags and set the timer for 12 hours. Cover your cooking vessel with plastic wrap or a lid to prevent water from evaporating. Check periodically; add water to the vessel, if necessary, to make sure the ribs are submerged the entire time.

5. When the ribs are done, remove them from the sous vide bags and pat them dry with paper towels. Sear them for 3 to 5 minutes, either under the broiler, on a very hot grill, or using a searing torch. Let them rest for 5 minutes, then serve.

DID YOU KNOW? Baby back ribs aren't actually from a baby pig. Rather, they come from the upper part of the back, where the ribs meet the spine, just beneath the pork loin. The name refers to their length; they're typically cut to 3 to 6 inches, quite a bit shorter than other rib cuts.

PORK TENDERLOIN WITH SUN-DRIED TOMATOES AND CAPERS

SERVES 4 | **PREP TIME:** 10 minutes | **COOK TIME:** 1 hour 30 minutes | **FINISHING TIME:** 5 minutes |
SOUS VIDE TEMPERATURE: 136°F | **FAMILY FRIENDLY, QUICK PREP**

I don't know about you, but I think sun-dried tomatoes bless everything they touch, adding a splash of happy color and intense flavor. For this recipe, we'll cook pork tenderloins with butter that's been infused with sun-dried tomatoes and piquant, salty capers. Then, because there just can't be too much of a good thing, we'll slather the finished pork with more of it. This one's a delight for the eyes as well as the palate.

2 (1-pound) pork tenderloins
Kosher salt
Freshly ground black pepper
1 to 2 tablespoons avocado
  or vegetable oil, for searing

1 stick
  (8 tablespoons) butter, at
  room temperature
¼ cup sun-dried
  tomatoes, chopped

2 tablespoons
  capers, chopped
2 tablespoons chopped fresh
  Italian parsley, for garnish

1. Preheat the water bath to 136°F. (See the differences in texture in the Pork cooking chart on page 242.)

2. Cut each of the 2 pork tenderloins into 4 pieces and season them generously with salt and pepper. In a skillet over high heat, warm the avocado oil. Sear the pieces of pork until the sides are just beginning to brown, about 2 minutes on each side. Lay the seared pieces of meat on a cutting board.

3. In a bowl, combine the softened butter, sun-dried tomatoes, and capers; using a fork, mix them well. Spread half of the infused butter mixture over the pork tenderloin.

4. Place the pieces of meat in a cooking bag. Vacuum-seal the bag or seal it using the water displacement method and place the bag into the water bath. Set the timer for 1 hour 30 minutes.

5. When the timer goes off, remove the pork from the cooking bag, spread the pieces with the remaining tomato-caper butter, sprinkle with chopped parsley, and serve.

ESSENTIAL PORK TENDERLOIN WITH PAN SAUCE

SERVES 4 | **PREP TIME:** 5 minutes | **COOK TIME:** 1 hour 30 minutes | **FINISHING TIME:** 20 minutes | **SOUS VIDE TEMPERATURE:** 136°F | **FAMILY FRIENDLY**

Pork tenderloin is a small, boneless, exceptionally tender cut of pork, as the name implies. It is also one of the leanest cuts of pork, comparable to boneless, skinless chicken breasts. Save the cooking juices for a simple, savory sauce to ladle over the pork, if you like.

2 (1- to 1½-pound) pork tenderloins

2 teaspoons kosher salt, plus more for the optional sauce

Freshly ground black pepper

6 to 8 herb sprigs (thyme, oregano, or rosemary, optional)

1 tablespoon cooking oil with high smoke point, for searing

2 tablespoons butter (1 tablespoon, optional)

2 garlic cloves, sliced

2 small shallots, sliced (optional)

1 tablespoon minced shallot (optional)

1 cup dry vermouth or dry white wine (optional)

1 heaping tablespoon whole-grain mustard (optional)

1. Preheat the water bath to 136°F. (Pork tenderloin can be cooked between 131°F and 158°F. Refer to the Pork cooking chart on page 242 for different textures and doneness.)

2. Season the pork generously on all sides with the salt and pepper. Place the tenderloin into a cooking bag and add the fresh herbs (if using). Vacuum-seal the bag or seal it using the water displacement method and place the bag into the water bath. Set the timer for 1 hour 30 minutes or up to 4 hours.

3. When the timer goes off, remove the pork from the bag, reserving the cooking liquid if you plan to make the sauce, and pat it dry with paper towels.

4. Heat the oil in a large skillet over high heat. When the oil is shimmering, add the pork tenderloins and turn them occasionally until browned, about 2 minutes.

5. Add 1 tablespoon butter, the garlic, and sliced shallots (if using) to the skillet; spoon the melting butter and aromatics over the pork as you continue to brown it, 1 more minute or so. Transfer the tenderloins to a cutting board.

6. If you choose to make a sauce, in the skillet, add the minced shallot and sauté for about 30 seconds. Add the vermouth and stir until it's reduced by about half. Add the mustard, the reserved cooking liquids, and the remaining 1 tablespoon butter. Stir until thickened and season with salt and pepper.

7. Slice the pork tenderloin and serve, with or without the sauce.

DID YOU KNOW? Pork tenderloin, also known as pork tender or pork fillet, is the most tender cut; it's very lean meat, and is always sold boneless, coming from the same part of the pig as pork chops—the part that extends from the hip to the shoulder. Don't confuse pork tenderloin with pork loin, which is a different cut, typically much larger and with different cooking requirements.

CUBAN-INSPIRED PORK TENDERLOIN

SERVES 4 | **PREP TIME:** 10 minutes, plus 30 minutes to 8 hours to marinate | **COOK TIME:** 1 hour 30 minutes | **FINISHING TIME:** 10 minutes | **SOUS VIDE TEMPERATURE:** 144°F | **FAMILY FRIENDLY**

This pork tenderloin chills out in a sunny spiced citrus marinade and then cooks in the sous vide to juicy pinkness. (See the *Change It Up* note if pink pork isn't your thing.) The marinade turns into a delectable glaze as you sear the pork around the edges. Crank up Buena Vista Social Club, mix the mojitos, and enjoy this quick and easy meal.

2 (1- to 1½-pound) pork tenderloins, cut into 6 to 8 chunks

4 garlic cloves, coarsely chopped

¼ cup cilantro, coarsely chopped

Juice of 1 orange

Juice of 2 lemons

2 teaspoons ground cumin

2 teaspoons dried oregano

1½ teaspoons kosher salt

1 teaspoon freshly ground black pepper

2 tablespoons avocado or vegetable oil, for searing

1. Place the pork pieces in a large zip-top bag. In a small bowl, mix the garlic, cilantro, orange juice, lemon juice, cumin, oregano, salt, and pepper and pour the marinade over the pork. Seal the bag, shake it up, and let it marinate in the refrigerator for at least 30 minutes or up to 8 hours.

2. Preheat the water bath to 144°F.

3. Remove the pork from the refrigerator. Open the bag and, using the water displacement method to remove the air, reseal it. Lower the bag into the water and set the timer for 1 hour 30 minutes.

4. When the timer goes off, remove the bag from the sous vide. Reserving the cooking juices, transfer the pieces of pork to a plate and pat them dry with paper towels.

5. Pour the cooking juices into a small saucepan and bring to a boil. Simmer, stirring, until slightly reduced, about 5 minutes.

6. Heat the avocado oil in a cast-iron skillet over high heat and sear the pork on all sides until the outside is golden brown, about 1 minute per side.

7. Transfer to a cutting board, slice the pork, and serve drizzled with sauce.

CHANGE IT UP: Cooking at 144°F will produce a pork tenderloin with a tender pink blush. If you like your pork medium-well, increase the temperature to 149°F, or to 158°F for well-done.

PERNIL

SERVES 8 | **PREP TIME:** 10 minutes | **COOK TIME:** 24 hours | **FINISHING TIME:** 1 hour 45 minutes |
SOUS VIDE TEMPERATURE: 154°F | **FAMILY FRIENDLY, PARTY READY**

Visit a Puerto Rican household at Christmas, and you're all but guaranteed to find *pernil*, a slow-roasted pork shoulder seasoned predominantly with garlic, oregano, and vinegar. This recipe adds a bit more spice with ancho chili powder and cumin, making the meat *muy delicioso*. Don't wait for Christmas, though—this is a pork shoulder for all seasons.

1 (3- to 4-pound) boneless
  pork shoulder
2 garlic cloves
1 medium onion, quartered
1 tablespoon fresh oregano
  leaves, or 1 teaspoon
  dried oregano

1½ teaspoons ground cumin
1½ teaspoons kosher salt
1 teaspoon freshly ground
  black pepper
½ teaspoon ancho chili
  powder (or add a pinch of

cayenne pepper to regular
  chili powder)
Extra-virgin olive oil,
  for drizzling
1½ teaspoons wine or apple
  cider vinegar
Lime wedges, for serving

1. Preheat the water bath to 154°F.

2. Score the skin side of the pork with a sharp knife, making strokes 1 inch apart in a diagonal pattern.

3. In a food processor, pulse the garlic, onion, oregano, cumin, salt, pepper, and ancho chili powder. Add oil in a drizzle as needed and scrape down the sides until the mixture is pasty. (Alternatively, mash the ingredients in a mortar and pestle.) Blend in the vinegar.

4. Rub this mixture well into the pork, coating every bit thoroughly. Put the meat into a sous vide bag. Vacuum-seal the bag and place it into the water bath. Set the timer for 24 hours.

5. Just before the timer goes off, preheat your oven to 300°F. When the pork is ready, remove it from the bag and pat it dry with paper towels. Place the shoulder on a foil-lined, rimmed baking sheet with a wire rack placed in it. Finish it in the oven until the exterior achieves a dark, mahogany bark, about 1 hour 30 minutes. Remove it from the oven and let it rest for 10 to 15 minutes.

6. Cut the pork into slices or chunks and serve with lime wedges.

NORTH CAROLINA-STYLE PULLED PORK

SERVES 10 | **PREP TIME:** 10 minutes, plus 24 hours to brine | **COOK TIME:** 24 hours |
FINISHING TIME: 10 minutes | **SOUS VIDE TEMPERATURE:** 154°F | **FAMILY FRIENDLY, PARTY READY**

There's no shortcut to authentic-tasting pulled pork. The good news is that it requires next to no effort. The pork marinates for a day in a cider-and-spice brine, and then the sous vide takes over, cooking the meat to precisely the texture you like. Just pull and serve, maybe with some traditional vinegary Carolina BBQ sauce, which whips up in a heartbeat.

4 cups water

4 cups apple cider

½ cup kosher salt, plus more for the optional barbecue sauce

½ cup dark brown sugar, plus ¼ cup more for the optional barbecue sauce

8 tablespoons Sassy Pig Rub (page 227), **divided**

2 bay leaves

Pinch red pepper flakes, plus more for the optional barbecue sauce

1 (5- to 8-pound) pork shoulder (also known as

pork butt), cut into 2- to 3-inch cubes

½ cup apple cider vinegar (optional)

½ cup white vinegar (optional)

½ teaspoon chili powder (optional)

1. In a large pot, mix the water, apple cider, salt, ½ cup brown sugar, 3 tablespoons Sassy Pig Rub, the bay leaves, and red pepper flakes.

2. Place the pork in the pot, ensuring that the brine covers it completely. Cover and refrigerate for about 24 hours.

3. Preheat the water bath to 154°F.

4. Remove the pork from the brine and pat the cubes dry. Set aside 2 tablespoons dry rub. Rub the remainder all over the pork, covering it thoroughly. Place the pork in a sous vide bag. Vacuum-seal the bag and place the bag into the water bath. Set the timer for 24 hours. Cover the water vessel with a lid or plastic wrap to prevent evaporation during cooking; check the water level from time to time and top it up, if necessary.

5. **Make the optional barbecue sauce:** In a jar combine the apple cider vinegar, white vinegar, remaining ¼ cup brown sugar, the chili powder, and remaining 2 pinches red pepper flakes, season with salt, and shake until mixed.

6. When the timer goes off, remove the bag from the water, and now it's pulling time! You can either separate the pork when it's still in the bag using just your fingers or remove the pork and pull it apart with two forks in the traditional way.

7. Season with the remaining dry rub, if you wish, and/or drizzle with barbecue sauce.

CHANGE IT UP: The brine recipe calls for 4 cups apple cider, not apple cider *vinegar*. If you misread it (or if you'd just like to try something different), rest assured, the vinegar works just fine. Some folks like it even better than the cider's flavor.

MAPLE-GLAZED HAM

SERVES 8 to 12 | **PREP TIME:** 5 minutes | **COOK TIME:** 3 to 8 hours | **FINISHING TIME:** 30 minutes | **SOUS VIDE TEMPERATURE:** 140°F | **PARTY READY**

Whether for the holidays or a big dinner party or buffet, a ham is one of the easiest things to bring to the table and makes an instant centerpiece. Just add to the festivity by topping it off with a sticky, sweet, and spicy maple glaze.

1 (7- to 10-pound) fully cooked bone-in ham	¾ cup brown sugar	½ teaspoon ground cinnamon
½ cup pineapple juice	¾ cup maple syrup	¼ teaspoon ground cloves
½ cup unsalted butter	2 tablespoons Dijon mustard	4 garlic cloves, smashed

1. Preheat the water bath to 140°F.

2. If the ham has a rind, remove the rind without cutting away the layer of fat beneath it. Score the surface with diagonal cuts.

3. Place the ham in an extra-large cooking bag and add the pineapple juice. Vacuum-seal the bag or seal it using the water displacement method and place it into the water bath. (If using a zip-top bag, double it up.) Set the timer for no less than 3 hours or up to 8 hours.

4. About 30 minutes before you want to serve the ham, preheat the oven to 500°F.

5. Meanwhile, in a small saucepan, heat the butter over medium heat until slightly browned. Add the brown sugar, maple syrup, mustard, cinnamon, and cloves, stirring to mix well until the brown sugar has dissolved, about 2 minutes. Reduce the heat to low, add the garlic, and bring to a simmer. Set the glaze aside and let it cool to luke-warm. It should be the consistency of room-temperature honey.

6. Remove the ham from the cooking bag, placing it, cut-side down, on a wire rack set on a rimmed baking sheet lined with foil. Pat the ham dry with paper towels and brush it with the glaze.

7. Put the ham in the oven for 5 minutes. Take it out, apply another coat of glaze, and return it to the oven. Repeat this 4 times, letting it roast for 5 minutes before applying a fresh layer of glaze. Remove the ham from the oven and allow it to rest for 5 minutes, then slice and serve.

BEER SAUSAGE

SERVES 6 | **PREP TIME:** 30 minutes | **COOK TIME:** 1 hour | **FINISHING TIME:** 5 minutes |
SOUS VIDE TEMPERATURE: 140°F | **FAMILY FRIENDLY, PARTY READY**

A cookout or Oktoberfest are great excuses to make this mouthwatering beer sausage, but after the first time, you won't wait for an excuse. The sausages cook completely but stay juicy and tender in a bath of caramelized onion and American pale ale. A quick visit to a cast-iron skillet or hot grill gives them a smoky char just ready for game night.

2 tablespoons butter

1 large red onion, thinly sliced

1 tablespoon brown sugar

¼ teaspoon kosher salt

12 ounces (1½ cups) American pale ale

1 pound raw bratwurst or Italian sausages (about 6 sausages)

1 to 2 tablespoons avocado or vegetable oil, for searing

6 toasted hot dog buns or split lengths of French bread

1. Preheat the water bath to 140°F.

2. In a large skillet over medium heat, melt the butter. Add the sliced red onion, brown sugar, and salt. Cook until the onions are browned and slightly caramelized, around 20 minutes. Reduce the heat to low and add the pale ale. Simmer for 5 minutes, then let cool.

3. Divide the sausages and the sauce evenly between two or more cooking bags. Vacuum-seal the bags or seal them using the water displacement method and place them into the water bath. Set the timer for 1 hour.

4. When the timer goes off, remove the cooking bags from the sous vide. Reserve the onion-beer cooking liquid and pat the sausages dry with paper towels. In either a hot, oiled cast-iron skillet (first heating the oil over high heat) or on a heated grill, give the sausages a good sear. Place them in the hot dog buns or French bread. Using tongs, top each sausage with the reserved beer-soaked, caramelized onions.

CHANGE IT UP: American pale ale has flavors of citrus and pine that work really well with this recipe, but don't hesitate to experiment. Pay a visit to your local craft brewery and see what other brews catch your fancy.

MAKE-AHEAD MAGIC: You could make the onion-beer sauce a day in advance; chill and refrigerate it until you're ready to cook the sausages.

SPICY LEMON PORK ROAST

SERVES 8 | **PREP TIME:** 10 minutes | **COOK TIME:** 3 hours | **FINISHING TIME:** 25 minutes |
SOUS VIDE TEMPERATURE: 138°F | **FAMILY FRIENDLY**

With this recipe, we're going to take a nice, mild-mannered piece of pork and spice it up, giving it a good rubdown with a smoky, zesty seasoning mixture before putting it into the sous vide. What can I say? A 10-minute sear in a hot oven will produce the crispy crackling that everyone adores.

1 (5- to 6-pound) center-cut
  pork loin
Leaves from 5 thyme
  sprigs, chopped

2 garlic cloves, crushed
2 teaspoons red
  pepper flakes
1 teaspoon smoked paprika

Zest and juice from ½ lemon
1 tablespoon extra-virgin
  olive oil

1. Preheat the water bath to 138°F.

2. Using a sharp knife, score the pork with diagonal cuts, about an inch apart, forming a diamond pattern.

3. In a bowl, mix together the thyme, garlic, red pepper flakes, paprika, lemon zest and juice, and olive oil, then rub the pork thoroughly, getting the rub deep into the cuts in the skin.

4. Place the pork in a cooking bag. Vacuum-seal the bag or seal it using the water displacement method and place the bag into the water bath. Set the timer for 3 hours.

5. Preheat the oven to 500°F. When the timer goes off, remove the pork from the cooking bag and pat it dry. Put the pork in a broiler pan and sear in the oven for 5 minutes; flip it over and sear the other side for another 5 minutes. Remove it from the oven and let it rest for 15 minutes.

6. Slice and serve.

TACOS DE CARNITAS

SERVES 6 | **PREP TIME:** 15 minutes | **COOK TIME:** 12 to 24 hours | **FINISHING TIME:** 20 minutes |
SOUS VIDE TEMPERATURE: 165°F | **FAMILY FRIENDLY**

Carnitas ("little meats") is Mexico's crispy variation on pulled pork. Fold it into tortillas with salsa and a whole array of toppings and pretend you're at your local taqueria.

1 (3-pound) skinless, boneless pork butt

1 tablespoon kosher salt

1 teaspoon freshly ground black pepper

1 tablespoon dried oregano

1 teaspoon ground cumin

1 tablespoon extra-virgin olive oil

2 medium white onions, divided (one coarsely chopped, and one finely chopped, for serving)

1 jalapeño, seeded and chopped

1 tablespoon minced garlic

1 medium orange, cut into wedges

12 taco-size flour or corn tortillas

Cilantro, finely chopped, for serving

Salsa of your choice, for serving

Lime wedges, for serving

1. Preheat the water bath to 165°F.

2. Cut the pork into 2- to 3-inch-thick slices.

3. In a large bowl, combine the pork, salt, pepper, oregano, cumin, olive oil, coarsely chopped onion, jalapeño, and garlic. Squeeze the juice from the orange wedges before adding the wedges to the bowl. Toss to mix well.

4. Put the mixture into a sous vide bag. Vacuum-seal the bag and place it in the water bath. Set the timer for 12 to 24 hours, as is convenient. You won't overcook the pork. Cover the water vessel with a lid or plastic wrap to prevent evaporation during cooking; check the water level from time to time and top it up, if necessary.

5. When the timer goes off, remove the sous vide bag and empty it into a large bowl. Using tongs, pick out the pieces of pork and place them on a rimmed baking sheet. When the meat has cooled adequately, shred it using either your hands or a pair of forks.

6. When ready to serve the tacos, preheat the broiler to high. Spread the shredded pork evenly across the baking sheet and place it about 3 inches below the broiler element for about 10 minutes. Flip the meat around a few times so that it can brown and crisp evenly. (You could also sear the pork in a cast-iron skillet, turning frequently.)

7. Pile the crispy pork onto the tortillas, add the finely chopped onion and cilantro, and serve with your favorite salsa and some lime wedges.

CHANGE IT UP: Some avocado slices in the tacos wouldn't go amiss.

MAKE-AHEAD MAGIC: The carnitas will keep beautifully in the fridge for up to 5 days. Allow the pork to cool completely after shredding it and store it in an airtight container. Just brown it under the broiler at serving time.

CHOUCROUTE GARNIE

SERVES 4 to 5 | **PREP TIME:** 20 minutes | **COOK TIME:** 24 hours | **FINISHING TIME:** 10 minutes |
SOUS VIDE TEMPERATURE: 150°F | **FAMILY FRIENDLY**

This choucroute garnie ("dressed sauerkraut") will indeed be exceptionally well-dressed, with perfectly cooked pork shoulder and bratwurst, not to mention the ham and hot dogs that will bake with and flavor the sauerkraut. This dish is a classic in Alsace, the region of France bordering Germany, and the German influence is obvious. Served with boiled potatoes, it will satisfy the heartiest appetites around your table.

1 (1½-pound) boneless
  pork shoulder, cut into
  3-inch chunks
2 tablespoons kosher salt
½ teaspoon freshly ground
  black pepper
1 tablespoon light
  brown sugar
2 bay leaves, divided
1 pound bratwurst, cut into
  2-inch pieces

2 tablespoons vegetable oil
  or duck fat
½ large onion,
  coarsely chopped
2 large garlic cloves,
  coarsely chopped
2 (2-pound) bags
  sauerkraut, drained
10 juniper berries
¼ teaspoon caraway seeds
1½ cups chicken stock

¾ cup Riesling or pinot
  gris wine
5 hot dogs
1 (1-pound) boneless ham
  steak, sliced
1 pound medium potatoes,
  peeled and quartered
  (about 5 potatoes)
Various types of mustard,
  for serving

1. Preheat the water bath to 150°F.

2. Place the pork shoulder chunks in a sous vide bag. Season with salt, pepper, and brown sugar, coating the meat well. Add 1 bay leaf to the bag, vacuum-seal it, and place it in the sous vide. Set the timer for 20 hours. Be sure to cover the sous vide water bath with a lid or plastic wrap to prevent evaporation; check the water level periodically and top it up, if necessary.

3. Place the bratwurst into a sous vide bag, vacuum-seal it, and put it in the refrigerator.

4. When the timer goes off, add the bratwurst to the sous vide, leaving the pork shoulder in place, and set the timer for another 4 hours.

5. About 1 hour before the meats are done, preheat the oven to 300°F.

6. In a Dutch oven on the stovetop, heat the vegetable oil over medium heat. Add the onion and garlic and sauté until softened, stirring, about 5 minutes. Stir in the sauerkraut, juniper berries, caraway seeds, chicken stock, wine, and the remaining 1 bay leaf. Increase the heat and bring to a rolling boil. Simmer for 5 to 10 minutes, until some of the alcohol evaporates.

7. Nestle the hot dogs and ham slices into the sauerkraut, cover the Dutch oven, and put it into the preheated oven for 30 minutes.

8. In a large saucepan, cover the potatoes with water, add a pinch of salt, and bring to a boil over high heat. Reduce the heat and simmer until the potatoes are fork-tender, 15 to 20 minutes. Drain them and cover to keep warm.

9. When the sous vide timer goes off, remove the pork shoulder and bratwurst from the sous vide bags and pat them dry with paper towels.

10. To serve, place a mound of the sauerkraut/hot dog/ham mixture in the center of each plate and arrange portions of pork shoulder, bratwurst, and boiled potato around it. Serve with an array of stone-ground, Dijon, yellow, or honey mustards.

CHANGE IT UP: Add a sliced apple, either red or green, to the sauerkraut mixture before baking for some color and sweetness. Feel free to add ¼ teaspoon cloves and/or allspice when sautéing the onion and garlic.

MAKE-AHEAD MAGIC: Cook the pork shoulder and bratwurst, remove the bags to an ice-water bath to chill them thoroughly, and then the sealed sous vide bags can stay in your fridge for up to 3 days. Cut the meats and add them to the Dutch oven before baking; they can reheat as the sauerkraut bakes.

Classic Rib Eye, page 176

BEEF AND LAMB

Perfect Burgers 168

Bacon Burgers with Guacamole 170

"Smoked" Brisket 172

Beef Barbacoa 174

Classic Pot Roast 175

Classic Rib Eye 176

California Steak Salad 177

Filet Mignon with Red Wine Sauce 178

Porterhouse with Spicy Mushroom Sauce 180

Beef Wellington 182

Beef Burgundy 184

Dijon-Herb Rubbed Prime Rib 186

Korean-Inspired Braised Short Ribs 187

Merguez Sausages with Vegetables and Herbed Yogurt Sauce 188

Italian-Style Meatballs 189

Lamb Kofta with Tzatziki Sauce 190

Essential Lamb Chops 192

48-Hour Moroccan-Inspired Lamb Shanks 195

Rack of Lamb with Rosemary-Balsamic Marinade 196

Curry Lamb 197

Spicy Asian-Inspired Lamb Stew 198

Mediterranean Leg of Lamb 200

Veal Osso Buco 201

PERFECT BURGERS

SERVES 4 | **PREP TIME:** 15 minutes | **COOK TIME:** 1 hour | **FINISHING TIME:** 25 minutes |
SOUS VIDE TEMPERATURE: 133°F | **FAMILY FRIENDLY, PARTY READY**

Cooking burgers in the sous vide isn't as loopy as it might sound at first. You're not tied down to the grill, watching and flipping, nor are you wondering if the oven's broiler is incinerating your beef patties. It reliably, predictably produces juicy, tender, thoroughly cooked burgers that want only a minute or two of browning just before serving.

2 pounds 80-percent lean
    ground beef
2 tablespoons finely
    chopped chives (optional)
2 teaspoons smoked
    paprika (optional)
2 dashes Worcestershire
    sauce (optional)

Kosher salt
Freshly ground black pepper
4 hamburger buns,
    for serving
1 tablespoon avocado or
    vegetable oil, for searing
2 tablespoons
    unsalted butter

Sliced cheese of your choice,
    for serving (optional)
1 large tomato, sliced,
    for serving
4 lettuce leaves, for serving
4 dill pickles, sliced,
    for serving
Ketchup, for serving

1. Preheat the water bath to 133°F.

2. Place the ground beef on a clean surface. If using the chives, smoked paprika, and/or Worcestershire, mix those in with clean hands. Form the mixture into four 1-inch-thick patties and season them on both sides with salt and pepper. Place each patty into a zip-top bag and seal the bags using the water displacement method. Immerse them in the water and set the timer for 1 hour.

3. When done, remove the burgers from the bags and place them on a large plate lined with paper towels. Pat them dry on both sides and season them with more salt and pepper. Let them rest for 15 minutes.

4. Toast the hamburger buns and have the toppings and condiments ready.

5. In a cast-iron skillet, heat the oil over high heat until it just begins to smoke. Place the burgers into the skillet and add the butter. Sear the burgers, shifting the skillet around to spread the butter, until the beef is browned on one side, no more than 1 minute.

6. Flip the burgers and place the sliced cheese on top (if using); cook for another 45 seconds or so, until the bottom edges of the burgers are browned and the cheese is nicely melted. Transfer the burgers to the buns. Top with tomato, lettuce, pickles, and ketchup as desired, and serve.

CHANGE IT UP: The list of potential toppings could go on for days—sautéed mushrooms, thinly sliced red onion (either raw or sautéed), bottled chile peppers, sliced avocado, Perfect Bacon (page 134).

CHANGE IT UP: The temperature I've suggested for this recipe, 133°F, will produce rosy-pink and very juicy burgers. For rarer meat, you can go as low as 126°F. For more well-done beef, set the temperature as high as 158°F.

MAKE-AHEAD MAGIC: If you like, shape and season the burgers, place them in the zip-top bags, and freeze them for a few days. When you're ready to cook, put them directly into the sous vide; there's no need to adjust the cooking time.

BACON BURGERS WITH GUACAMOLE

SERVES 4 | **PREP TIME:** 10 minutes | **COOK TIME:** 1 hour | **FINISHING TIME:** 25 minutes |
SOUS VIDE TEMPERATURE: 133°F | **FAMILY FRIENDLY, PARTY READY**

I admit, this recipe sounds quirky at first glance. (Spiced pineapple yogurt—seriously?) But it's seriously scrumptious. Add guacamole, cheese, and bacon to juicy, medium-rare sous vide burgers and get ready for delighted gasps. These burgers are showstoppers for neighborhood get-togethers; just double or quadruple the recipe and thrill the whole gang.

2 pounds 80-percent lean ground beef

1 teaspoon kosher salt, plus more for seasoning

Freshly ground black pepper

½ cup (4 to 5 ounces) pineapple yogurt

1 tablespoon smoked paprika

3 ripe avocados

2 tablespoons freshly squeezed lime juice (from 1 lime)

½ teaspoon garlic powder

¼ cup finely diced onion

1 large Roma tomato, finely diced

Cilantro, for the guacamole (optional)

4 hamburger buns, for serving

½ cup shredded Monterey Jack cheese or more, for serving

8 slices Perfect Bacon (page 134), halved crosswise, for serving

1 tablespoon avocado or vegetable oil, for searing

4 curly lettuce leaves, for serving

1. Preheat the water bath to 133°F.

2. Place the ground beef on a clean surface. Form 4 patties and season them on both sides with salt and pepper. Place each patty into a zip-top bag and seal the bags using the water displacement method. Immerse them in the water and set the timer for 1 hour.

3. When the timer goes off, remove the burgers from the bags and place them on a large plate lined with paper towels. Pat them dry on both sides and season with more salt and pepper. Let them rest for 15 minutes.

4. In a small bowl, combine the pineapple yogurt and smoked paprika. Set aside.

5. In another bowl, make the guacamole by mashing the avocados with a fork and mixing in 1 teaspoon salt, the lime juice, and garlic powder. Mix in the onion, tomato, and cilantro to taste (if using).

6. Toast the hamburger buns and have the shredded cheese and bacon ready.

7. In a cast-iron skillet, heat the oil over high heat until it just begins to smoke. Place the burgers into the skillet, searing them until the beef is browned on one side, no more than 1 minute. Flip the burgers and cook another 45 seconds or so, until the bottom edges are browned.

8. Spread the yogurt mixture on the bottom halves of the hamburger buns and the guacamole on the top halves. Place the burgers on the bottom buns; top them with grated cheese, bacon strips, and lettuce, then cover them with the top halves of the buns. Serve.

CHANGE IT UP: If you'd like your burgers rarer or more well-done, see the *Change It Up* tip for the Perfect Burgers recipe (page 168).

"SMOKED" BRISKET

SERVES 8 to 10 | **PREP TIME:** 10 minutes, plus 2 to 3 hours to marinate | **COOK TIME:** 24 to 72 hours | **FINISHING TIME:** 3 to 4 hours | **SOUS VIDE TEMPERATURE:** 135 or 155°F | **FAMILY FRIENDLY, PARTY READY**

Normally, the first step to making smoked brisket is acquiring a smoker, but we'll skip that, instead incorporating smoked salt, smoked paprika, and liquid smoke into the rub. After a few hours of dry-brining, the meat will have a distinctively smoky flavor. The classic brisket cooking rule is "low and slow," but it's worth the wait.

1 (5-pound) beef brisket, point cut with fat cap

¼ cup smoked salt or kosher salt

⅓ cup freshly ground black pepper

¼ cup brown sugar

2 tablespoons smoked paprika

1 tablespoon mustard powder

2 teaspoons onion powder

1 teaspoon garlic powder

¼ teaspoon liquid smoke (optional)

1. Slice the brisket in half crosswise to fit into large sous vide bags.

2. In a small bowl, combine the salt, black pepper, brown sugar, smoked paprika, mustard powder, onion powder, and garlic powder and mix well. Rub two-thirds of the mixture over the brisket, and reserve the remaining third.

3. Place each brisket half in a sous vide bag. Add 4 drops liquid smoke (about ⅛ teaspoon), if using, in each bag. Vacuum-seal the bags and let the brisket rest for 2 to 3 hours in the refrigerator.

4. Preheat the water bath to 135°F for tender brisket with a steak-like texture or 155°F for a shredding consistency.

5. When the water has reached temperature, submerge the bags. If you're cooking at 135°F, set the timer for 36 to 72 hours. At 155°F, set it for 24 to 36 hours. Cover the water vessel with a lid or plastic wrap to prevent evaporation during cooking; check the water level from time to time and top it up, if necessary.

6. When the sous vide timer goes off, put an oven rack in the lower-middle position and preheat the oven to 250°F.

7. Remove the brisket from the sous vide bags and pat the meat dry with paper towels. Apply the remaining rub to the whole surface of the brisket and place it on a baking rack. Place it in the oven and allow it to roast until it develops a nice crust, 3 to 4 hours.

8. Remove the brisket from the oven, allow it to rest for 10 minutes, then slice and serve.

CHANGE IT UP: If you are short on time when it comes to the oven finish, roast the meat for 1 hour at 300°F, then crank up the oven to 400°F for another 5 to 10 minutes to help the bark develop.

DID YOU KNOW? A full cut of brisket is typically 12 to 16 pounds. From that, butchers produce flat and point cuts. The former is typically rectangular and is ideal for corned and smoked beef recipes. The point cut is irregularly shaped and more marbled; it works well for braised and shredded beef recipes. For this recipe, I recommend using a point cut with the fat cap intact and plenty of intramuscular marbling.

MAKE-AHEAD MAGIC: If you like, when you remove the brisket from the sous vide, cool it in an ice-water bath; you can then keep it in the fridge, vacuum-sealed, for up to 1 week before finishing it.

BEEF BARBACOA

SERVES 8 | **PREP TIME:** 5 minutes | **COOK TIME:** 24 hours | **FINISHING TIME:** 5 minutes |
SOUS VIDE TEMPERATURE: 175°F | **FAMILY FRIENDLY, PARTY READY, QUICK PREP**

This barbacoa will make for the best homemade beef tacos, all for less than 10 minutes of effort, leaving you plenty of time to mix that pitcher of margaritas. If there are leftovers, fear not. Burrito bowls, quesadillas, taco salads, or Chilaquiles Eggs Benedict (page 20) beckon.

1 (3- to 4-pound) beef
  chuck roast

1 medium onion, sliced

3 or 4 chipotle peppers in
  adobo sauce

1 cup beef bone broth or
  low-sodium beef broth

4 garlic cloves

1½ tablespoons
  ground cumin

1 tablespoon dried oregano

2 teaspoons kosher salt

½ teaspoon freshly ground
  black pepper

¼ teaspoon ground cloves

¼ cup freshly squeezed lime
  juice (from 2 large limes)

3 bay leaves

Tortillas, warmed,
  for serving

Chopped white onion,
  for serving

Chopped tomatoes,
  for serving

Chopped fresh cilantro,
  for serving

Chopped avocado,
  for serving

1. Preheat the water bath to 175°F.

2. Cut the beef into 1- to 2-inch cubes and place them into one or more sous vide bags. Add the sliced onion.

3. In a food processor, combine the chipotle peppers, broth, garlic, cumin, oregano, salt, black pepper, cloves, and lime juice. Pulse until blended. Carefully pour the mixture over the beef and add the bay leaves. Vacuum-seal the bag(s) and place them into the water bath. Set the timer for 24 hours.

4. When the timer goes off, remove the bags from the sous vide and transfer the contents to a large bowl. Using two forks, shred the beef. Wrap it in the tortillas and serve topped with the chopped onion, tomato, cilantro, and avocado (or other toppings of your choice).

DID YOU KNOW? A barbacoa was a wooden structure that the Taino people in the Caribbean used to smoke meat. The Spaniards took it back to Europe with them in the 16th century, and it became the root for our word *barbecue*. Beef barbacoa is a classic Mexican dish.

CLASSIC POT ROAST

SERVES 4 to 6 | **PREP TIME:** 10 minutes | **COOK TIME:** 18 hours | **FINISHING TIME:** 15 minutes |
SOUS VIDE TEMPERATURE: 133°F | **FAMILY FRIENDLY**

Chuck roast is one of the most flavorful beef cuts, and bonus, it's also a lean cut. With scant marbling, it could be chewy, but not if you slow-cook it in your sous vide, which gives you prime-rib flavor and tenderness at a fraction of the price.

1 (3-pound) beef chuck roast

2 to 3 tablespoons
extra-virgin olive oil

1½ teaspoons kosher salt,
plus more for seasoning

1½ teaspoons freshly ground
black pepper, plus more
for seasoning

2 teaspoons sugar

1 tablespoon garlic powder

2 teaspoons chopped
fresh rosemary

2 tablespoons avocado or
vegetable oil, for searing

1 tablespoon cornstarch

2 tablespoons water

1. Preheat the water bath to 133°F.

2. Truss the roast with several lengths of kitchen twine to hold it in a nice, uniform shape during cooking, and then rub it all over with the olive oil.

3. In a small bowl, combine the salt, pepper, sugar, garlic powder, and rosemary. Rub the roast on all sides with the seasoning mixture.

4. Put the roast into a cooking bag (if using a zip-top bag, double it up). Vacuum-seal the bag or seal it using the water displacement method and place the bag into the water bath. Set the timer for 18 hours. Cover the water vessel with a lid or plastic wrap to prevent evaporation during cooking; check the water level from time to time and top it up, if necessary.

5. When the timer goes off, remove the roast from the bag, reserving the cooking juices for the gravy. Pat the meat dry with paper towels and remove the twine.

6. In a skillet over medium-high heat, warm the avocado or vegetable oil; sear the roast on all sides until browned, about 1 minute per side. Remove the meat and set it aside to rest.

7. In a small bowl, whisk the cornstarch and water together. Pour the reserved cooking juices into the same skillet over medium-high heat and bring them to a simmer, scraping up any browned bits. Whisk in the cornstarch mixture and simmer, stirring, until the gravy is thickened, about 5 minutes. Season to taste with salt and pepper.

8. Slice the pot roast, ladle some gravy over it, and serve.

CLASSIC RIB EYE

SERVES 4 | **PREP TIME:** 5 minutes | **COOK TIME:** 1 hour | **FINISHING TIME:** 5 minutes |
SOUS VIDE TEMPERATURE: 133°F | **FAMILY FRIENDLY, QUICK PREP**

You don't need to visit a steakhouse or, for that matter, be a grill guru to enjoy a perfect rib eye. This quick and stress-free rib eye is guaranteed to wow gourmets, grill gurus, and your family . . . basically everyone with the good fortune to be at your table. Serve with Garlic-Herb Mashed Potatoes (page 52).

2 pounds bone-in or boneless rib eye steak, 1-inch thick (about 2 steaks)	2 tablespoons kosher salt Freshly ground black pepper 2 tablespoons extra-virgin olive oil	1 bay leaf or 1 rosemary or thyme sprig, plus more for finishing (optional) 2 tablespoons butter

1. Preheat the water bath to 133°F.

2. Season the steaks on both sides with the salt and pepper.

3. Place the steaks in a cooking bag with the olive oil and bay leaf (if using). Vacuum-seal the bag or seal it using the water displacement method and place the bag into the water bath. Set the timer for 1 hour.

4. When the timer goes off, remove the steak from the cooking bag and pat it dry with paper towels.

5. Preheat a skillet over high heat and add the butter. When the butter has stopped bubbling, add the steak, and if you like, some fresh herbs. Baste the meat with the butter while it sears, for 1 to 2 minutes on each side, just long enough to develop a good crust. You can also sear the meat under the broiler, on a hot grill, or using a kitchen torch.

6. Thinly slice the steak and serve.

CHANGE IT UP: The time and temperature in this recipe will produce a medium-rare dry-aged rib eye; see the chart on page 244 for different levels of doneness with different thicknesses.

CALIFORNIA STEAK SALAD

SERVES 8 | **PREP TIME:** 5 minutes | **COOK TIME:** 2 hours | **FINISHING TIME:** 10 minutes |
SOUS VIDE TEMPERATURE: 131°F | **FAMILY FRIENDLY, QUICK PREP**

Like a Hollywood star, this meal-size salad boasts both looks and wealth: A rainbow of color, it's absolutely loaded with nutrients and flavor. Succulent slices of medium-rare flank steak and ripe avocado are surrounded by grilled onions and mushrooms, all sitting on a bed of fresh baby greens and cherry tomatoes. The kicker is the bold, eye-opening chimichurri drizzled over the top.

2 pounds flank steak

1 tablespoon kosher salt

Freshly ground black pepper

2 tablespoons extra-virgin olive oil

2 tablespoons butter

8 ounces (about 2½ cups) cremini mushrooms, quartered

2 red onions, cut into 1-inch-thick slices

2 (5-ounce) packages baby spinach and/or spring green mix

2 pints cherry tomatoes, halved

2 avocados, sliced

1 cup Chimichurri (page 229)

1. Preheat the water bath to 131°F.

2. Season the steak on both sides with the salt and pepper. Slide it into a cooking bag and add the olive oil. Vacuum-seal the bag or seal it using the water displacement method and place the bag into the water bath. Set the timer for 2 hours.

3. When the steak is done, remove it from the cooking bag and pat it dry. Preheat a skillet over medium-high heat and add the butter. When the butter is melted, add the steak. Baste the meat with the butter while it sears, 1 to 2 minutes on each side, just long enough to develop a good crust. Remove the steak from the skillet and set aside.

4. Put the mushrooms and the red onion slices in the skillet, still over medium-high heat. With a spatula, stir the mushrooms and flip the onion slices until the onion is slightly charred and the mushrooms are well browned, 3 to 4 minutes. Remove the skillet from the heat.

5. To assemble the salad, arrange the baby spinach on a large serving plate, followed by the onion and mushrooms. Slice the steak and place it on top of the vegetables. Top with cherry tomatoes and sliced avocado. Drizzle the chimichurri over the steak salad and serve.

MAKE-AHEAD MAGIC: If you'd like to cook the steak ahead of time, use a vacuum-sealed sous vide bag. When it's finished cooking, transfer it to an ice-water bath to chill it thoroughly. It will then keep in the fridge for up to 2 days or in the freezer for up to 6 weeks.

FILET MIGNON WITH RED WINE SAUCE

SERVES 4 | **PREP TIME:** 5 minutes | **COOK TIME:** 45 minutes | **FINISHING TIME:** 10 minutes |
SOUS VIDE TEMPERATURE: 129°F | **FAMILY FRIENDLY, QUICK PREP**

French for "dainty fillet," the filet mignon is cut from a non-working muscle in the tenderloin area, so it is supremely tender. The price is not so dainty, though, and many home cooks are skittish to give it a go. Fear not; the sous vide produces buttery-textured beef in under an hour. Add a simple red wine sauce, and you're putting top-tier steakhouse fare on your table. This is divine served over Crispy Smashed Potatoes (page 53).

FOR THE FILETS:

4 (8-ounce) filets mignon,
   1-inch thick
Kosher salt
Freshly ground black pepper
1 tablespoon garlic powder

Extra-virgin olive oil, for
   drizzling and searing
2 or 3 fresh thyme
   sprigs (optional)
1 bay leaf (optional)
2 tablespoons butter

FOR THE RED WINE SAUCE:

2 garlic cloves
1 teaspoon fresh thyme
1 cup red wine
4 tablespoons (½ stick)
   butter, cubed

1. Preheat the water bath to 129°F.

2. **Prepare the filets:** Season the filets with salt, pepper, and garlic powder on all sides. Place the meat into one or more cooking bags and drizzle with the olive oil. Add the thyme and bay leaf to the bag (if using). Vacuum-seal the bag(s) or seal them using the water displacement method and place the bag(s) into the water bath. Set the timer for 45 minutes.

3. When the timer goes off, remove the beef from the bag(s), reserving the cooking juices, and pat it dry with paper towels.

4. Heat a skillet over medium-high heat. When it's hot (water drops sizzle when they hit the surface), add some olive oil, the steaks, and the butter. Baste the meat with the butter while it sears, about 1 minute on each side, or until the filets have a crisp, darkened crust. Remove them from the pan.

5. **Make the wine sauce:** Add the reserved cooking juices to the still-hot skillet. Bring them to a simmer, scraping up any browned bits, and add the garlic and thyme. Cook, stirring, until the garlic begins to brown, taking care not to let the sauce burn or stick. Add the wine and then the butter, stirring continuously until the sauce thickens a bit, about 5 minutes. Remove the pan from the heat and pour the sauce through a fine-mesh sieve.

6. Slice the filet mignon and drizzle the wine sauce over it.

CHANGE IT UP: Go ahead and experiment with different herbs in the cooking bag: Rosemary, oregano, parsley, sage, and tarragon are all good candidates. Each will lend its distinct personality to the meat.

DID YOU KNOW? If you are starting with frozen steaks, no worries! There's no need to defrost them before putting them into the sous vide. Just multiply the cooking time by 1½. If you're pulling filets mignon out of your freezer, for example, just set the timer for 68 minutes rather than 45.

PORTERHOUSE WITH SPICY MUSHROOM SAUCE

SERVES 4 | **PREP TIME:** 5 minutes | **COOK TIME:** 1 hour | **FINISHING TIME:** 20 minutes |
SOUS VIDE TEMPERATURE: 129°F | **FAMILY FRIENDLY**

If a first glance at this recipe suggests that it's a weekend project, wait! You can indeed serve up a thick, superbly finished porterhouse topped with a zesty portobello and bacon sauce on any weeknight. What's more, it's jaw-droppingly delicious. Serve with any kind of potato, asparagus, or Cauliflower Puree (page 65).

FOR THE PORTERHOUSE STEAK:

2 (1½- to 2-pound) porterhouse steaks

2 tablespoons kosher salt

Freshly ground black pepper

2 fresh thyme sprigs (optional)

2 fresh rosemary sprigs (optional)

1 tablespoon avocado or vegetable oil, for searing

1 tablespoon butter

FOR THE SPICY MUSHROOM SAUCE:

4 slices thick-cut bacon, cut into ½-inch pieces

8 ounces (about 3 cups) sliced baby portobello mushrooms (or creminis)

½ cup diced onion

2 garlic cloves

½ teaspoon freshly ground black pepper

½ teaspoon red pepper flakes

1 cup tomato-basil pasta sauce

¼ cup finely chopped fresh Italian parsley

½ cup shredded Parmesan cheese (optional)

1. Preheat the water bath to 129°F.

2. **Prepare the porterhouse:** Season the steaks on both sides with salt and pepper. Slide them into a cooking bag; add the thyme and rosemary (if using), placing some on either side of the meat. Vacuum-seal the bag or seal it using the water displacement method and place the bag into the water bath. Set the timer for 1 hour.

3. When the timer goes off, remove the steak from the cooking bag, reserving the cooking juices. Pat the meat dry with paper towels.

4. In a cast-iron skillet, heat the oil over high heat. Add the steak and the butter to the skillet. Baste the meat with the butter while it sears, 1 to 2 minutes on each side, just long enough to develop a good crust. Use tongs to rotate the meat and sear all the edges too. Remove the steak from the skillet to rest and reduce the heat to medium-high.

5. **Make the mushroom sauce:** Cook the bacon pieces in the skillet until they are crisp, stirring frequently, about 5 minutes, then transfer them to a plate covered with a paper towel.

6. In a food processor, finely chop the mushrooms, onion, and garlic. Add this mixture to the skillet with the black pepper and red pepper flakes. Cook for about 4 minutes, until fragrant. Add the reserved cooking juices and pasta sauce to the mushroom mixture. Reduce the heat to low and cook for 4 to 5 minutes, stirring occasionally. Stir in the parsley.

7. Slice the steak and top it with the mushroom sauce, cooked bacon, and some Parmesan cheese (if using).

DID YOU KNOW? Porterhouse and T-bone steaks are cut from the same part of the cow, the short loin. So, what's the difference? It's the thickness: A porterhouse steak must be at least 1¼ inches thick. If it's less than that, the USDA classifies it as a T-bone. If you're looking for a heftier cut of meat, reach for the porterhouse.

BEEF WELLINGTON

SERVES 6 to 8 | **PREP TIME:** 20 minutes | **COOK TIME:** 1 hour 30 minutes | **FINISHING TIME:** 1 hour | **SOUS VIDE TEMPERATURE:** 131°F | **FAMILY FRIENDLY, PARTY READY**

Chef Gordon Ramsay characterizes beef Wellington as the ultimate indulgence, and I agree. This isn't something to whip up on a casual weeknight, but it's still a very approachable dish that will elevate any occasion to magical. Pour a dry red, light some candles, and indulge!

1 (2- to 3-pound, about 6-inch long) center-cut beef tenderloin roast, fat trimmed

1 tablespoon kosher salt plus more for sprinkling

Freshly ground black pepper

4 tablespoons extra-virgin olive oil, divided

1 pound cremini mushrooms

2 large shallots

¼ cup dry red wine

4 tablespoons Dijon mustard

2 teaspoons minced fresh thyme leaves

1 or 2 sheets frozen puff pastry dough, thawed

¼ pound prosciutto, thinly sliced

1 large egg, beaten

1. Preheat the water bath to 131°F. Season the beef tenderloin with 1 tablespoon salt and pepper on all sides.

2. In a large skillet, heat 2 tablespoons olive oil over medium-high heat; place the roast in the pan and brown it on all sides, flipping it periodically, about 3 minutes total.

3. Remove the meat from the skillet and place it in a cooking bag. Vacuum-seal the bag or seal it using the water displacement method and place the bag into the water bath. Set the timer for 1 hour 30 minutes.

4. Meanwhile, in a food processor, pulse the mushrooms and shallots on and off, about 10 times, until finely chopped. Don't overprocess.

5. In the same large skillet from step 2, heat the remaining 2 tablespoons olive oil over medium-high heat until hot. Add the mushrooms and shallots and cook until tender and all liquid is evaporated, stirring often, 4 to 6 minutes. Add the wine and cook for 2 to 3 minutes, until all liquid is evaporated. Stir in the mustard, thyme, and a pinch of pepper. Cook for 2 to 3 minutes. Transfer from the skillet to a medium bowl and cool.

6. Shortly before the timer goes off, preheat the oven to 425°F. When the beef is done, remove it from the cooking bag and pat it dry.

7. Lay a double layer of plastic wrap, about 2 feet long and 1 foot wide, on your work surface. Lay one sheet of the pastry dough on it. Roll it into a 16-by-16-inch square. Place slightly overlapping pieces of prosciutto on the dough, shingle-fashion, leaving a 2-inch border at the top and bottom edges. Spread the cooled mushroom mixture evenly over the prosciutto.

8. Place the tenderloin along the very bottom edge of the prosciutto and mushroom layer. Carefully roll the beef in the puff pastry until it is completely wrapped, using the plastic wrap to help tighten it as you go. Trim any excess pastry with a sharp knife. Fold the sides of puff pastry protruding from either end of the beef roll toward the center, then fold the flaps down to seal it completely. Once the beef is completely rolled up, wrap it with more plastic wrap, twisting the ends to make sure the roll is very tight; put it into the freezer for at least 30 minutes.

9. Adjust an oven rack to the center position, transfer the Wellington to a foil-lined baking sheet, and brush it all over with the beaten egg. Use a sharp paring knife to score a decorative pattern in the pastry (if you haven't created the latticework decoration described in the *Change It Up* tip). Sprinkle with salt. Bake until the pastry is golden brown, about 10 minutes. Remove the Wellington from the oven and let it rest for 10 minutes. Slice and serve.

CHANGE IT UP: For a decorative latticework pattern on your Wellington, dust your work surface lightly with flour. Spread out a second sheet of puff pastry and, using a lattice pastry cutter, cut a strip of pastry as long as your beef and drape it over the roll, spreading the pieces to form the lattice.

DID YOU KNOW? Beef Wellington may hold the record for bogus stories about its origins, including that it was created to honor Lord Wellington's victory at Waterloo, or that it resembles a Wellington boot. More likely it was adapted from a French recipe and just given a proper English name.

BEEF BURGUNDY

SERVES 8 | **PREP TIME:** 50 minutes | **COOK TIME:** 16 hours | **FINISHING TIME:** 15 minutes | **SOUS VIDE TEMPERATURE:** 140°F | **FAMILY FRIENDLY**

Beef Burgundy (or bœuf Bourguignon) hails from the French region beloved for both its wines and its Charolais beef cattle. The French excel at devising recipes to turn the leaner, less expensive cuts of meat into culinary masterpieces, and this is a fine example. Serve with Cauliflower Puree (page 65) or mashed potatoes for a hearty yet elegant meal.

6 slices bacon, cut into ¼-inch pieces

1 (5-pound) boneless beef chuck eye roast, cut into 1-inch cubes

3 teaspoons kosher salt, divided

1 teaspoon freshly ground black pepper

¼ cup cornstarch

Vegetable oil, as needed, for searing

2 medium carrots, peeled, halved lengthwise, and sliced

2 large onions, halved and sliced

6 medium garlic cloves, minced

1 (750 mL) bottle pinot noir, or any medium-bodied red wine

1 cup beef broth

2 teaspoons fresh thyme leaves

2 bay leaves

4 tablespoons unsalted butter, at room temperature, divided

10 ounces (about 3 cups) cremini mushrooms, thinly sliced

1 cup sweet peas, fresh or frozen

2 tablespoons all-purpose flour

Chopped parsley, for garnish

1. Preheat the water bath to 140°F.

2. In a large sauté pan, cook the bacon over medium heat, stirring occasionally, until lightly browned, about 10 minutes. Transfer the bacon with a slotted spoon to a large cooking bag, leaving the fat in the pan.

3. Pat the beef cubes dry with a paper towel and, in a bowl, season them with 2 teaspoons salt, the pepper, and cornstarch, tossing them until evenly coated. Working in batches, sear the beef in the bacon fat (adding vegetable oil, if needed) over medium-high heat until browned on all sides, 3 to 5 minutes per side. As the seared cubes are done, add them to the bag with the bacon.

4. Put the carrots, onion, and remaining 1 teaspoon salt in the pan and cook, over medium-high heat, stirring occasionally, until the onion is slightly browned, about 10 minutes. Add the garlic and cook for 1 more minute. Use a slotted spoon to transfer the vegetables to the cooking bag; discard the fat left in the pan.

5. In the same pan, heat the wine over medium heat, scraping up any browned bits with a spoon. Add the broth and simmer until the liquid has reduced by one-quarter, about 15 minutes.

6. Add the wine mixture, thyme, and bay leaves to the bag. Vacuum-seal the bag, or seal it using the water displacement method, and place the bag into the water bath. (If using a zip-top bag, double it up.) Set the timer for 16 hours. Cover the water vessel with a lid or plastic wrap to prevent evaporation during cooking; check the water level from time to time and top it up, if necessary.

7. Just before the timer is finished, in the pan, melt 2 tablespoons butter and cook the mushrooms until tender, about 5 minutes. Set aside.

8. When the timer goes off, remove the bag, cut a small opening in it, pour the cooking liquid into the pan with the mushrooms, and warm it over medium heat. Skim off any fat that's visible on the surface. Add the peas to the pan.

9. In a small bowl, mash together the remaining 2 tablespoons butter and the flour with a fork. Whisk this into the sauce. Bring the sauce to a simmer, stirring frequently, and cook until it thickens and the peas are cooked, 5 to 8 minutes.

10. Add the meat and vegetables left in the bag to the pan and mix thoroughly.

11. Garnish with chopped parsley and serve.

DIJON-HERB RUBBED PRIME RIB

SERVES 6 to 8 | **PREP TIME:** 5 minutes, plus 1 to 12 hours to marinate | **COOK TIME:** 6 hours |
FINISHING TIME: 40 minutes | **SOUS VIDE TEMPERATURE:** 132°F | **FAMILY FRIENDLY, PARTY READY**

It's your turn to host the holiday meal. Put all your apprehensions aside and enjoy both the company and the food with this gorgeously seasoned, medium-rare, exquisitely tender prime rib au jus. Consider serving with potatoes of any kind, green beans, or Parmesan and Balsamic Brussels Sprouts (page 49).

3 tablespoons Dijon mustard	2 tablespoons minced fresh rosemary leaves	1 (6- to 8-pound) bone-in, backbone removed beef rib roast (2 to 4 ribs)
1 tablespoon steak seasoning blend of your choice		4 cups beef stock

1. In a small bowl, combine the Dijon mustard, steak seasoning, and rosemary. Mix well and rub onto each side of the rib roast. Place the roast in a cooking bag. (If using a zip-top bag, double it up.) Vacuum-seal the bag or seal it using the water displacement method. Place it in the refrigerator to marinate for at least 1 but up to 12 hours.

2. Preheat the water bath to 132°F.

3. When the water has reached temperature, immerse the roast and set the timer for 6 hours.

4. Shortly before the sous vide finishes, preheat the oven to 425°F.

5. When the timer goes off, remove the beef from the cooking bag, reserving the cooking liquid, and pat it dry with paper towels.

6. Place the meat on a sheet pan fitted with a baking rack and roast for 10 to 15 minutes, until the crust is dark golden brown. Remove the roast from the oven and let it rest for 10 to 15 minutes.

7. In a large saucepan, bring the cooking liquid and beef stock to a boil, reduce the heat, and simmer until reduced by half. Skim off and discard any solids that float to the top.

8. Slice the roast and serve it with the sauce.

KOREAN-INSPIRED BRAISED SHORT RIBS

SERVES 4 to 6 | **PREP TIME:** 15 minutes | **COOK TIME:** 24 hours | **FINISHING TIME:** 2 minutes |
SOUS VIDE TEMPERATURE: 167°F | **FAMILY FRIENDLY**

Don't wait for the Korean lunar new year to make this version of *galbi jjim*; it's a delicious and auspicious meal no matter the time of year. Jujubes (aka red dates or Chinese dates) and ginkgo nuts are beloved items in traditional Chinese medicine. Include them for extra nutrition and added flavor.

3½ to 4 pounds bone-in beef short ribs	2 tablespoons rice wine (mirin)	2 carrots, cut into 1-inch pieces
1 tablespoon kosher salt	1 tablespoon minced garlic	8 dried jujube or red dates (optional)
Freshly ground black pepper	1 teaspoon sesame oil	10 ginkgo nuts, peeled (optional)
2 to 3 tablespoons avocado or vegetable oil, for searing	1½ cups peeled, cored, and chopped red apple or Asian pear	10 chestnuts, peeled (optional)
6 tablespoons soy sauce	½ cup chopped onion	
2 tablespoons brown sugar	5 whole black peppercorns	
2 tablespoons honey		

1. Preheat the water bath to 167°F.

2. Season the ribs on all sides with the salt and pepper. In a pan, heat the avocado oil over medium-high heat. When it's very hot, add the ribs and sear until golden brown, about 2 minutes per side. Set the ribs aside and let them cool.

3. In a blender or food processor, blend the soy sauce, sugar, honey, rice wine, garlic, sesame oil, apple, onion, and peppercorns together.

4. Place the seared ribs into a sous vide bag (use more bags, if necessary). Add the carrot and jujube (if using), ginkgo nuts (if using), and chestnuts (if using). Pour the sauce into the bag(s). Vacuum-seal the bag(s) and set the timer for 24 hours. Cover the water vessel with a lid or plastic wrap to prevent evaporation during cooking; check the water level from time to time and top it up, if necessary.

5. When the timer goes off, remove the ribs from the sous vide bag(s) and serve.

MERGUEZ SAUSAGES WITH VEGETABLES AND HERBED YOGURT SAUCE

SERVES 4 | **PREP TIME:** 5 minutes | **COOK TIME:** 1 hour 30 minutes | **FINISHING TIME:** 5 minutes | **SOUS VIDE TEMPERATURE:** 150°F | **FAMILY FRIENDLY, QUICK PREP**

Long, thin sausages featuring lamb, mutton, beef, or a combination, seasoned with cumin, coriander, fennel, and chili—thank you, North Africa! While your first inclination might be to grill these guys as the Moroccans do, turn instead to your sous vide, which will produce sausages much juicier and more flavorful than your grill can manage. A quick sear will give the skin the proper snap. Serve with tomato, onion, and red bell pepper and, of course, pita bread.

1 pound fresh merguez sausages	2 tablespoons avocado or vegetable oil, for searing	Kosher salt
1 cup Greek yogurt	1 red onion, cut into wedges	Freshly ground black pepper
1 to 2 tablespoons chopped fresh Italian parsley	4 Roma tomatoes, cut into wedges	Pita bread, for serving
1 tablespoon chopped fresh mint leaves	2 red bell peppers, cut into wide strips	

1. Preheat the water bath to 150°F.

2. Place the sausages into a zip-top bag and seal it using the water displacement method. Submerge the bag and set the timer for 1 hour 30 minutes.

3. In a bowl, mix the yogurt, parsley, and mint. Set aside.

4. When the sausages are done, remove them from the bag and pat them dry. Reserve the cooking juices. In a skillet, heat the avocado oil over medium-high heat and give the sausages a good sear, 1 to 2 minutes per side. Remove the sausages from the skillet and pour the reserved cooking juices into it. Add the onion, tomato wedges, and bell pepper strips and season with salt and black pepper. Flip the vegetables as needed until you see a nice char on both sides.

5. Serve the sausage with the grilled onions, tomatoes, and bell peppers, a generous dollop of the herbed yogurt, and pita bread to mop it all up.

CHANGE IT UP: Merguez also makes a fine breakfast sausage if you like some spice to kick off the day.

ITALIAN-STYLE MEATBALLS

SERVES 4 to 6 | **PREP TIME:** 15 minutes, plus at least 1 hour to freeze | **COOK TIME:** 1 hour | **FINISHING TIME:** 15 minutes | **SOUS VIDE TEMPERATURE:** 145°F | **FAMILY FRIENDLY**

These are no ordinary meatballs. A colorful array of Mediterranean spices and herbs seasons them and the sous vide holds in all the moisture while cooking. Any Italian grandmother would be proud.

1 pound 80-percent lean
    ground beef
½ pound ground veal
½ pound ground pork
2 teaspoons kosher salt
½ teaspoon freshly ground
    black pepper

2 teaspoons onion powder
2 teaspoons garlic powder
2 teaspoons sweet paprika
1 teaspoon dried thyme
1 teaspoon coriander
1 teaspoon ground cumin
2 tablespoons butter

Tomato sauce, for
    serving (optional)
Freshly grated
    Parmesan cheese, for
    serving (optional)
Italian parsley, chopped,
    for serving (optional)

1. In a large bowl, mix the ground beef, ground veal, ground pork, salt, pepper, onion and garlic powders, paprika, thyme, coriander, and cumin thoroughly using your clean hands. Don't overmix.

2. Roll the mixture into roughly 32 (2-inch) meatballs and place them on a baking sheet.

3. Freeze the meatballs for at least 1 hour; this will help them keep their round shape during the vacuum-sealing and cooking.

4. Preheat the water bath to 145°F.

5. Place the frozen meatballs into multiple sous vide bags, maintaining 1 inch of space between them. Vacuum-seal the bags and lower them into the heated water. Set the timer for 1 hour.

6. When the timer goes off, remove the meatballs from the sous vide bags and pat them dry with paper towels. In a cast-iron skillet, heat the butter over high heat. Working in batches, carefully place the meatballs in the skillet, maintaining space between them. Gently roll them around to brown all sides, about 5 minutes per batch.

7. Serve as desired, perhaps with tomato sauce, a sprinkling of freshly grated Parmesan, and/or some chopped Italian parsley.

LAMB KOFTA WITH TZATZIKI SAUCE

SERVES 6 to 8 | **PREP TIME:** 20 minutes, plus 1 or more hours to freeze | **COOK TIME:** 3 hours |
FINISHING TIME: 10 minutes | **SOUS VIDE TEMPERATURE:** 140°F | **FAMILY FRIENDLY, PARTY READY**

You'll find variations on kofta throughout the Near and Middle East, occasionally made with ground beef but more often with mutton or lamb. This recipe is redolent with aromatic spices—cumin, cinnamon, smoked paprika, and allspice—enriched by red bell pepper and cilantro, and it gets a pleasant kick from a jalapeño. A cool, classic tzatziki is the perfect foil to tie everything together.

1 small onion,
coarsely chopped

3 garlic cloves, coarsely
chopped

1 small red bell pepper,
coarsely chopped

1 small jalapeño pepper,
stem and seeds removed,
coarsely chopped

½ cup gently packed cilantro
or parsley leaves

2 pounds ground lamb

¾ teaspoon ground cumin

¼ teaspoon
ground cinnamon

½ teaspoon smoked paprika

½ teaspoon allspice

1½ teaspoons kosher salt

¼ teaspoon freshly ground
black pepper

2 to 3 tablespoons avocado
or vegetable oil, for searing

Tzatziki Sauce (page 235),
for serving

Pita bread, for serving

1. In a food processor, combine the onion, garlic, bell pepper, jalapeño pepper, and cilantro and pulse until the vegetables are finely minced but not pureed. Transfer the minced vegetables to a fine-mesh sieve and use a spatula to press out as much liquid as possible. Add the vegetable mixture to a mixing bowl.

2. Add the lamb, cumin, cinnamon, smoked paprika, allspice, salt, and pepper to the mixing bowl. Using your hands, mash the mixture together until combined. Form it into slightly flattened meatballs, 2 inches in diameter, and place them on a baking sheet. Freeze for at least 1 hour; this will help them keep their shape.

3. Preheat the water bath to 140°F.

4. Place the frozen kofta into multiple sous vide bags, keeping them in a single layer with about 1 inch between them. Vacuum-seal the bags and place them into the sous vide. Set the timer for 3 hours.

5. When the kofta are done, remove them from the bags and pat them dry with paper towels. In a cast-iron skillet over high heat, warm the avocado oil. Working in batches, sear the kofta on both sides until browned, 2 to 3 minutes per side. Serve with the tzatziki sauce and pita bread.

CHANGE IT UP: As you make your way around the Mediterranean, the kofta seasonings (as well as the spellings—kofte, köfte) change. Mint, thyme, cloves, cardamom, and sumac often pop up in recipes. Experiment with the seasonings and see what grabs your fancy.

MAKE-AHEAD MAGIC: You can shape the kofta and then, when they're frozen, transfer them to an airtight bag or container and keep them in the freezer up to 3 months before putting them into the sous vide.

ESSENTIAL LAMB CHOPS

SERVES 4 | **PREP TIME:** 15 minutes | **COOK TIME:** 2 hours | **FINISHING TIME:** 10 minutes |
SOUS VIDE TEMPERATURE: 134°F | **FAMILY FRIENDLY**

You and your family will love this go-to lamb chop recipe. It uses very basic seasonings, it's simple to prepare, and the sous vide draws out the organic and natural flavor of the lamb. Broccoli steamed in the lamb juice is an ideal accompaniment.

FOR THE LAMB:

8 (3-ounce) lamb chops

Kosher salt

Freshly ground black pepper

½ teaspoon ground cumin

½ teaspoon cayenne pepper

2 to 3 tablespoons avocado
   or vegetable oil, for
   searing, divided

2 rosemary sprigs

4 garlic cloves

Lemon slices (optional)

**FOR THE STEAMED BROCCOLI
(OPTIONAL):**

2 tablespoons extra-virgin
   olive oil

2 garlic cloves, minced

1 pound (about 2 heads)
   broccoli florets

¼ cup reserved lamb juice

Kosher salt

1. Preheat the water bath to 134°F.

2. **Prepare the lamb:** Season the lamb chops on both sides with salt and black pepper, cumin, and cayenne pepper. Set aside.

3. Heat a large cast-iron skillet over medium-high heat for 3 to 5 minutes. Add 1 tablespoon avocado oil and swirl to coat the bottom. Sear the lamb chops on both sides, about 30 seconds per side. While the lamb is searing, toss in the rosemary sprigs and garlic.

4. Prepare two sous vide bags and place 4 lamb chops into each in a single layer. Transfer the rosemary and garlic from the skillet to the sous vide bags and add the lemon slices (if using). Vacuum-seal the bags and lower them into the heated water. Set the timer for 2 hours.

5. Once the timer goes off, remove the lamb from the bags and transfer it to a plate. Pat the chops dry with paper towels. Reserve the lamb juice for the broccoli, if you're making it.

6. In a skillet, heat the remaining 1 to 2 tablespoons avocado oil over high heat to sear the lamb chops, about 30 seconds per side, until well-browned. Transfer the lamb chops to serving plates and let them rest for 5 minutes.

7. **Make the broccoli (optional):** In the same skillet, heat the olive oil over medium-high heat. Add the garlic and stir until fragrant, about 30 seconds. Add the broccoli florets to the skillet and sauté for about 1 minute. Pour the reserved lamb juice over the broccoli and cover to steam for 5 minutes, or until the broccoli is tender. Taste and season with salt, as desired.

8. Serve the lamb chops with the broccoli or your favorite vegetable sides.

48-HOUR MOROCCAN-INSPIRED LAMB SHANKS

SERVES 4 | **PREP TIME:** 10 minutes | **COOK TIME:** 48 hours | **FINISHING TIME:** 5 minutes |
SOUS VIDE TEMPERATURE: 140°F | **FAMILY FRIENDLY, QUICK PREP**

Although this Moroccan-inspired recipe cooks for 48 hours, you can while away those two days, just anticipating fall-off-the-bone tender lamb. Serve with Spicy Honey-Glazed Parsnips (page 61) or Cauliflower Puree (page 65) for a complete meal.

2 teaspoons
   ground cinnamon

2 teaspoons
   ground coriander

2 teaspoons kosher salt

1 teaspoon freshly ground
   black pepper

1 teaspoon ground cumin

1 teaspoon ground nutmeg

1 teaspoon cayenne
   pepper (optional)

4 (1½-pound) bone-in
   lamb shanks

4 thyme sprigs (optional)

1 tablespoon unsalted butter

1. Preheat the water bath to 140°F.

2. In a small bowl, mix the cinnamon, coriander, salt, black pepper, cumin, nutmeg, and cayenne (if using), then place the spice rub on a large plate. One by one, put the lamb shanks on the plate and roll them around to cover them thoroughly with the rub.

3. Carefully slide each seasoned shank into its own sous vide bag. Add a sprig of thyme to each bag (if using), then vacuum-seal the bags and place them into the sous vide. Set the timer for 48 hours. Cover the water vessel with a lid or plastic wrap to prevent evaporation during cooking; check the water level from time to time and top it up, if necessary.

4. When the lamb is done, remove the lamb shanks from the bags and pat them dry. In a large skillet, melt the butter over medium-high heat. When the butter stops foaming, add the shanks. Sear them until well-browned on all sides, 3 to 5 minutes, and serve.

DID YOU KNOW? The shank is the lower part of the lamb's leg, from the knee down. As you'd imagine, these muscles are heavily used, and this makes for some of the toughest meat on the sheep, which is why these shanks are slow-cooked to tenderness. The upside is the flavor, which is stronger than beef and utterly distinctive.

RACK OF LAMB WITH ROSEMARY-BALSAMIC MARINADE

SERVES 4 | **PREP TIME:** 3 minutes | **COOK TIME:** 2 hours | **FINISHING TIME:** 5 minutes | **SOUS VIDE TEMPERATURE:** 131°F | **FAMILY FRIENDLY, QUICK PREP**

A rack of lamb is visually arresting and a treat for the taste buds. The recipe is a simple one; the balsamic vinegar and rosemary complement the lamb's distinctive flavor without overpowering it. Serve with Sous Vide Kale (page 63).

2 (1¼- to 2-pound) lamb rib racks (7 to 8 ribs each), Frenched or not

1 tablespoon kosher salt

Freshly ground black pepper

2 tablespoons extra-virgin olive oil

¼ cup balsamic vinegar

1 tablespoon finely chopped fresh rosemary leaves

2 to 3 tablespoons avocado or vegetable oil, for searing

1. Preheat the water bath to 131°F.

2. If there is a layer of surface fat on the lamb, score it with a sharp knife, making cuts in the surface fat about 1 inch apart and no deeper than the depth of the fat. Season the meat on both sides with the salt and pepper and place the racks in one or more sous vide bags. Add the olive oil, balsamic vinegar, and chopped rosemary. Ensure that the meat is well-coated, and vacuum-seal the bag(s). Put the lamb into the sous vide and set the timer for 2 hours.

3. When the timer goes off, remove the lamb racks from the bag(s) and pat them dry with paper towels.

4. Heat the avocado oil in a cast-iron skillet over high heat. When the pan is hot, add the rack of lamb, fat-side down, and gently press it down; sear the fat side until golden-brown and crispy, 2 to 3 minutes. Then turn off the heat and turn the lamb onto the meat side. Let it rest there for 30 seconds, then remove it from the pan.

5. Cut the rack into chops and plate them or bring the racks to the table whole and carve there for a more dramatic presentation.

DID YOU KNOW? Lamb, mutton, and goat have a distinctive, bold flavor thanks to a type of fatty acid not found in other meats. If that gamey flavor doesn't do it for you, buy only the very freshest lamb and cook it with antioxidant-rich spices, herbs, and flavorings—think mustard, rosemary, and balsamic vinegar. The antioxidants serve to slow oxidation down, giving the meat a subtler flavor.

CURRY LAMB

SERVES 4 | **PREP TIME:** 5 minutes | **COOK TIME:** 24 hours | **FINISHING TIME:** 40 minutes |
SOUS VIDE TEMPERATURE: 140°F | **FAMILY FRIENDLY**

Here, a bottled vindaloo curry paste seasons the lamb chunks as they cook to buttery tenderness in the sous vide. Baby spinach added at the last moment makes this an extravagantly tasty and nutritious one-pot meal.

2 pounds boneless lamb shoulder, cut into bite-size pieces

¾ cup vindaloo curry paste, divided

2 tablespoons extra-virgin olive oil

2 small onions, finely chopped

2 garlic cloves, finely chopped

2 teaspoons grated fresh ginger

2 cups low-sodium chicken stock or water

⅓ cup tomato paste

2 cups baby spinach

1 tablespoon coconut aminos

2 tablespoons chopped cilantro, for garnish

Plain yogurt, for serving

Steamed basmati rice or naan bread, for serving

1. Preheat the water bath to 140°F.

2. Place the lamb in a large cooking bag. Add ¼ cup vindaloo paste and shift the meat around in the bag until it's well-coated. Vacuum-seal the bag or seal it using the water displacement method, and place it into the water bath. (If using a zip-top bag, double it up.) Set the timer for 24 hours. Cover the water vessel with a lid or plastic wrap to prevent evaporation during cooking; check the water level from time to time and top it up, if necessary.

3. About 40 minutes before the lamb is finished, prepare the sauce. In a large sauce-pan, heat the olive oil over medium-high heat. When it's shimmering, add the onions and cook until softened, 3 to 5 minutes. Add the garlic and ginger and cook until aromatic, about 1 minute. Add the remaining ½ cup vindaloo paste and cook until fragrant, 1 to 2 minutes. Stir in the stock or water and tomato paste and bring to a simmer. Reduce the heat to low, cover, and simmer for 30 minutes.

4. Stir the spinach and coconut aminos into the sauce and stir until the spinach is wilted. Turn off the heat, cover, and keep warm.

5. When the timer goes off, remove the lamb from the cooking bag and add them directly to the sauce on the stovetop. Stir to mix, and transfer the curry to a serving bowl. Garnish with cilantro and serve with yogurt and rice or naan bread.

SPICY ASIAN-INSPIRED LAMB STEW

SERVES 4 | **PREP TIME:** 10 minutes | **COOK TIME:** 24 hours | **FINISHING TIME:** 20 minutes |
SOUS VIDE TEMPERATURE: 145°F | **FAMILY FRIENDLY**

This is winter comfort food done right. A lamb stew flavored with soy sauce, Thai chiles, and star anise will warm you up from the inside. Daikon (or "winter radish") is crisp and slightly sweet, a welcome switch from potato. After all, the Irish aren't the only ones who make a mean lamb stew.

2 tablespoons avocado or
vegetable oil, for searing

2 pounds lamb stew meat or
boneless lamb leg, cut into
2-inch pieces

5 garlic cloves, peeled
and smashed

¼ cup Shaoxing wine
or sherry

1 cup chicken bone broth or
chicken stock

2 Thai chiles, sliced

2 to 3 tablespoons peeled
and sliced fresh ginger

3 tablespoons dark
soy sauce (or mix
2 tablespoons
light soy sauce,
1 teaspoon molasses, and
2 teaspoons water)

2 tablespoons light soy
sauce, like Kikkoman

1 tablespoon brown sugar

2 teaspoons ground cumin

3 whole star anise

1 pound daikon radish,
peeled and cubed

1 tablespoon cornstarch

2 tablespoons cold water

Chopped scallions,
for garnish

1. Preheat the water bath to 145°F.

2. In a cast-iron skillet, heat the avocado oil over medium-high heat; sear the lamb pieces until golden-brown on all sides, 1 to 2 minutes per side, working in batches if necessary. Add the garlic cloves to the skillet to roast at the same time. Put the pre-seared lamb and roasted garlic into a large cooking bag.

3. Add the wine and stock to the skillet, scraping up any browned bits, followed by the chiles, ginger, dark and light soy sauces, brown sugar, cumin, and star anise. Bring the sauce to a boil and let the alcohol evaporate, about 5 minutes. Then scoop the sauce into the cooking bag. Vacuum-seal the bag or seal it using the water displacement method and place the bag into the water bath. (If using a zip-top bag, double it up.) Set the timer for 24 hours. Cover the water vessel with a lid or plastic wrap to prevent evaporation during cooking; check the water level from time to time and top it up, if necessary.

4. When the timer goes off, remove the bag from the water bath. Pour the cooking liquid into a large saucepan and leave the lamb in the bag.

5. Add the daikon to the saucepan and bring the mixture to a boil. Simmer over medium heat until the daikon is tender, about 15 minutes. Mix the cornstarch with the water and add it to the sauce. Stir until the sauce is thickened.

6. Return the lamb to the saucepan just long enough to warm it, and then serve it garnished with the chopped scallions.

MEDITERRANEAN LEG OF LAMB

SERVES 6 to 8 | **PREP TIME:** 10 minutes | **COOK TIME:** 2 to 6 hours | **FINISHING TIME:** 5 minutes |
SOUS VIDE TEMPERATURE: 135°F | **PARTY READY, QUICK PREP**

This leg of lamb is dressed to impress a crowd, getting a double punch of flavor from garlic and lemon rubbed on the inside and paprika, cumin, and coriander on the outside. If you like, reserve the cooking juices and braise some sliced fennel, onion or leek, and potato wedges to accompany the lamb.

1 tablespoon minced garlic
(3 or 4 cloves)

1 tablespoon finely
grated lemon zest (from
2 medium lemons)

1 tablespoon extra-virgin
olive oil

4 teaspoons kosher
salt, divided

1 tablespoon paprika

2 teaspoons
ground coriander

1 teaspoon ground cumin

1 (3½- to 4-pound) boneless
leg of lamb

Freshly ground black pepper

2 to 3 tablespoons avocado
or vegetable oil, for searing

1. Preheat the water bath to 135°F.

2. In one small bowl, mix the garlic, lemon zest, olive oil, and 2 teaspoons salt. In another small bowl, mix the remaining 2 teaspoons salt, paprika, coriander, and cumin.

3. Have a few 20-inch lengths of kitchen twine ready. Unroll the lamb and lay it flat, fat-side down. Rub the lemon-garlic mixture evenly over the surface of the lamb, then season it with pepper. Roll the lamb back into a tight cylinder and truss it with the twine; trim off any excess twine. Rub the outside of the lamb evenly with the dry spice mixture.

4. Slide the seasoned meat into a cooking bag. Vacuum-seal the bag or seal it using the water displacement method and place the bag into the water bath. (If using a zip-top bag, double it up.) Set the timer for 2 hours or up to 6 hours.

5. When the timer goes off, remove the leg of lamb from the water bath and pat it dry with paper towels. Reserve the cooking juices for some braised vegetables to serve with the lamb or another use. In a cast-iron skillet over medium-high heat, warm the avocado oil. Sear the lamb on all sides until nicely browned and crisped, about 4 minutes in total. Remove the lamb from the skillet.

6. Remove the twine from the lamb, slice, and serve.

VEAL OSSO BUCO

SERVES 4 | **PREP TIME:** 30 minutes | **COOK TIME:** 24 hours | **FINISHING TIME:** 2 minutes |
SOUS VIDE TEMPERATURE: 176°F | **FAMILY FRIENDLY**

Veal shanks are loaded with flavor, but they need a long cooking time to reach that falling-off-the-bone quality that we all crave. So just set it and forget it! This traditional Milanese dish, originally prepared using cinnamon, makes a delightfully hearty meal that will certainly hit the spot on a cold winter's night. Serve with Simple Polenta (page 40) or Cauliflower Puree (page 65).

4 (1-pound) cross-cut
  veal shanks
Kosher salt
Freshly ground black pepper
3 tablespoons extra-virgin
  olive oil, divided

1 large onion, diced
1 cup diced carrots
1 cup diced celery
4 garlic cloves, crushed
1 tablespoon tomato paste
1 tablespoon ground cumin

1 tablespoon fresh
  thyme leaves
2 cups dry white wine
Chopped fresh parsley,
  for garnish

1. Preheat the water bath to 176°F.

2. Season the veal shanks thoroughly with salt and pepper. In a large cast-iron skillet, heat 2 tablespoons olive oil over medium-high heat and sear the meat, about 2 minutes on each side. Remove the veal from the pan and set it aside.

3. In the same skillet, heat the remaining 1 tablespoon olive oil, onion, carrots, celery, garlic, tomato paste, cumin, thyme, and a pinch of salt and cook, stirring often, until the onions have softened, 8 to 10 minutes.

4. Stir in the wine, scraping up any browned bits; bring to a simmer and cook until the mixture has reduced to about 3 cups, 10 to 12 minutes.

5. Place the veal shanks in one or more sous vide bags and pour the sauce over them. Vacuum seal the bag(s), lower into the sous vide, and set the timer for 24 hours. Cover the water vessel with a lid or plastic wrap to prevent evaporation during cooking; check the water level from time to time and top it up, if necessary.

6. When the timer goes off, your veal shanks are good to go! Spoon some of the sauce over them, garnish with parsley, and serve.

Matcha Ice Cream, page 211

CHAPTER 8

DRINKS AND DESSERTS

EDIBLE AND BAKEABLE COOKIE DOUGH

MAKES 4 cups | **PREP TIME:** 10 minutes | **COOK TIME:** 1 hour 15 minutes | **FINISHING TIME:** 1 hour 40 minutes | **SOUS VIDE TEMPERATURE:** 135°F | **FAMILY FRIENDLY, PARTY READY**

Who didn't sneak some cookie dough out of the bowl as a child? Now that you're grown up, you don't have to sneak. Just pasteurize the egg in the sous vide and the flour in the oven or microwave and you can eat all the raw dough you want with none of the salmonella risks.

1 large egg

4 cups all-purpose flour

1¼ cups butter, at
    room temperature

¾ cup granulated sugar

¼ cup packed light
    brown sugar

2 tablespoons milk

1 teaspoon vanilla extract

2 teaspoons baking powder

½ teaspoon kosher salt

1. To pasteurize the egg, preheat the water bath to 135°F while you bring the egg to room temperature. (This is important; if you start with chilled eggs, the yolk may not reach the temperature necessary for pasteurization. You can pasteurize extra eggs as well; just chill them rapidly in an ice water bath for 30 minutes and return them to the refrigerator when finished.)

2. Gently submerge the egg in the water bath and set the timer for 75 minutes. In a large bowl, prepare an ice-water bath with a 50/50 mixture of cold water and ice cubes. When the egg is done, remove it with a slotted spoon and immediately submerge it in the ice-water bath for 30 minutes.

3. To pasteurize the flour, spread the flour on a rimmed baking sheet and toast it in a preheated 375°F oven for 6 minutes. Alternatively, microwave the flour for 1 minute 15 seconds on high, stirring in 15-second intervals. Allow the flour to cool to room temperature.

4. In a large bowl, cream the butter, granulated sugar, and brown sugar until light and fluffy, about 5 minutes. Beat in the egg, milk, and vanilla.

5. In another large bowl, whisk together 3½ cups of the pasteurized flour, the baking powder, and salt; gradually beat the dry ingredients into the wet ingredients, adding the remaining flour if necessary. Stir in your favorite toppings and divide the dough into four 1-cup portions. Refrigerate, covered, to chill for at least 1 hour.

6. If you choose to make cookies, drop the dough in 1-tablespoon portions onto a baking sheet, leaving at least 1 inch between the cookies. Bake at 350°F for 11 to 13 minutes.

RED WINE-POACHED PEARS

SERVES 4 | **PREP TIME:** 10 minutes | **COOK TIME:** 1 hour | **FINISHING TIME:** 5 minutes |
SOUS VIDE TEMPERATURE: 175°F | **QUICK PREP**

While you're eating dinner, these Bosc pears can have a happy hour of their own in the sous vide, basking in red wine and vermouth. Orange and vanilla also contribute generously to the flavor palette. Served with a scoop of vanilla ice cream, this is an ultra-easy, guest-impressing, visually stunning, and, of course, delicious dessert.

1 vanilla bean	½ cup granulated sugar	3 (3-inch) strips orange peel
4 Bosc pears, peeled	¼ cup sweet vermouth	Vanilla ice cream,
1 cup red wine	1 teaspoon kosher salt	for serving

1. Preheat the water bath to 175°F.

2. Cut the vanilla bean in half crosswise, then split each half lengthwise. Inside the pod, you'll see the tiny, dark seeds; use the point of your knife to scrape them out. Put both the pods and the seeds into a cooking bag.

3. Add the pears, wine, sugar, vermouth, salt, and orange peel to the bag. Vacuum-seal the bag or seal it using the water displacement method, and place the bag into the water bath. Set the timer for 1 hour.

4. When the timer goes off, remove the bag from the sous vide. Take the pears out of the bag and core and slice them, then place them into 4 bowls. Top each bowl with a scoop of vanilla ice cream, drizzle with some of the cooking liquid, and serve.

CHANGE IT UP: Will other kinds of pears work with this recipe? Absolutely, but they'll absorb the seasonings in their own ways, giving the finished dish a different flavor. Try Anjou or Bartlett.

CLASSIC CHOCOLATE PUDDING

SERVES 5 | **PREP TIME:** 20 minutes | **COOK TIME:** 1 hour | **FINISHING TIME:** 15 minutes, plus 8 to 12 hours to chill | **SOUS VIDE TEMPERATURE:** 176°F | **FAMILY FRIENDLY**

When I say "classic" chocolate pudding, I'm talking about the rich, satiny pudding made on stovetops long before the advent of the instant stuff. Your sous vide will give you the same depth of flavor and the sublime creaminess without the constant stirring and fussing. You'll see: The proof is in the pudding.

¼ cup cornstarch

8 tablespoons sugar, divided

2 tablespoons cocoa powder

2 cups whole milk

¾ cup light cream (30% fat)

2 large egg yolks

½ teaspoon salt

1. Preheat the water bath to 176°F.

2. In a small bowl, combine the cornstarch and 6 tablespoons sugar and mix well with a fork, breaking up any lumps.

3. In a medium saucepan over medium-low heat, whisk together the cocoa powder and the cornstarch-sugar mixture. Gradually add the milk and cream, whisking to mix. Heat until the mixture reaches a boil, stirring frequently with a rubber spatula to avoid scorching. The mixture should thicken slightly.

4. In a large mixing bowl, combine the egg yolks, remaining 2 tablespoons sugar, and the salt. Whisk until smooth. Begin slowly pouring the hot milk mixture into the egg mixture; adding the milk mixture slowly will avoid causing the eggs to curdle. You can increase the pour rate gradually as you go.

5. Strain this mixture through a fine-mesh strainer.

6. Pour the mixture into five 8-ounce Mason jars and close them fingertip-tight.

7. Place the jars gently into the heated sous vide bath and set the timer for 1 hour. When the pudding is done, remove the jars from the water using tongs and allow them to cool at room temperature for 15 to 30 minutes. Refrigerate the jars overnight before serving.

CHANGE IT UP: How about pouring the pudding into a pie shell? Graham cracker crust, anyone? Or reach for your favorite toppings: whipped cream, chopped nuts, chocolate or peanut butter chips, coconut flakes, strawberries, granola, crushed cookies . . .

ARBORIO RICE PUDDING

SERVES 4 | **PREP TIME:** 3 minutes | **COOK TIME:** 5 hours | **FINISHING TIME:** 2 minutes |
SOUS VIDE TEMPERATURE: 180°F | **FAMILY FRIENDLY, QUICK PREP**

This won't be your typical rice pudding because here you'll use Arborio rice. It's not just for risotto. In fact, the short, stout, starchy grains make an exceptionally luxurious and creamy pudding. Be sure to check the *Change It Up* tip for variations on this tasty pudding.

¾ cup Arborio rice

1½ cups water

¼ teaspoon salt

4 cups whole milk

½ cup granulated sugar

½ teaspoon vanilla extract

Ground cinnamon, for
  topping (optional)

1. Preheat the water bath to 180°F.

2. Combine the rice, water, salt, milk, sugar, and vanilla in a zip-top bag. Double it up and seal using the water displacement method. When the water reaches temperature, submerge the bag and set the timer for 5 hours.

3. When the timer goes off, remove the bag and serve the pudding immediately or chill it and serve it cold later, topping it with ground cinnamon (if using).

CHANGE IT UP: Oh, the things you can do with this recipe! Use brown sugar instead of white, try nondairy milks or a splash of rum, add other spices like cardamom or ground ginger, or toss in some raisins. Versatility is rice pudding's middle name.

DID YOU KNOW? Both India and China claim to have invented rice pudding. In either case, it's been a beloved comfort food for many centuries.

MAKE-AHEAD MAGIC: If you wish, when the pudding is cooked, chill the bag in an ice-water bath for 15 minutes, then put it in the refrigerator, where it will keep for 2 days.

CRÈME ANGLAISE OR VANILLA ICE CREAM

MAKES 2 cups | **PREP TIME:** 5 minutes | **COOK TIME:** 1 hour | **FINISHING TIME:** 15 minutes |
SOUS VIDE TEMPERATURE: 180°F | **FAMILY FRIENDLY, PARTY READY**

Crème anglaise is essentially a thick and sublimely creamy pourable custard that also happens to be the base for excellent vanilla ice cream. Drizzle it on berries, pies, waffles, or cake to gild the lily in the best possible way. Cognac and vanilla liven up this version of a classic recipe.

1¾ cups milk	1 teaspoon cornstarch	1½ teaspoons cognac
4 large egg yolks	1 teaspoon pure	Seeds of ½ vanilla bean
½ cup granulated sugar	vanilla extract	pod (optional)

1. Preheat the water bath to 180°F.

2. In a saucepan, heat the milk over medium heat until a skin forms on the surface, but don't let it boil. When the skin forms, remove the pan from the heat.

3. In a blender or food processor, puree the milk, egg yolks, sugar, cornstarch, vanilla, cognac, and vanilla bean seeds (if using) until smooth and frothy, about 30 seconds.

4. Pour the mixture into a large zip-top bag. Double it up, seal it using the water displacement method, and place it into the heated water. Set the timer for 1 hour. On and off throughout the hour, agitate the bag to prevent clumping.

5. In a large bowl, prepare an ice-water bath with a 50/50 mixture of cold water and ice cubes. When the timer goes off, move the bag from the sous vide to the ice-water bath and then to the fridge to thoroughly chill the mixture before serving or churning. The crème anglaise will keep in the fridge for up to 3 days.

6. If you are making ice cream, follow the instructions for your ice-cream maker at this point, using a well-chilled bowl. It will depend on your particular machine, but 15 to 20 minutes is an average churning time. Transfer the ice cream to a freezer-safe container and let it harden for at least 1 hour. The ice cream will keep for 1 week.

CHANGE IT UP: Feel free to raid the spice rack and liquor cabinet for this recipe, adding freshly ground nutmeg, cloves, or cinnamon and replacing the cognac with rum or bourbon.

CHOCOLATE ICE CREAM

MAKES 1 quart | **PREP TIME:** 5 minutes | **COOK TIME:** 1 hour | **FINISHING TIME:** 2 hours 30 minutes |
SOUS VIDE TEMPERATURE: 185°F | **FAMILY FRIENDLY, PARTY READY**

This dark and wickedly creamy homemade ice cream is bliss in a bowl. Better yet, it whips up in a flash. It's fabulous as-is, but who can resist a sundae bar or some favorite mix-ins?

6 large egg yolks
1 cup granulated sugar
Pinch kosher salt

½ cup unsweetened
   cocoa powder
1 cup whole or
   2 percent milk

2 cups heavy (whipping)
   cream or light
   whipping cream

1. Preheat the water bath to 185°F.

2. In a large bowl, whisk together the egg yolks, sugar, salt, cocoa powder, and milk until well combined, then whisk in the cream. If any foam or bubbles form, eliminate them with a very brief pass with your hand torch or carefully remove them with a spoon.

3. Pour the ice-cream mixture into a zip-top bag. Double it up and seal it using the water displacement method. Put it into the sous vide and set the timer for 1 hour.

4. In a large bowl, prepare an ice-water bath with a 50/50 mixture of cold water and ice cubes. When the timer goes off, transfer the bag to the ice-water bath to cool for 15 to 20 minutes, then put it into the fridge to chill for about 1 hour.

5. Follow the instructions for your ice-cream maker, using a well-chilled bowl. It will depend on your particular machine, but 15 to 20 minutes is an average churning time. Transfer the ice cream to a freezer-safe container and let it harden for at least 1 hour. The ice cream will keep for 1 week.

CHANGE IT UP: Oh, the possibilities. Fold some dark chocolate chips, chopped walnuts or macadamia nuts, cookie bits, or Reese's Pieces into the ice cream just after churning. Give your decadence free rein here!

TEMPERED CHOCOLATE

MAKES 2 cups | **PREP TIME:** 2 minutes | **COOK TIME:** 20 minutes | **FINISHING TIME:** 5 minutes |
SOUS VIDE TEMPERATURES: 115°F, 81°F, and 90°F | **FAMILY FRIENDLY, PARTY READY, QUICK PREP**

When making candies and other dipped foods, you need to temper the chocolate so it will pour
and set smoothly, with a snap and a sheen and the richest imaginable flavor. It's a massive pain
to do—unless you use your sous vide, which is the best, most foolproof way to temper chocolate.
You can temper even small amounts perfectly and store leftovers easily in a ready-to-use form.
Get ready for chocolate truffles and chocolate-coated strawberries, pretzels, nuts, apple and
pear slices . . . heck, just host a fondue party!

1 pound dark chocolate,
semisweet or bittersweet

1. Preheat the water bath to 115°F.

2. Place your chocolate in a sous vide bag and vacuum-seal it. When the water
   is heated, immerse the bag and set the timer for 5 minutes. This step will melt
   the chocolate.

3. Reduce the sous vide temperature to 81°F and drop a few ice cubes into the bath
   until the water reaches that temp.

4. Once the water is at 81°F, increase the setting to 90°F and let the water warm back up
   with the bag still in the water. The bag should stay in the water for at least 5 minutes
   at 90°F. During this 5-minute period, take the bag out of the water every minute or so
   and squeeze it to move the chocolate around within the bag. Agitating the chocolate
   at this point in the process is necessary to avoid a spotted, streaky finished product.

5. When you're ready to use the tempered chocolate, remove the sous vide bag from
   the water and snip off a corner, *et voilà!* Your sous vide bag is now a piping bag,
   and you can drizzle the chocolate wherever you like. If you've not used all of it,
   simply squeeze the chocolate away from that corner and reseal it. Now that it's
   vacuum-sealed again, store it indefinitely at room temperature and just re-temper
   it the next time you want melted chocolate.

DID YOU KNOW? Water is the archenemy of tempered chocolate, causing it to seize, so
be sure to keep any splashes and drips well away from the finished product.

MATCHA ICE CREAM

MAKES 1 quart | **PREP TIME:** 5 minutes | **COOK TIME:** 1 hour | **FINISHING TIME:** 2 hours 30 minutes | **SOUS VIDE TEMPERATURE:** 185°F | **FAMILY FRIENDLY, QUICK PREP**

Most people who order matcha ice cream in Japanese restaurants are instantly smitten with the powerful green-tea flavor, the moderate sweetness, and the vivid, verdant color. This ultra-easy four-ingredient recipe aims to top off your take-out sushi nights.

2 cups half-and-half	3 tablespoons matcha (green tea powder)	½ cup granulated sugar
		⅛ teaspoon kosher salt

1. Preheat the water bath to 185°F.

2. In a large bowl, whisk together the half-and-half, matcha, sugar, and salt. If any foam or bubbles form, eliminate them with a very brief pass with your hand torch or carefully remove them with a spoon.

3. Pour the ice-cream mixture into a zip-top bag. Double it up and seal it using the water displacement method. Put it into the sous vide and set the timer for 1 hour.

4. In a large bowl, prepare an ice-water bath with a 50/50 mixture of cold water and ice cubes. When the timer goes off, transfer the bag to the ice-water bath to cool for 15 to 20 minutes, then put it into the fridge to chill for 1 hour.

5. Follow the instructions for your ice-cream maker, using a well-chilled bowl. It will depend on your particular machine, but 15 to 20 minutes is an average churning time. Transfer the ice cream to a freezer-safe container and let it harden for at least 1 hour. The ice cream will keep for 1 week.

DID YOU KNOW? The better the matcha powder you use, the better your ice cream will be. There are several different grades of matcha, depending upon the quality and color of the tea leaves, processing method, and so on. Ceremonial is the top grade, then culinary grade, which is further divided into premium, café, ingredient, kitchen, and classic grades (in diminishing levels of quality). Look for matcha powder in the best grades; it will be sold in tins.

CRÈME BRÛLÉE

SERVES 6 to 10 | **PREP TIME:** 50 minutes | **COOK TIME:** 1 hour | **FINISHING TIME:** 1 hour 40 minutes |
SOUS VIDE TEMPERATURE: 176°F | **FAMILY FRIENDLY, PARTY READY**

Crème brûlée (literally "burnt cream") is a sumptuously creamy custard crowned with a crisp layer of caramelized sugar. It's an absolute classic in the French dessert repertoire. Make this Crème Brûlée a day or two ahead, caramelize the sugar just before serving, and . . . voilà. You can make this either in jars or in a bag, to be transferred into ramekins. Jars are a bit simpler to make, but you need to be very careful when torching the sugar to be sure you don't shatter them. Ramekins offer more surface area for the crunchy sugar topping and are more heat-tolerant. Your choice.

⅔ cup (4 to 6) large egg yolks
½ cup granulated sugar, plus extra for dusting

1 teaspoon vanilla extract
Pinch kosher salt

2½ cups heavy (whipping) cream

1. Preheat the water bath to 176°F.

2. In a mixing bowl, combine the egg yolks, sugar, vanilla, and salt and whisk until smooth.

3. Slowly pour the cream into the egg mixture, whisking constantly. You can increase the pour rate gradually as you go, but don't stop whisking.

4. Pour the mixture through a fine-mesh strainer, then allow it to rest for 30 minutes. Bubbles will form and dissipate; skim off any remaining ones.

5. **Mason jar option:** Pour the mixture into six 8-ounce Mason jars, pouring in a slow, low, steady stream. Pouring too quickly or from too high above will cause bubbles to form on the surface of the custard. (If bubbles do form as you pour, lightly and quickly flash the surface with a hand torch to remove them or carefully remove them with a spoon.) Close the jars fingertip-tight.

   Cooking bag (ramekin) option: Using a funnel if needed, pour the custard into a zip-top bag. Double it up and seal it using the water displacement method.

6. Carefully place the jars or the bag into the sous vide and set the timer for 1 hour. When the timer goes off, remove the jars or the bag. If you're using the bag, snip one corner and pipe the custard into eight to ten 4- to 6-ounce ramekins. Allow the jars or ramekins to cool at room temperature, about 30 minutes, then move them to your fridge to chill for at least 1 hour or up to 2 days.

7. **Before serving the jars:** Remove the lids; if there is any condensation on the surface of the custard, gently dab it up with a paper towel. Sprinkle a layer of sugar over the surface of the custard: the more sugar, the crunchier your top layer will be. Set your hand torch to its lowest level. Control the heat by moving the torch closer and farther from the custard—the distance should be about 10 inches from the jar. Keeping the flame at this distance is necessary to avoid cracking the glass.

    Before serving the ramekins: Top each custard with about 1 teaspoon sugar in a thin, even layer. Place the ramekins in the oven, 2 to 3 inches from the broiler element, and turn on the broiler. Cook until the sugar caramelizes, about 5 minutes.

8. Allow the sugar to set for five minutes to fully harden before serving; serve within 2 hours.

CHANGE IT UP: Replace the vanilla extract with a liqueur such as anisette, cognac, Grand Marnier, or Bailey's.

LEMON CURD

MAKES 10 (8-ounce) Mason jars | **PREP TIME:** 20 minutes | **COOK TIME:** 1 hour | **FINISHING TIME:** 30 minutes | **SOUS VIDE TEMPERATURE:** 167°F | **FAMILY FRIENDLY**

The English have long made lemon curd out of lemons, so to speak, and slathered it on crumpets and scones. Give this homemade version of the thick, sunny, citrusy custard a try on pancakes, muesli, or fresh berries, in layered cakes, or simply eat it with a spoon. A jar of lemon curd makes a great gift, too.

1½ cups granulated sugar	1 cup freshly squeezed	10 large egg yolks
¼ cup lemon zest (from	lemon juice (from about	1½ sticks (12 tablespoons)
about 6 lemons)	8 lemons)	butter, melted and cooled

1. Preheat the water bath to 167°F.

2. In a food processor, blend the sugar and the lemon zest until the sugar is a fine powder and the zest has completely infused it.

3. With the food processor running, slowly pour in the lemon juice.

4. Add the egg yolks, one at a time, allowing the mixture to blend thoroughly after each.

5. Again, with the food processor still running, pour the melted butter into the bowl.

6. Once blended, slowly pour the mixture into ten 8-ounce Mason jars and close them fingertip-tight.

7. Carefully place the jars into the sous vide and set the timer for 1 hour.

8. When the timer goes off, remove the jars from the water and allow them to cool to room temperature, about 30 minutes. You can then store them in the refrigerator for up to 2 weeks.

CHANGE IT UP: Lemons don't have the corner on the curd market. Follow the recipe using the zest and juice of either limes or grapefruit when you're ready for something different.

DULCE DE LECHE

MAKES 12 ounces | **PREP TIME:** 5 minutes | **COOK TIME:** 12 hours | **FINISHING TIME:** 2 minutes |
SOUS VIDE TEMPERATURE: 185°F | **FAMILY FRIENDLY, QUICK PREP**

Ahhh, Dulce de Leche, "milk candy" indeed! This effortless, one-ingredient confection transforms condensed milk into a thick, smooth, caramelized sauce that can be poured into cocoa or coffee, drizzled on ice cream, dolloped onto pancakes, or spread on toast. You could also just dig in with a spoon.

1 (12-ounce) can sweetened
   condensed milk

1. Preheat the water bath to 185°F.

2. Pour the sweetened condensed milk into one or more Mason jars. I usually use three 4-ounce jars, but you can use larger jars. Close the lids fingertip-tight. Place them in the heated water bath and set the timer for 12 hours. Cover the water vessel with a lid or plastic wrap to prevent evaporation during cooking; check the water level from time to time and top it up, if necessary.

3. When the timer goes off, remove the jars from the sous vide. Serve immediately or allow the jars to cool to room temperature, after which you can store them in the refrigerator for up to 2 weeks.

CHANGE IT UP: Try stirring 1 teaspoon vanilla extract or ½ teaspoon ground cinnamon into the milk before it goes into the sous vide to tweak the flavor.

CLASSIC CHEESECAKE IN A JAR

MAKES 5 single-serving cheesecakes | **PREP TIME:** 10 minutes | **COOK TIME:** 60 or 90 minutes |
FINISHING TIME: 8 hours 30 minutes | **SOUS VIDE TEMPERATURE:** 176°F | **FAMILY FRIENDLY, PARTY READY**

I think the answer to many of life's problems can be found in a jar of cheesecake. This is a simple, classic recipe, and depending on the cooking time you choose, the cake will have either a creamy or custard-y texture. Using buttermilk produces a nice tang, but heavy cream is a fine substitute. The hardest thing about making these cheesecakes is deciding on the toppings.

2 (8-ounce) packages
   cream cheese, at
   room temperature
½ cup granulated sugar

¼ teaspoon kosher salt
3 medium eggs
1 teaspoon vanilla
   extract (optional)

½ cup plus 1 tablespoon
   buttermilk or heavy
   (whipping) cream

1. Preheat the water bath to 176°F.

2. In the bowl of a food processor, combine the cream cheese, sugar, and salt. Blend the mixture until smooth, periodically scraping down the sides of the bowl.

3. Add the eggs and vanilla (if using) to the cream cheese mixture. Blend, again scraping the sides of the bowl as needed.

4. With the food processor running, slowly pour in the buttermilk. Blend the mixture just until everything is smoothly combined, with no chunks of cheese remaining.

5. Fill each of the five Mason jars with the batter, leaving some room for toppings. Close the jars fingertip-tight.

6. Lower the jars carefully into the water. Set the timer for 90 minutes for a firm, creamy, traditional cheesecake, or for 60 minutes to produce a smoother, more custard-like texture.

7. When the timer goes off, remove the jars from the sous vide and allow them to cool at room temperature for 30 minutes, then place them in the refrigerator to chill for at least overnight.

8. At serving time, remove the lids and add some toppings, if you like: fresh fruit, fruit compote, cookie crumble, or whatever strikes your fancy.

CHILE-INFUSED HONEY

MAKES 16 ounces | **PREP TIME:** 5 minutes | **COOK TIME:** 2 hours | **FINISHING TIME:** 5 minutes |
SOUS VIDE TEMPERATURE: 95°F or 122°F | **FAMILY FRIENDLY, QUICK PREP**

This is an exquisite balance of sweetness and heat. When it comes to flavored honeys, your sous vide cuts the infusion time from several weeks to a couple of hours. Just try this jalapeño honey once, and you'll be sold! You'll be spreading it on sourdough bread, drizzling it over fried chicken or goat cheese, swizzling it into cocktails, and giving it as gifts, if you can bear to part with it.

1 fresh jalapeño pepper

16 ounces (2 cups) raw or pasteurized honey

1. Preheat the water bath to 95°F for raw honey or 122°F for pasteurized honey (see the *Did You Know?* tip). Slice the jalapeño and put it into a 16-ounce Mason jar, including the seeds. Reduce or eliminate the seeds to decrease the spiciness. Pour the honey over the pepper and seal the jar fingertip-tight.

2. Gently lower the jar into the sous vide and set the timer for 2 hours.

3. When the timer goes off, remove the jar from the sous vide and strain the jalapeño slices from the honey. Store the honey in the Mason jar in a cool, dry place, where it will keep indefinitely.

DID YOU KNOW? The process of pasteurization heats honey to destroy harmful micro-organisms; it also changes the honey's composition, eliminating beneficial enzymes and degrading the flavor. If you're starting with raw honey and wish to keep it unpasteurized, use the lower temperature, 95°F (the maximum temperature within a beehive).

CHANGE IT UP: Although jalapeños are certainly one of the more interesting flavors to mix with honey, they're far from the only one. For every cup of honey, you could also choose from the following infusion ideas: 1 vanilla bean pod (with or without the zest from ½ orange), 2 tablespoons fresh thyme, 2 chopped rosemary sprigs, 1 tablespoon grated lemon peel plus a couple of lemon slices, 1 tablespoon chopped fresh ginger, or 5 cinnamon sticks. Enjoy experimenting.

BLUEBERRY-INFUSED SYRUP

SERVES 4 | **PREP TIME:** 5 minutes | **COOK TIME:** 1 hour | **FINISHING TIME:** 20 minutes |
SOUS VIDE TEMPERATURE: 135°F | **PARTY READY**

When you're trying to think of a resort-worthy drizzle, here you are. You won't find this maple syrup infused with blueberries and lemon at your typical pancake house. Savor it on pancakes, waffles, cheesecake, or ice cream. Or stir 2 tablespoons of it into a jug of red sangria for an unforgettable drink.

1 cup maple syrup

¾ cup blueberries, fresh
   or frozen

2 tablespoons freshly
   squeezed lemon juice
   (from 1 lemon)

1½ teaspoons lemon zest
   (from 1 lemon)

¼ teaspoon kosher salt

1. Preheat the water bath to 135°F.

2. In a zip-top bag, combine the maple syrup, blueberries, lemon juice, lemon zest, and salt. Seal the bag using the water displacement method and immerse it in the heated water. Set the timer for 1 hour or for up to 3 hours.

3. When the timer goes off, remove the bag from the water bath. Let it cool to room temperature, about 20 minutes.

MAKE-AHEAD MAGIC: When the blueberry syrup has cooled after the sous vide, you can transfer it to an airtight container and refrigerate it for up to 2 weeks.

LEMON AND ROSEMARY INFUSED VODKA

MAKES 750mL | **PREP TIME:** 5 minutes | **COOK TIME:** 3 hours | **FINISHING TIME:** 8 hours |
SOUS VIDE TEMPERATURE: 145°F | **PARTY READY**

Among the countless flavors with which to infuse vodka (including bacon—yes, really), this lemon and rosemary combination is sophisticated and intriguing, turning the vodka an eye-catching chartreuse. Using your sous vide cuts the infusion time from 3 to 5 days to a mere 3 hours, so you can enjoy happy hour today. Mix it with soda or serve it on the rocks. Cheers!

750mL high-quality
vodka, like Tito's
Handmade Vodka

Zest of 6 large lemons
6 rosemary sprigs

1. Preheat the water bath to 145°F.

2. In a large zip-top bag, combine the vodka, lemon zest, and rosemary. Double it up and seal using the water displacement method. When the sous vide reaches temperature, submerge the bag in the water. Set the timer for 3 hours.

3. When the timer goes off, remove the bag and strain the contents through a fine-mesh strainer into a large bowl. Cool to room temperature and transfer to a storage bottle. Refrigerate overnight before serving. The vodka will keep in an airtight bottle for up to 6 months.

CHANGE IT UP: Swap out the lemon zest for the zest of 3 grapefruits for a different citrus flavor.

DID YOU KNOW? Using a reasonably good vodka for your infusions will pay off. The infused flavors can't smooth a low-end vodka's rough edges.

PEAR AND CRANBERRY CHAMPAGNE COCKTAILS

SERVES 8 | **PREP TIME:** 5 minutes | **COOK TIME:** 30 minutes | **FINISHING TIME:** 40 minutes |
SOUS VIDE TEMPERATURE: 175°F | **PARTY READY**

This alluring cocktail is full of zing and lower in sugar than most fruity drinks. The vibrant dark pink color is perfect for brunch, the holidays, a festive evening, or even a girls' night in.

1½ cups whole cranberries, fresh or frozen

1 medium ripe pear, peeled, cored, and halved

2 teaspoons lemon zest (from 1 lemon)

2 tablespoons water

3 tablespoons honey or maple syrup

1 bottle champagne, like Argyle Brut from Trader Joe's

Fresh mint leaves, for garnish (optional)

Lemon slices, for garnish (optional)

Fresh cranberries, for garnish (optional)

1. Preheat the water bath to 175°F.

2. In a cooking bag, combine the cranberries, pear, lemon zest, water, and honey. Vacuum-seal the bag, or seal it using the water displacement method, and place the bag into the water bath. (If using a zip-top bag, double it up.) Set the timer for 30 minutes.

3. When the timer goes off, remove the bag from the sous vide and transfer the contents to a food processor. Process on high until the mixture is pureed. Taste and add more honey or your preferred sweetener, if desired. Add water if the puree is too thick.

4. Refrigerate the fruit puree until it's completely chilled, about 30 minutes.

5. When ready to serve, pour ¼ cup of the fruit puree into a wineglass; stir in a little bit of champagne until well mixed, then top it with more champagne until the glass is three-quarters full. Repeat for the rest of the servings.

6. Garnish with fresh mint, lemon slices, or a few fresh cranberries as desired and serve. Any left-over fruit puree will keep in an airtight container in the fridge for up to 2 weeks.

CHANGE IT UP: Use sparkling water instead of champagne to turn this into a fabulous mocktail.

CUCUMBER-INFUSED GIN

MAKES 16 ounces | **PREP TIME:** 5 minutes | **COOK TIME:** 2 hours | **FINISHING TIME:** 35 minutes | **SOUS VIDE TEMPERATURE:** 150°F | **PARTY READY**

There's no denying it, gin and cucumbers make a beautiful pair. When Hendrick's came on the scene, most of us fell head over heels for the whole cucumber-infused thing but were less infatuated with the price tag. This is a quick, simple, and wallet-friendly way to enjoy the soothing, cooling essence of cucumber in your gin on a hot summer evening.

1 medium cucumber, unpeeled	16 ounces (2 cups) London dry gin

1. Preheat the water bath to 150°F.

2. Slice 4 inches of the cucumber crosswise into very thin slices; a mandoline is handy here. The formula is 1 inch of cucumber for every 4 ounces gin, in case you want to adjust the yield. In a zip-top bag sealed using the water displacement method or Mason jars sealed fingertip-tight, combine the sliced cucumbers and the gin. Place the sealed bag or jar(s) into the sous vide and set the timer for 2 hours.

3. When the timer goes off, strain the gin, and allow it to cool at room temperature for about 30 minutes. Store it in an airtight container. It makes an especially refreshing summertime G&T!

DID YOU KNOW? The best thing, of course, is to use a cucumber that you've just picked from your garden. If you're using one from the store, be sure to wash off any wax coating. Waxy residue in your gin is not a good thing.

SPICY HOT TODDIES

SERVES 6 | **PREP TIME:** 5 minutes | **COOK TIME:** 1 hour | **FINISHING TIME:** 5 minutes |
SOUS VIDE TEMPERATURE: 135°F | **PARTY READY, QUICK PREP**

If the thought of a hot toddy on a cold night is heavenly, make that hot toddy with chile-and-cinnamon-infused maple syrup and celestial choirs will sing. Subtly spiced, perfectly sweet, slightly tart, and blissfully boozy, a mug of this stuff will banish the chill for sure. Double the recipe when the gang gathers in front of your fireplace on a snowy night.

1 cup maple syrup

2 whole cinnamon sticks, plus more for garnish

1 dried red chile pepper

½ teaspoon red pepper flakes

3 lemons, cut in half crosswise

12 ounces (1½ cups) bourbon

Lemon slices, for garnish (optional)

1. Preheat the water bath to 135°F.

2. In either a zip-top bag sealed using the water displacement method or a Mason jar closed fingertip-tight, combine the maple syrup, cinnamon sticks, chile pepper, and red pepper flakes. Place the sealed bag or jar into the heated sous vide and set the timer for 1 hour or for up to 3 hours. When the timer goes off, remove the infused maple syrup from the sous vide and strain it into a jar or small pitcher.

3. For each toddy, combine the juice of ½ lemon, 3 to 4 tablespoons infused maple syrup, 2 ounces (about 4 tablespoons) bourbon, and enough hot water to top it up (less water for a stronger drink, more for a weaker one).

4. Garnish with a cinnamon stick and lemon slice (if using) and serve.

MAKE-AHEAD MAGIC: You can make the infused maple syrup in advance; it will keep in an airtight container in your fridge for up to 2 weeks. Just reheat it when you're ready to mix your toddies.

Counterclockwise from top right:
Honey-Spiced Barbecue Sauce, page 230;
Spicy Cilantro-Lime Sauce, page 228;
Chimichurri, page 229; Tzatziki Sauce,
page 235; Lemon Vinaigrette (in ramekin and
bowl), page 226; and Sassy Pig Rub, page 227

RUBS, SAUCES, AND SEASONINGS

LEMON VINAIGRETTE

MAKES 1 cup | **PREP TIME:** 5 minutes | **QUICK PREP**

A good vinaigrette is so much more than a salad dressing; drizzle it over cooked vegetables, eggs, or fish. And let's be honest, it's really the make-or-break component of any salad. This lemon vinaigrette has just five wholesome ingredients and takes 5 measly minutes to throw together. No store-bought bottled dressing can come close.

Juice of 2 large lemons	2 tablespoons Dijon mustard	½ teaspoon freshly ground black pepper
⅓ cup extra-virgin olive oil	1 teaspoon kosher salt	

In a small bowl, whisk together the lemon juice, olive oil, mustard, salt, and pepper until well blended. Transfer to an airtight container. Store this dressing in the fridge for up to 5 days; shake well to reincorporate before using.

CHANGE IT UP: Add a pinch of fresh herbs, such as mint, basil, dill, or cilantro. To jazz it up, add some lemon zest, maple syrup, orange juice, or garlic. Make it a honey-mustard dressing by whisking in some raw honey and coconut. For a spicy kick, drop in a bit of jalapeño, red pepper flakes, or cayenne.

SASSY PIG RUB

MAKES ½ cup | **PREP TIME:** 5 minutes | **QUICK PREP**

This rub is a key ingredient in the North Carolina–Style Pulled Pork (page 156), where it serves two functions: It adds flavor and also helps the meat stay moist during cooking. Also, no need to limit yourself to using it on the other white meat. It also perks up plain chicken, tofu, and even vegetables—try it on butternut squash!

- 2 tablespoons packed light brown sugar
- 2 tablespoons paprika
- 2 teaspoons ground coriander
- 2 teaspoons onion powder
- 2 teaspoons garlic powder
- 2 teaspoons mustard powder
- 2 tablespoons kosher salt
- ½ teaspoon freshly ground black pepper

Combine the brown sugar, paprika, coriander, onion powder, garlic powder, mustard powder, salt, and pepper in a clean jar or zip-top bag. Mix or shake thoroughly to combine and store in a cool, dark place to use as needed. It will keep for up to 6 months.

DID YOU KNOW? Salt penetrates meat; other spices and herbs do not. If you are using a rub on small pieces of meat or are concerned about sodium intake, eliminate or reduce the salt from the rub and apply it separately.

SPICY CILANTRO-LIME SAUCE

MAKES 1 cup | **PREP TIME:** 5 minutes | **QUICK PREP**

Simple to make, this sauce offers a zesty and complex range of flavors and a fresh green color. Drizzle it over cooked meats, fish, or vegetables or use it as a salad dressing. You'll find yourself blending up another batch in no time.

1 cup firmly packed fresh cilantro leaves

1 jalapeño pepper, coarsely sliced (remove the seeds for less kick)

2 garlic cloves

¼ cup extra-virgin olive oil

¼ cup freshly squeezed lime juice (from 2 limes)

1 tablespoon coconut aminos, or ½ teaspoon kosher salt

1. In a food processor or blender, combine the cilantro, jalapeño, garlic, olive oil, lime juice, and coconut aminos and blend on high speed for 30 seconds, until thoroughly mixed.

2. Pour into an airtight container and refrigerate for up to 1 week.

DID YOU KNOW? The coconut aminos are the secret ingredient in this recipe that brings it all together. Made from the fermented sap of coconut palm, coconut aminos are a magical combination of sweet, salty, and savory. It has about a third of the sodium of soy sauce and is also wheat- and gluten-free, making it an excellent choice for those on restrictive diets.

CHIMICHURRI

MAKES 1 cup | **PREP TIME:** 5 minutes | **QUICK PREP**

Chimichurri (it's just so much fun to say, isn't it?) originated in Argentina and Uruguay, where it is often made to accompany their Pampas-fed beef. With a lush base of parsley blended with other herbs, spices, and vinegar, this sauce complements fish and vegetables just as well as it does steak.

1 cup lightly packed fresh parsley

2 large garlic cloves

1 teaspoon dried thyme

¼ teaspoon red pepper flakes

¼ cup beef bone broth or regular beef broth

¼ cup red wine vinegar

¼ cup extra-virgin olive oil

½ teaspoon kosher salt

⅛ teaspoon freshly ground black pepper

1. In a food processor, blend the parsley, garlic, thyme, red pepper flakes, broth, vinegar, olive oil, salt, and black pepper until well combined, about 30 seconds.

2. Pour the sauce into an airtight container and refrigerate it for up to 2 weeks.

CHANGE IT UP: Replace the parsley in this classic recipe with a cup of fresh cilantro for a change in the herbal notes. Also, if you like your chimichurri a bit thicker—and if you're serving it immediately—add ¼ small ripe avocado.

DID YOU KNOW? The beef bone broth in this recipe is not merely for flavor; compared to regular broths, bone broths are packed with nutrients, including oh-so-beneficial collagen.

HONEY-SPICED BARBECUE SAUCE

MAKES 2 cups | **COOK TIME:** 15 minutes | **QUICK PREP**

Whether you're grilling pork ribs, chicken legs, swordfish fillets, or even tofu, the key to it all is the sauce. Try this recipe, and I am wagering there will never be a bottled barbecue sauce in your kitchen again.

½ cup water or reserved
    meat cooking juice
½ cup apple cider vinegar
1½ cups ketchup
2 tablespoons dark
    soy sauce (or mix

2 tablespoons
    light soy sauce,
    1 teaspoon molasses, and
    2 teaspoons water)
¼ cup honey
2 teaspoons
    mustard powder

1½ teaspoons garlic powder
2 teaspoons
    Worcestershire sauce
1 teaspoon freshly ground
    black pepper
1 teaspoon cayenne pepper

In a saucepan, combine the water or reserved meat cooking juice with the vinegar, ketchup, soy sauce, honey, mustard powder, garlic powder, Worcestershire sauce, black pepper, and cayenne pepper. Bring to a simmer over medium heat and cook until thickened, about 15 minutes.

CHIPOTLE-PECAN PESTO

MAKES 1¼ cups | **PREP TIME:** 10 minutes | **FAMILY FRIENDLY, PARTY READY, QUICK PREP**

What happens when you send a proper Italian basil pesto to Mexico? The most wonderful mayhem! The basil and pine nuts get the boot, replaced by smoky chipotle chiles in adobo sauce and pecans. Warning: This stuff is habit-forming, and there's no end to the things you can do with it.

3 large garlic cloves	4 or 5 chipotle peppers in adobe sauce	½ cup freshly grated Parmesan cheese
⅓ cup extra-virgin olive oil	½ cup pecans	

1. In a food processor, combine the garlic and olive oil and pulse until the garlic is minced.

2. Add the chipotle peppers and some of the adobo sauce to taste, along with the pecans, and blend until smooth.

3. Transfer the mixture to a bowl, add the Parmesan, and stir until thoroughly blended.

CHANGE IT UP: For a vegan pesto, leave out the Parmesan and add 3 to 4 tablespoons nutritional yeast.

MAKE-AHEAD MAGIC: This pesto will keep in the refrigerator for up to 2 weeks.

GREMOLATA

MAKES ⅓ cup | **PREP TIME:** 10 minutes | **QUICK PREP**

When you want a condiment to brighten and freshen a dish, think gremolata, a vivid green dose of parsley-lemon-garlic goodness. The Italians famously serve it with Veal Osso Buco (page 201), but keep it in mind for fish, pasta, soups, and more.

4 bunches Italian flat-leaf parsley, leaves removed and finely minced (about 4 to 5 tablespoons)

4 garlic cloves, finely minced or grated

4 teaspoons lemon zest (from about 1½ lemons)

Kosher salt

Freshly ground black pepper

In a mixing bowl, combine the parsley, garlic, and lemon zest. Mix thoroughly and season with salt and pepper to taste. If you'd like a finer texture, you can use a mortar and pestle to crush the ingredients further. Gremolata is best when absolutely fresh, but it will keep in an airtight container in the refrigerator for 1 or 2 days.

CHANGE IT UP: Go nuts! Add ¼ cup unsalted almonds, very finely diced.

DID YOU KNOW? A Microplane is your best friend when it comes to making gremolata. Use it to grate both the lemon zest and the garlic. It takes a lot of knifework to achieve the fine mince that this tool can provide.

BLUE CHEESE SAUCE

MAKES about 1 cup | **PREP TIME:** 5 minutes | **QUICK PREP**

Mention blue cheese sauce and everyone thinks of Buffalo Wings (page 101), but it makes an equally happy marriage with beef, spooned over steak or burgers. Why stop there? Baked potatoes, steamed or grilled veggies—just about anything that calls out for a rich, intense splash of flavor will revel in this sauce.

⅓ cup crumbled blue cheese

¼ cup light sour cream

¼ cup mayonnaise

1 teaspoon freshly squeezed lemon juice

1 garlic clove, crushed

In a blender, combine the blue cheese, sour cream, mayonnaise, lemon juice, and garlic and blend until smooth. Stored in an airtight container, the sauce will keep for 5 to 6 days in the refrigerator.

CHANGE IT UP: There are many types of blue cheese, each with its own flavor nuances. Gorgonzola, Cashel Blue, Buttermilk Blue, and Maytag Blue are a few of the varieties you're likely to see. Gorgonzola is most often recommended for sauces, but really, any of them will do nicely. Try a few and see which you like best.

AIOLI

MAKES ¾ cup | **PREP TIME:** 10 minutes, not including egg pasteurization, plus 30 minutes to chill | **QUICK PREP**

Aioli is, more or less, a fancy French name for a garlicky, lemony mayonnaise. It's a traditional and popular sauce across the Mediterranean and is made with raw egg, so make sure to use an egg that's been pasteurized in the sous vide.

1 garlic clove, minced

1 teaspoon kosher salt

1 large egg yolk (from a pasteurized egg; for egg pasteurization steps, see page 204)

1 teaspoon Dijon mustard

¾ cup extra-virgin olive oil

½ teaspoon freshly ground black pepper

1 tablespoon freshly squeezed lemon juice

In a medium bowl, mix together the garlic, salt, egg yolk, mustard, olive oil, black pepper, and lemon juice. Cover the bowl and refrigerate for at least 30 minutes before serving.

TZATZIKI SAUCE

MAKES 2 cups | **PREP TIME:** 10 minutes | **QUICK PREP**

Whenever you're whipping up a Greek or Middle Eastern dish, tzatziki is a great option for topping or dipping. This cool, refreshing mixture of yogurt, cucumber, and herbs is just the accompaniment for kebabs or stuffed vine leaves, or simply sprinkle on some feta and scoop it up with wedges of pita bread.

1 cup Greek yogurt

1 cup grated cucumber, water squeezed out

2 tablespoons freshly squeezed lemon juice

2 garlic cloves, pressed

1 teaspoon kosher salt

¼ teaspoon freshly ground white pepper

2 tablespoons chopped fresh mint leaves

2 tablespoons chopped fresh dill

1. In a medium bowl, stir together the yogurt, cucumber, lemon juice, and garlic and season with salt and white pepper. Add the mint and dill and gently stir to combine.

2. Cover and refrigerate. This sauce will keep in the refrigerator for 3 days.

SOUS VIDE COOKING CHARTS

These charts will allow you to come up with your own creations, no matter what you're excited to eat. Go wild!

EGGS

ITEM	TEXTURE	TEMPERATURE	TIME
Pasteurized eggs	Raw	135°F	1 hour 15 minutes
Poached eggs	Just opaque whites, runny yolks	147°F	1 hour
Soft-boiled eggs	Creamy, runny yolks, opaque whites	162°F / 194°F	35 minutes / 8 minutes
Hard-boiled eggs	Firm yolk but still creamy, not chalky; completely opaque whites	170°F / 194°F	1 hour / 20 minutes
Egg bites	Soft and airy	172°F / 185°F	1 hour / 25 minutes

VEGETABLES

ITEM	PREP	TEMPERATURE	TIME
Asparagus, bell peppers	Asparagus left whole, bottoms trimmed and peeled if stalks are large; bell peppers cored and cut into strips	183°F	15 to 20 minutes
Brussels sprouts, broccoli	Brussels sprouts stemmed trimmed and halved; broccoli cut into florets	183°F / 194°F	45 minutes to 1 hour / 30 minutes
Hearty root vegetables (carrots, parsnips, beets)	Sliced or cut into chunks	183°F / 194°F	1 to 3 hours / 30 minutes
Winter squash (butternut, acorn, delicata)	Peeled and sliced into evenly-sized pieces like half moons	185°F / 194°F	1 to 3 hours / 30 minutes
Fingerling potatoes	Whole, if small; halved, if large	194°F	1 hour
Red, yellow, or Yukon Gold potatoes	Sliced or cut into evenly-sized pieces	190°F	1 hour
Russet potatoes	Peeled and sliced into evenly-sized pieces like half moons	183°F / 194°F	1 hour 30 minutes to 3 hours / 1 hour
Sweet potatoes, yams	Peeled and sliced into evenly sized pieces like half moons	194°F	30 minutes
Cauliflower	Cut into florets	183°F	1 hour
Corn on the cob	Whole	183°F	30 minutes

FISH AND SHELLFISH

ITEM	TEXTURE	TEMPERATURE	TIME
Fish fillets	Very tender	104°F to 113°F	40 minutes to 1 hour 10 minutes
	Tender and flaky	122°F to 124°F	40 minutes to 1 hour 10 minutes
	Firm, well-done	131°F to 134°F	40 minutes to 1 hour 10 minutes
Shrimp	Translucent, soft and buttery	125°F	15 minutes to 1 hour
	Very tender with a hint of firmness	130°F	15 minutes to 1 hour
	Moist, juicy and tender	135°F	15 minutes to 1 hour
	Opaque, juicy with a good bouncy bite	140°F / 158°F	15 minutes to 1 hour / 10 minutes
Scallops	Smooth, silky	113°F	30 minutes
	Soft and buttery	123°F	30 minutes
	Firm, structured	131°F	30 minutes

ITEM	TEXTURE	TEMPERATURE	TIME
Lobster tails	Translucent and soft	120°F	20 minutes to 1 hour
	Succulent and tender	130°F	20 minutes to 1 hour
	Firm and traditional	140°F	20 minutes to 1 hour
Lobster claw	Firm	150°F	20 minutes to 1 hour
Octopus	Tender, structured	140°F	24 hours
	Tender, silky	171°F to 175°F	5 hours
	Very tender	185°F	24 hours
Squid	Juicy and tender	136°F	2 to 4 hours
Soft-shell crab	Tender	154°F / 145°F	45 minutes / 3 hours

POULTRY

ITEM	TEXTURE	TEMPERATURE	TIME
Chicken breast	Very soft and juicy	140°F	1 to 3 hours
	Soft and juicy	146°F to 150°F	1 to 3 hours
	Firm and juicy	160°F	1 to 3 hours
Chicken wings	Fall-off-the-bone tender	160°F	2 hours
	Juiciest and most tender	165°F	1 hour
Chicken legs	Very juicy, firm	149°F	1 to 4 hours
	Very juicy and tender	165°F	1 to 4 hours
	Fall-off-the-bone tender	165°F	4 to 8 hours
Whole chicken (divided into pieces)	Juicy and tender	155°F	3 hours
Whole chicken	Juicy and tender	150°F	6 to 7 hours
Turkey breast	Tender	131°F	8 hours
	More tender	131°F	18 hours
	Most tender	131°F	24 hours

ITEM	TEXTURE	TEMPERATURE	TIME
Turkey legs	Tender, firm	140°F	24 to 28 hours
	Tender and juicy	149°F to 150°F	24 to 28 hours
	Fall-off-the-bone tender	158°F	24 to 28 hours
	Tender but less moist	167°F	7 to 8 hours
Duck breast	Tender and juicy	136°F	1 hour 30 minutes to 4 hours
	Totally tender, slightly less juicy	144°F	1 hour 30 minutes to 4 hours
	Firm, less juicy	149°F	1 hour 30 minutes to 4 hours
	Well-done	158°F	1 hour 30 minutes to 4 hours
Duck legs	Firm	140°F	16 to 20 hours
	Tender, moist	158°F	16 to 20 hours
	Fall-off-the-bone tender	176°F	16 to 20 hours

PORK

PORK CUT	TEXTURE	TEMPERATURE	TIME
Pork chops	Soft and rosy Pink and juicy Blushing and tender Springy and barely pink Firm and light brown	126°F 131°F 135°F 140°F 149°F	½-inch-thick: 30 minutes ¾-inch-thick: 45 minutes 1-inch-thick: 1 hour 1½-inch-thick: 1 hour 30 minutes 2-inch-thick: 2 hours
Pork shoulder/butt	Firm Steak-like Structured Easy to pull Super-shreddable	133°F 138°F to 140°F 147°F 154°F to 158°F 167°F to 176°F	24 hours
Bacon	Tender and steak-like Juicy and luscious Succulent and fork-tender Rich and braise-y	147°F	8 hours 16 hours 24 hours 48 hours
Sausages	Extra juicy and soft Extra juicy and firm Springy and juicy Juicy, firm, and tender	140°F 150°F 160°F 176°F	1 to 4 hours 1 to 4 hours 1 to 4 hours 20 minutes

PORK CUT	TEXTURE	TEMPERATURE	TIME
Center-cut loin	Blushing pink	131°F	2-inch diameter: 45 minutes
	Pink	136°F	2½-inch diameter: 1 hour 15 minutes
	Pinkish	144°F	3-inch diameter: 1 hour 30 minutes
	Pinkish gray	149°F	3½-inch diameter: 2 hours
	Gray	158°F	4-inch diameter: 2 hours 30 minutes
Tenderloin	Rosy and soft	131°F	1 hour 30 minutes to 4 hours
	Pink and juicy	136°F	
	Blushing and tender	144°F	
	Barely pink and springy	149°F	
	Fibrous and firm	158°F	
Pork belly	Tender and steak-like	154°F	24 hours
	Succulent and braise-y	176°F	7 hours
Pork ribs	Firm	145°F for extra meaty ribs	36 hours
	Pull-off-the-bone	165°F for traditional textured ribs	12 hours
Ham	Juicy and soft	140°F	3 to 8 hours

BEEF AND LAMB

CUT	DONENESS	TEMPERATURE	TIME
Rib eye steak **T-bone steak** **New York strip steak** **Top sirloin steak**	Rare Medium-rare Medium Medium-well Almost-well	126°F 129°F 133°F 140°F 147°F	¾-inch-thick: 45 minutes 1-inch-thick: 1 hour 1½-inch-thick: 1 hour 30 minutes 2-inch-thick: 2 hours
Tenderloin steak	Rare Medium-rare Medium Medium-well Well-done	122°F 129°F 136°F 147°F 154°F	45 minutes
Flank steak	Medium-rare Medium Medium-well Well-done	131°F 136°F 144°F 154°F	2 to 8 hours
Chuck steak	Medium-rare Medium Medium-well Well-done	131°F 136°F 144°F 154°F	24 hours
Tenderloin roast	Very rare (blue) Rare Medium Medium-well Well-done	126°F 133°F 140°F 149°F 167°F	2-inch-thick: 2 hours 2½-inch-thick: 2 hours 30 minutes 3-inch-thick: 3 hours 3½-inch-thick: 4 hours 30 minutes

CUT	DONENESS	TEMPERATURE	TIME
Prime rib roast	Rare	122°F	4- to 5-inch-thick: 4 hours
	Medium-rare	129°F	5- to 6-inch-thick: 6 hours
	Medium	136°F	
	Medium-well	144°F	
	Almost-well	154°F	
Beef short ribs	Firm	149°F	
	Tender	158°F	
	Succulent	167°F	24 hours
	Fall-apart	176°F	
Brisket	Steak-like	135°F	36 to 72 hours
	Moist and tender	155°F	24 to 36 hours
Beef burger	Rare	126°F	½-inch-thick: 15 minutes
	Medium-rare	133°F	¾-inch-thick: 22 minutes
	Medium	140°F	1-inch-thick: 30 minutes to 1 hour
	Medium-well	147°F	
	Well-done	158°F	
Lamb chops	Rare	126°F	¾-inch-thick: 30 minutes
	Medium-rare	131°F	1-inch-thick: 45 minutes
	Medium	140°F	1½-inch-thick: 1 hour
	Medium-well	149°F	2-inch-thick: 1 hour 30 minutes
	Well-done	158°F	

CUT	DONENESS	TEMPERATURE	TIME
Rack of lamb	Rare	126°F	2-inch-thick: 2 hours
	Medium-rare	131°F	2½-inch-thick: 2 hours 30 minutes
	Medium	140°F	
	Medium-well	149°F	3-inch-thick: 3 hours
	Well-done	158°F	3½-inch-thick: 4 hours 30 minutes
Boneless lamb leg	Very rare	122°F	2 to 3 hours
	Medium-rare	126°F	3 hours
	Medium	135°F	2 to 6 hours
	Medium-well	149°F	2 to 6 hours
	Well-done	158°F	2 to 6 hours
Lamb shank	Medium	140°F	24 hours to 48 hours
	Shreddable but firm	150°F	18 to 24 hours
	Fork-tender	167°F	18 to 24 hours
	Fall-off-the-bone	176°F	12 to 18 hours
Lamb shoulder	Medium-rare	131°F	24 hours to 48 hours
	Medium	140°F	

MEASUREMENT CONVERSIONS

Volume Equivalents (Liquid)

US STANDARD	US STANDARD (OUNCES)	METRIC (APPROXIMATE)
2 tablespoons	1 fl. oz.	30 mL
¼ cup	2 fl. oz.	60 mL
½ cup	4 fl. oz.	120 mL
1 cup	8 fl. oz.	240 mL
1½ cups	12 fl. oz.	355 mL
2 cups or 1 pint	16 fl. oz.	475 mL
4 cups or 1 quart	32 fl. oz.	1 L
1 gallon or 4 quarts	128 fl. oz.	4 L

Oven Temperatures

FAHRENHEIT	CELSIUS (APPROXIMATE)
250°F	120°C
300°F	150°C
325°F	165°C
350°F	180°C
375°F	190°C
400°F	200°C
425°F	220°C
450°F	230°C

Volume Equivalents (Dry)

US STANDARD	METRIC (APPROXIMATE)
⅛ teaspoon	0.5 mL
¼ teaspoon	1 mL
½ teaspoon	2 mL
¾ teaspoon	4 mL
1 teaspoon	5 mL
1 tablespoon	15 mL
¼ cup	59 mL
⅓ cup	79 mL
½ cup	118 mL
⅔ cup	156 mL
¾ cup	177 mL
1 cup	235 mL
2 cups or 1 pint	475 mL
3 cups	700 mL
4 cups or 1 quart	1 L

Weight Equivalents

US STANDARD	METRIC (APPROXIMATE)
½ ounce	15 g
1 ounce	30 g
2 ounces	60 g
4 ounces	115 g
8 ounces	225 g
12 ounces	340 g
16 ounces or 1 pound	455 g

RESOURCES

If you are interested in starting or leveling up your sous vide game, here is a list of the gear that I recommend. All of these items are available on Amazon, though you can also sometimes buy items directly from the company's website, especially when looking at the various sous vide machines.

Sous Vide Machines: I use an Anova Precision Cooker, though the Breville Joule Sous Vide is also very well regarded.

Vacuum Sealers: Geryon, Anova, and FoodSaver all make good models. It's useful to have both dry and moist food modes, and some of them have an attachment you can use on large bags.

Sous Vide Bags: AsianiCandy sells a hand pump that also comes with reusable silicone bags, sealing clips, and sous vide clips for about $20 on Amazon. It's worth seeking out. Nutri-Lock makes 8- and 11-inch vacuum seal bag rolls that cost less than the ones the vacuum sealer company sells. These are useful because you can choose how big the bag is, and who doesn't like saving money?

Hand Torches: The Bernzomatic TS8000 combined with the Searzall attachment are the gold standard for hand torches, but I also really like the Zoocura Refillable Industrial Butane Torch.

Sous Vide Containers: EVERIE's 12-quart container and Anova's 16-quart one will work for almost any cooking project; choose one depending on the capacity you need.

Sous Vide Silicone Lids for Stockpot: Several brands sell silicone lids to prevent water from evaporating, but I like the ones EVERIE and Anova make.

REFERENCES

These are some of the sources I used in researching this book, which are well worth perusing yourself.

ChefSteps.com

CooksIllustrated.com/articles/1131-is-sous-vide-safe

DouglasBaldwin.com/sous-vide.html

FDA.gov/media/90663/download

Recipes.AnovaCulinary.com

SeriousEats.com

INDEX

ACKNOWLEDGMENTS

I would like to acknowledge and express my deepest gratitude to the following people for their great support in my life journey and their contributions to the creation of this book:

For generously sharing their knowledge and experiences, I pay homage to the experts in sous vide cooking and wish to thank every one of them in person: Douglas Baldwin, J. Kenji López-Alt, the ChefSteps team and community, and the Anova community.

My precious family and friends for their love and support: Han Chang, Tina Chen, Allen Cheng, Ashlee Lukoff, Amanda Coffin, Katherine Sonoda, Brian Knoll, Stephanie Pai, Felix Chang, and Irene Agcaoili.

To my editor, Cecily McAndrews, for the superb outline and editing of this book; Joe Cho, for presenting the opportunity to share my sous vide cooking journey with the world; the magnificent team at Callisto Media for the layout, graphics, design, photographs, and everything in between that went into this book you hold in your hands; and Caryn Abramowitz, for polishing this book to a high sheen.

Finally, to my son, Marcus, who is responsible for the beginning of my life and its true journey. Thank you for giving me the strength and hope to carry on during one of the most difficult times in my life. You illuminate every breath I take through your very existence.

ABOUT THE AUTHOR

Sharon Chen is a former corporate "yes" girl turned cookbook author, food blogger, and avid sous vide fanatic. She is deeply versed in content creation and content marketing, especially in the food industry.

Born and raised in Shanghai, China, Sharon is heavily influenced by her mother's home cooking. It was not until Sharon started her own family in the United States in 2013 that she realized how important cooking and eating at home are in order to foster a vibrant and healthy family life. She soon became a self-taught home chef and has been extending her culinary journey from simple Chinese recipes passed down by her mother to a variety of authentic cuisines she learned through her extensive travels and blogging.

Sharon started cooking sous vide when she moved to Hong Kong in 2018, as a way to work around her tiny kitchen that lacked an oven. This modern method of cooking was a life-changing experience that quickly turned into an obsession, which she plans to continue exploring. You can learn more about Sharon and her work on her blog at StreetSmartKitchen.com.